BACKSTAGE PASS

BACKSTAGE PASS

A Life in Show Business

PAT EGAN

RS
RED STRIPE
PRESS

Published by
Red Stripe Press
an imprint of
Orpen Press
Upper Floor, Unit B3
Hume Centre
Hume Avenue
Park West Industrial Estate
Dublin 12
Ireland

email: info@orpenpress.com
www.orpenpress.com

Paperback ISBN 978-1-78605-158-5
ePub ISBN 978-1-78605-159-2

Printed in Dublin by SPRINTprint Ltd

This book is dedicated to my wife,
the beautiful Helena,
and also to my wonderful daughters, Deborah and Layla.

'You may take my happiness to make you happier,
Even though you never know I gave it to you –
Only let me hear sometimes, all alone,
The distant laughter of your joy.'
Edmond Rostand, Cyrano de Bergerac

Foreword

To whom it may concern, Pat Egan is a friend of mine, and has been since I first toured Ireland in the 70s. Being a friend of mine, he gets a free pass on things that he may have done, things that you would hate your mother to know. Pat's most outstanding feature, and the reason he gets all the successful tours again and again, is that he is honest, maybe the most honest promoter in the world!

I introduced him to Indian food, which he attacked rather bravely, like a man not knowing how much of it he would have to eat, as the tours and the years rolled by. He has all of the right stances. He knows when to shut up, and when to be cheery. I have sat in silence in my dressing room with him for company and have been as happy as a clam. I have sat in the same dressing room, surrounded by Irish friends and legends, and been really glad that Pat was there, witnessing it all. We have sat up late in a Chinese restaurant, singing songs with Donovan.

What else would you need from a promoter? I am proud to say that Pat Egan is a friend of mine.

Billy Connolly

Acknowledgements

Over my 75 long years I have received so much help and support both on a personal and professional level from family, friends, and music business contacts.

Some have been mentioned in the pages of my story but many friends I cherish with great love and affection have not.

There are too many to mention but you know who you and how much I value your love and friendship.

Thank you to my brother Jim Egan, an inspiration.

Deepest gratitude to Caroline O'Neill, Garrett Delaney and Áine Carmody for keeping our business afloat the last twenty years.

Extra special thanks to Tony Clayton-Lee, Donard Duffy, Noel Mazie Clifford and Brian McMahon for kick-starting the whole idea.

Thanks to Bill Cooper for the many photos and also to the other photographers I could not identify.

And thank you to Eilish Maher and all the kids at St Audeon's, Ireland's greatest primary school.

To the song publishers for the use of their lyrics, greatly appreciated:

- Jimmy MacCarthy, Universal Music, 'Adam at the Window' and 'Bright Blue Rose'.
- Hal Leonard, Universal Music, 'Speak Softly, Love'.
- James Last/Carl Sigman, Universal Music, 'Music from Across the Way'.
- Doc Pomus/Mort Shuman, Warner Chappell, 'Save the Last Dance for Me'.
- Charles Aznavour/Herbert Kretzmer, Berlin Associates, 'Yesterday When I Was Young'.

Contents

Preface

It was the Covid outbreak that led me to attempt to write my memories of a life in showbusiness. The biggest obstacle facing me was that I am not a writer – nor am I pretending to be. I left school at thirteen unable to read or write properly and the only exam I ever sat was my Primary Certificate, and somehow I passed. The rest of my education was, as they say, perfected at the University of Life on some of north inner-city Dublin's most famous streets. I was, however, determined to write this book myself, warts and all.

My story is not unique – there are many guys from the rough streets of 1950s Dublin who have gone on to make their names and fortunes in business, politics, movies and the arts. All these people, including some of our most acclaimed literary figures like Joyce and Shaw, walked the same streets as I did as a kid. But none of them was ever as lucky as I was.

Introduction: FROM DORSET STREET TO WINDSOR CASTLE

*T*t's a hell of a long way from being a penniless corner boy – my ma's phrase – hanging out around Lower Dorset Street in the 1960s, whistling at young wans and pulling their pixie-tails, to being a VIP guest at Her Majesty Queen Elizabeth's Diamond Jubilee at Windsor Castle.

I'm not suggesting for one moment that no one else from Dublin's inner city has ever been invited to Windsor Castle, but I'd bet my bottom dollar I was the only 1950s street urchin by the name of Paddy (a street urchin without an arse in his trousers, no less) to have lunch in the Queen's presence. Of all the magical events I've attended in my fifty-plus years as a music fan and a music promoter – and there have been many, many incredible experiences, believe me – this day above all others was the highlight.

Not that I am any kind of a royalist. Far from it. How could I be when my mother's first cousin was Cathal Goulding, Chief of Staff of the Official IRA? Cousin Cathal went around raiding Irish Army ammunition stores in Phoenix Park in the late 1930s, and blowing up customs huts along the border in the 1950s, much to my grandmother's disapproval. She called him 'a right blackguard' for bringing the family's good name to the attention of the local Garda Superintendent and the Special Branch. Truth be told, my grandmother's sister and Goulding's mother were diehard Republicans; nonetheless, my grandmother was having none of it.

It was Sunday, 13 May 2012, when myself and the beautiful Helena were picked up at Heathrow Airport by a driver from – seriously – the

Queen's Cavalry. The Range Rover had a Royal Jubilee emblem on its doors, and as we drove the hour or more journey to Windsor Castle, our driver asked would we mind if he listened to the end of the match. It was the Manchester City vs Queens Park Rangers Premiership clincher, where the brilliant Sergio Aguero scored that sensational late goal to give City the 2012 Premiership title. As a Man City fan, I was only too glad to agree. Honestly, what isn't to like about listening to your favourite soccer team winning a Premiership title while being driven to a castle?

So how on earth did this happen to corner boy Paddy?

A week or two before the event, I had received a call from Universal Records in London to inform me that I was to be the Canadian Tenors' special (and only invited) guest at a Royal Command Performance for Her Majesty Queen Elizabeth. However, it was not the West End theatre show I had imagined but an equestrian and musical pageant held in the grounds of Windsor Castle to celebrate her Diamond Jubilee.

Following their Dublin concert in 2010, I had become friendly with the Canadian Tenors and their agent, Richard Mills. Very few people in Ireland had ever heard of them, but I had managed to get them a 1,200-seat sell-out audience at Dublin's National Concert Hall. The singers and their agent were very impressed by my efforts. The Tenors (as they later called themselves) happened to be the favourite adopted musical group of the Royal Canadian Mounted Police, who were also appearing at the Queen's Diamond Jubilee event. The boys had kindly invited me and Helena as their only two permitted VIP guests.

Following submission of our passports, we underwent at least a half-dozen other security checks (no questions about any particular relative of mine, thank God!). We had individual instamatic photographs taken, which were pinned to a security wall with a handful of others, and then made our way to the Queen's personal backstage enclosure area. Here, she was to meet various bigwigs from the Canadian Mounted Police, the Canadian Diplomatic Corps and their guests. It was a backstage area that even the Rolling Stones or U2 would have appreciated. I have seen many, and this was like nothing I had ever experienced before. We dined in a super deluxe marquee at the same table as the Canadian Ambassador to the UK, his wife and a bunch of generals and majors, all covered from head to toe in medals, stars and military paraphernalia. Other than the ambassador and his wife, the only other non-uniformed people at our table were billionaire couple Hilary and Galen Weston (Galen died in the spring of 2021). Hilary owned Brown Thomas and was Ireland's and Canada's richest woman. They were both courteous and charming and were delighted to know we were from Ireland.

Over the decades, I have met a lot of very famous people, but I was never one to try to be too familiar or friendly with them, not even the artists whose shows I was presenting. Being a concert promoter operating at the highest level gave me a unique insight into the behaviours and personalities of artists who were idolised by millions. My job was never about hanging out with the stars, but this trip to Windsor Castle was really the stuff of dreams. I had met royalty previously, at Billy Connolly's sixtieth birthday party at his castle in the Scottish Highlands. I had met a British prime minister and an American president. Obviously, none of these people had a donkey's notion as to who I was, but still, the invitation to Windsor Castle was one for my own history books.

At the pageant, which was hosted by Dame Helen Mirren (who, of course, had portrayed Queen Elizabeth II in the 2006 film *The Queen*), there were over 550 horses and 1,100 performers. They came from almost every country in the world that Queen Elizabeth had visited in her (then) 60-year reign. The show featured South African stars from *The Lion King* musical, Cossacks from Russia, cowboys from Oklahoma, dancers from the Cook Islands, and on stage, Il Divo, Susan Boyle, and my friends the Canadian Tenors. It was also one of the last VIP appearances by the Australian entertainer Rolf Harris, who had painted an official portrait of Queen Elizabeth in 2005. (His career ended in 2014 when he was convicted of the sexual assault of four underage girls.)

When Helena and I were escorted to our seats we were amazed to be sitting just two rows behind Queen Elizabeth, almost within touching distance. At first we thought we must be in the wrong seats, but no, our special Jubilee blankets pinned with our names, Pat and Helena Egan, were spread across our cushioned chairs. I think we would have pinched ourselves if we hadn't been so dazzled by the sense of occasion.

Ireland was one of the few countries whose contribution to the event did not involve horses. Instead, it was represented by a *Riverdance* dance troupe. This was quite odd, I thought. No one would have been more aware than Her Majesty that Ireland is recognised worldwide for its legendary racehorses, celebrated showjumpers and acclaimed racing trainers. It was a spectacular event, needless to say, and as guests we were taken to the stables where 50 Canadian horses were housed. I was amazed at the attention to detail that went into bringing the animals over from Canada – it was a bigger operation than a major touring rock show! The horses had their own specially converted 707 jumbo jet, with dozens of stable hands and riders in tow. And this was just the Canadian contribution – over forty other countries flew in horses for the event.

Late into the evening, when the plush after-party was over, our royal car and the friendly driver was waiting to take us back to our hotel. Helena and I looked at each other as we made our way into London city centre. Part of us still couldn't believe what a day it had been. It was, by a long stretch, one of the most interesting of the many incredible days in my concert promoting career.

So how did this all come about for a snotty-nosed kid for Dublin's inner city, a kid who left school at thirteen and started his first job as a messenger boy on less than two Irish pounds a week? Not for the first time, I had stepped out of Dorset Street into the pages of *Hello!* magazine. It was one of those events that, when you see the splendour and affluence of the people in the photographs, you might say to yourself, mostly without any shred of envy, 'Isn't it well for them, with their Cristal champagne and strawberries.' And so it was for Paddy Egan from Dorset Street, Dublin.

It's a long story from nothing to somewhere, and for no apparent reason, it seems the good Lord chose to bless me with a life of extreme joy and adventure.

1: 'PATRICK EGAN HAS LIMITED POTENTIAL AS A STUDENT'

*T*never met my dad. In 1942, in the middle of World War II, James Egan went to England to find work, leaving my mother and their three kids to fend for themselves. My mam, Mary Cox from Summerhill, always hoped he would return. When he did, it was for just one night in August 1945, the night I was conceived. That was the last she ever heard of him until his death in 1978.

A single mother with four kids in late 1940s Dublin just shouldn't happen. Not only that, it simply wasn't allowed. There was only so long a woman alone with one kid, never mind four, married or single, could stay under the radar. A nosey neighbour, a local busybody and a supposed social call from Bishop John Charles McQuaid's Gestapo (disguised as the local, apparently friendly, parish priest) were all it took for the woman in question to have her name noted and discussed with the local Sisters of the Cross. For what reason, you might ask. For this: as a suitable candidate for imprisonment in a mother and baby home or the local Magdalene laundry. In the year of my birth, 1946, however, the local Catholic influencers had not reckoned with the fiery determination of one Margaret Elizabeth Cox, my grandmother. She was herself the mother of eight children, my mother, who was then 31, being the eldest.

'Over my dead body. My grandchildren are going nowhere,' she told Father Hurley, the parish priest of Berkley Road, when the first approaches were made in the late 1940s to have me, my older brother, Jim, and my sisters, Margaret and Carmel, split up and sent to state institutions. 'We are making arrangements for Mary and the kids to have a home near us,,'

1

she lied to the authorities, not knowing for a second where she was going to raise the one pound a week rent needed to move us into 13 Eccles Place (little more than a rebuilt stable with only four tiny rooms, no kitchen and in the back yard a very dodgy galvanised tin-roofed toilet, complete with its bum-wiping scissored newspaper squares hanging by a nail on just half a wooden door.)

At thirteen stone, Grandma Cox was an imposing heavy-set lady who wore her hair in a bun and seemed to be forever dressed in a floral apron. She was a kind and caring woman but took no nonsense from any of her offspring. 'That's for your own good,' she would say after clobbering me across the head with a plastic slipper. 'You'll remember that the next time you step out of line, ye little brat, how dare you!' I can remember her having a confrontation with the coal man for messing up her clean hallway. My eldest sister, Carmel, told me Granny Cox was the only woman on the street who stood up to the men. Sure, didn't she tell Father Hurley that her granddaughters won't be going anywhere near the Sacred Heart home for little girls and he could, if he liked, ask the Blessed Virgin for confirmation of that! At that time, women were supposed to be seen and not heard, and despite Margaret Cox's good faith she most certainly was not one to genuflect at the raised velvet-gloved iron fist of John Charles McQuaid in his attempts to interfere with her family. Thankfully for the young fatherless Egan clan, she was never going to let that happen.

No. 13 Eccles Place was just across the street from my grandmother's house at 22 Leo Street. The house in Leo Street was just one of 26 built behind the Mater Hospital, right across the road from Mountjoy Prison on the North Circular Road. It was a slightly larger four-roomed house with an outside toilet. There was no bathroom, and just two bedrooms, shared by my grandparents and their eight children. My childhood home in Eccles Place was eventually bought by my mother in the mid-60s for £340. Like so much of my past, it no longer exists, having been demolished to make way for the Mater Private Hospital. Gone it may be, but nothing can demolish the wonderful childhood memories buried in my heart and mind for the last seventy-odd years. If Grafton Street in the 50s could be 'Heaven at Eleven' for Noel Purcell, one of Dublin's most famous sons, then north inner-city Dublin was, for me, the boulevard of magical dreams.

The back lanes of Dorset Street, Eccles Street, Leo Street, Synnott Place, North Circular Road and Gardiner Street were my playground from the time I was five years of age. Our two-bedroomed house at Eccles Place

2

backed on to Eccles Street, with my back bedroom window overlooking the schoolyards of two girls' schools. Right next to our back yard was the Bertrand and Rutland High School for Girls, and beside that the Dominican Convent Girls' school, both of which were far too hoity-toity and upmarket for my sisters to attend. At that age, though, girls were the last thing on my mind. I was far too busy kicking a ball and swapping comics and hanging out around Dorset Street or up at the Royal Canal at the back of Mountjoy Prison.

When I was ten, one of my school pals, Sean Burke, who lived around the corner from me in St Joseph Street, tragically drowned while skating on thin ice on the canal near Binns Bridge. Almost 70 years later, the tears of Sean's inconsolable, broken-hearted mother are as real and raw in my mind as if it were yesterday. I knew nothing of life, never mind grief and death. I kept thinking Sean must be coming back sometime soon, that he was just in hospital, that he couldn't be gone for good. How could he die at such a young age? Dying was for old people, wasn't it? But dead and gone he was, and at that early age I learned my first cruel reality: life is here today and gone tomorrow. After Sean's death, the canal became a no-go area. I was under strict orders not to play any games near it or take short-cuts across the canal. There was really no need for the warnings because the tears of Sean's mam would be for ever engraved on my memory. To this day, I can't drive across Binns Bridge without thinking of him and how he never got to do or enjoy so many of the simple things I took for granted. We all know we are going to die at some point, but I don't think anyone ever really believes it will happen to them.

Every day, I walked to and from school, St Patrick's in Drumcondra. It was a penny for the bus fare but I rarely had it. Mam gave me tuppence every Sunday to buy sweets, and the only other money I ever saw was in her purse when she counted out the one shilling and sixpence for me to give to the insurance man from the Royal Liver Society. In later years, I often nicked two shillings out of that same purse to go to the Drummer (Drumcondra Grand cinema). I knew it was wrong, but I always told myself it was just a loan and I would repay it when I started working.

Despite ending up as a right eejit, barely able to read or write, I enjoyed my school years at St Pats. In a class of twenty-eight, I usually came in at twenty-second or twenty-third, always one place ahead of my partner in crime, Shay Hession. Two complete dunces, my mother would call us. Even at eleven, Shay had the archetypal Del Boy touch. He knew

3

how to wheel and deal in comics, Dinky cars, chestnuts and marbles. There was no fluff on Shay, but he dragged me into one scam too many and landed me up in front of headmaster Baldy O'Brien for six of his very best lashes. On top of that, my mother was summoned to the school and put on notice that any further such incidents involving Pádraig Mac Aodhgáin would result in my dismissal.

Speaking of scams, I was the one who got caught by the manager of Lemon's sweet factory for receiving stolen goods. The Lemon's building, built in the late 40s, ran alongside the Tolka River, right next to St Pats. But the thing was, Your Honour, they weren't stolen sweets, they were swaps! Shay had set up a swap for sweets deal with a couple of the young wans who worked at the factory. At 1 p.m. every Friday, Shay and I would head for Lemon's. The deal worked like this: Shay would knock three times on a factory window, which was in a lane behind the houses on Millmount Avenue. The window would open and we'd hand in a bunch of a particular type of comics – they had to be the 64-page pocket-style, *True Romance* or *Jackie*-type love stuff, absolutely no cowboys or *Roy of the Rovers*. A few minutes later, the window would open again and a box of Lemon's Fruit Gems, with 36 packets of sweets, would be handed out. The window would slam shut and Shay and I would tear down the lane with our big box of goodies. After a few weeks, however, I was fed up with fruit gems – I wanted some chocolate instead. That escapade, however, was to be our downfall. For the Easter eggs, we had to go to a different window that was next to a rear emergency door. It was on that fateful day our scam was exposed. I had just collected four big eggs from the new delivery window when with a loud crash-bang the emergency door swung open and out jumped the Lemon's manager, who grabbed me by the neck, shouting, 'Gotcha, you little gurrier!' Shay dropped his eggs and took off like Road Runner, leaving me to face the music. What happened next? Shay did alright for himself and has kept in touch with me over the years. He was a Ford Motors International Salesman of the Year in the 80s, selling more than one car a day over an entire year. Like I said, a real Del Boy.

In the 50s my mam was never home between 9 a.m. and 6 p.m. because she worked two jobs. In the morning, she was at Dublin Corporation dispensing free milk to the mothers of newborn babies. In the afternoon, she worked as a cleaner for a kind lady, Mrs McMahon, who lived in a big house overlooking Palmerston Park in Upper Rathmines. Mrs McMahon lived alone in the six-bedroom house and would pay my mother one pound and two shillings a week, way over what house cleaners normally earned then. Plus, mam never left for home on a Friday without a basket of fruit, freshly cooked scones or, sometimes, chocolates. Little acts of kindness like this are imprinted in my childhood memories: my aunt Theresa bringing home cream buns every Thursday after she got her wages; my godmother Ita giving me two and sixpence at Christmas and on my birthdays; and postal orders from Brother Xavier Cox OFM, my uncle, all the way from southern Africa. This was unusual, as the front of the postal order featured a photo of the Queen of England. Brother Cox was my mother's brother, and he was a Capuchin missionary stationed in Rhodesia (now Zimbabwe). All these little acts of kindness taught me from an early age that sharing brings joy. Two or more people end up happy when you share your good fortune around. Everyone's a winner, I thought. I have tried from my pre-teenage years to perfect the art of sharing. I have found it the most satisfying way of showing appreciation. What you give and share with those you know and love is returned tenfold time and time again. Not just in personal relationships but with strangers and in business too. You may have everything money can buy, but if you don't share it you have nothing.

When I left school at just fourteen, having just about scraped through my Primary Certificate, I could barely read or write. My mother was very disappointed and often in tears over my primary school grades. The school reports from St Patrick's Drumcondra always went something like, 'Patrick Egan has limited potential as a student, he spends much of his class-time daydreaming and his attention to the basic subjects is way short of what is required to progress beyond primary level. Unless he improves, he may well face being held back for another year in 5th class.' And held back I was, along with my ever-present school buddy, Shay Hession. Thankfully, it never impacted either of us in any harmful way. 'What am I going to do with you?' mam asked me numerous times, never really knowing the answer. 'You won't be able to make your way in the world if you can't read or write simple English.'

The only thing I got good marks in was simple multiplication and sums. That was thanks to Shamie 'Two Horses' Woods, who lived at No. 8 on our street and who taught me a few hard business facts. Shamie was sixteen, the local hardchaw, and he got his nickname because he kept horses in his back yard. He was obsessed with '50 per cent'. I'm not sure he knew half the time what he was talking about, but I was well impressed. One time he took a box of Smarties off me and emptied most of the contents into his pocket. Handing me back the almost empty box he says, 'Now we both have 50 per cent.' All I could think of was that my 50 per cent looked a hell of a lot less than his. Then he said I should have put 50 per cent in my pocket before I handed over the box. I was getting mighty confused now, but the idea of having more Smarties hidden away in the first instance seemed to make better sense to me. Another day, he asked for a bite of my apple. 'I'll only take 50 per cent,' he said. I had already eaten a chunk of it, so when he gobbed a big bite and said, 'I only took fifty per cent', I realised that 50 per cent is half of anything you have, but not half of what you started with. (Now, when I do a deal, I always take the first 20 per cent off the top for Pat Egan, and make my figures work on 80 per cent. As far as the opposition is concerned I'm putting 100 per cent on the table. My mentor, Oliver Barry, who set me up in business in the 70s, told me, 'You don't have to be a college whizz kid to cut a good deal, just ensure from the beginning to put your cut to one side.')

If grappling with school wasn't bad enough, I was grounded on a regular basis, with no street play, no football, no hanging around with pals after school. As my mother worked afternoons it was up to my granny to impose the punishment, and no better woman to ensure I spent the hours locked away in her front parlour slaving over my school work. Well, that's what granny presumed I was doing when I was actually reading *Roy of the Rovers* and *Hotspur* comics, and singing at the top of my voice songs such as 'Báidín Fheilimí' and 'Oró Sé do Bheatha 'Bhaile', trying to impress her with my non-existent vocal skills.

A newspaper seller who lived in Dorset Row used to drop a free newspaper into my mother every day. She was a single woman, and I think he fancied her. He was, I am sad to say, wasting his free newspaper because my mother had eyes only for one man – the man who broke her heart by never returning home when the war ended. After tea every evening, she would sit down at the table with me and spread out the big broadsheet newspaper, the *Irish Press*. She did not like Éamon de Valera, but since the paper was free she was happy to take what she called 'Dev's rag'. She would read me the headlines.

'Frank Aiken, Ireland's ambassador to the United Nations, says that the world must never again go to war.'
'Ronnie Delaney wins Olympic Gold.'

'Manchester United in Air Crash.'

Then it was into the hard stuff. She would give me ten lines of the headline story to learn off by the following night. I seldom got all the complicated words right, but I loved knowing what was going on in the big wide world outside Eccles Place. It was also a great introduction to a lifelong addiction – my love of newspapers. At the age of twelve, I got my very first real reading book, *No Rest for Biggles*. It felt great to hold with its shiny cover and brilliant artwork drawing of a German Messerschmitt in flames with Biggles in his Spitfire reaching for the stars. I still love to hold new books. The joy of having something that was created in someone else's mind and yet is still totally yours to have and cherish. Despite my lack of early reading skills, I have progressed to become a collector of great books, including several first editions by my near neighbour of the 1950s at 7 Eccles Street – the legendary Mr James Joyce. I have spent my entire life as an entertainment agent and promoter, and I have been privileged to present some of the world's greatest stars in concert, but I have no doubt that the simple reading skills taught to me by my mother all those years ago have helped me to become the person I am today. Without them, my life would have been less rich.

Speaking of James Joyce, when I was growing up around Eccles Place I had no awareness of the history that surrounded me in the likes of Gardiner Street, Temple Street, Eccles Street, North Circular Road, North Frederick Street and Dorset Street. Simply put, I knew nothing of my surroundings. I was aware that the Mater Hospital was next door to us, Mountjoy Prison was around the corner, Temple Street Children's Hospital was across the road and Croke Park was about five minutes away on foot. Like so many other kids, I had good reason to remember Temple Street. I had been a patient on two occasions before I was ten: first with a broken leg sustained when I fell over a skipping rope (while my sisters laughed – the cruelty!); and a more serious second visit resulting from a severe case of scarlet fever. Myself and my best pal, Paddy Byrne, were street-shore adventurers. Paddy would hold the shore up with his two hands and I would dig deep down with my bare hands into the dirty black street shit and slime and drag up a handful of mouldy grit which I would dump on the footpath. What was the purpose of such a disgusting carry-on? Well, everyone at some time or other has dropped keys or watched a penny, a shilling or maybe even a half-crown roll down the path and into a street shore. Paddy and I were after hidden treasures to spend on Patsy Pops, as you do when you're a kid. We always picked up a penny or two, sometimes more, in our searches of muddy drains, but in my case, I picked up something a whole lot worse. After investigating one dirty drain too many, I caught the dreaded fever and spent three weeks in Temple Street Children's Hospital. A lesson too late for the learning.

As a kid, I ran in and out of big tenement doorways in Dorset Street and Eccles Street, which were very rarely locked. I robbed apples from the nuns' orchard, climbed over back walls between the Dominican Convent and the Bertrand Russell schools. I played kick the can and rolled discarded car tyres around the roads. I sat playing marbles on the tenement steps and at the age of twelve I got my first goodnight kiss from my street sweetheart Rachel outside her front door at 7 Eccles Street. In 1958, Rachel's big family was one of six occupying the three-storey crumbling house. Little did I know it then, but 7 Eccles Street was the home of Leopold Bloom, star of Joyce's masterpiece *Ulysses*. To think I could have nicked that front door knocker long before New York tourist Fred Seiden stole it from the derelict building in 1966!

As we passed through local streets, my mother would always try to broaden my horizons by telling me titbits of interesting information about our neighbourhood. She would stop outside 6/7 North Fredrick Street and say, 'Harry Clarke has his workshop in that house. He makes the most beautiful church windows.' At St. George's Church in Temple Street, she told me that the Duke of Wellington, who defeated Napoleon at Waterloo and became the first prime minister of Great Britain, had been baptised and married in the church. She also told me that Kevin Barry was hanged in Mountjoy Prison and that my grandmother's nephew and her first cousin was Cathal Goulding, the IRA leader who had also spent time in Mountjoy. She pointed out the house at the end of Lucky Lane on the corner of the

• •

'Pat, for God's sake what are you on about? I only took three bottles of wine and a plate of sandwiches for the lads.' – Legendary guitarist Philip Donnelly on being caught lifting some refreshments for the support act (Freddie White Band) out of Eric Clapton's dressing room.

• •

North Circular Road where Sean O'Casey wrote many of his great literary works.

Eccles Place, just off Dorset Street, runs parallel with Eccles Street at the back of the Mater Hospital. I watched with schoolboy curiosity some of the elite of our society – Presidents Éamon de Valera and Seán T. O'Kelly, Bishop John Charles McQuaid – being greeted at the entrance by the Reverend Mother as they entered what seemed, at least in my innocent eyes, a plush and important place to be sick. In the 1950s, there were thirteen houses in Eccles Place, although at least four of them were hard to find as they were in a back lane and had been converted into a stables, a sewing shop and a two-bit printing works, the Fleet Printing Company. The Fleet, as everyone called it, was run by Flash Hugh McLaughlin, so-called because he drove a Mercedes, wore fancy wide pinstriped suits and had a blonde girlfriend who wore a fur coat and looked like Mae West. My mother called her a fashion peg. One of McLaughlin's partners was another stylish flash Harry by the name of Gerry McGuinness, who later started the *Sunday World* newspaper.

Because my mother worked mornings and afternoons in two different jobs I spent a great deal of my pre-teens and early teens, winters and summers, hanging out around Dorset Street, Eccles Street and Leo Street. I was generally just being a nuisance and sticking my nose into things that didn't concern me. That was how it happened that a very large Arabic-looking gentleman, Dr Paul Singer, hired me to keep an eye on his Bristol 404 tailfin Cadillac. That was some car! It was the first one I ever saw with silver fins like you'd see on a Dan Dare space rocket. Not at all the kind of car you'd park in a rundown back alley. To be fair, Flash Hughie drove a lovely old silver Mercedes, but it looked poor beside the Bristol 404 tailfin. Yet there it was, parked up against Shamie's front door, right in the centre of Eccles Place.

The Arab, as I called him, was larger than life. He would have been perfectly cast as the baddie in a *Sinbad the Sailor* B-movie or in the likes of *Casablanca* or *The Maltese Falcon*. An immaculate suit, black oily hair, sallow skin, at least 18 stone, with squinting eyes and a tiny goatee beard.

'Now, young lad, I have a job for you,' he said. 'I want you to keep a close eye on this new car and ensure that it comes to no harm. There's sixpence now and the rest when I get back.'

Yes, mister,' I said, 'you can count on me. Who will I ask for if there is any trouble?'

'There'd better not be or you won't get paid.'

'Yes, mister, don't worry,' I answered meekly as I watched him roll down Eccles Place and around the lane into the Fleet printing works.

'What are you doing sitting there beside that yoke?' shouted Shamie, looking for all the world like Harold Steptoe, as his horse and cart, loaded with Varian brushes, pulled up alongside the gleaming Bristol tailfin.

'Be careful, be careful! Don't hit it!' I screamed. 'I'm doing security on it for the Arab.'

'Who the fuck is the Arab, ya stupid eejit?' he asked without waiting for a reply.

The Woods family lived in the biggest house on the street. Like my mam's family, there were five boys and three girls. Father and mother Woods originally came from Tipperary. The front door of No. 8 was always open and any old Tom, Dick or Harry passing by seemed to just drop in for a mug of tea and a chat. The Woods threw the best Saturday night parties anywhere in the north inner city, especially if Tipperary were playing in Croke Park the next day. Half of County Tipp seemed to converge on Eccles Place, much to the distress of the cranky neighbours. The singing and dancing went on into the early hours and it was open house for anyone wearing a blue and amber scarf, many of them sleeping on the floorboards before heading to the big game, no doubt with a sizeable hangover to match.

Mrs Woods kept livestock in the back yard – horses, goats, hens, a duck and a couple of roosters. The hens and duck spent more time in her kitchen than the yard, perching on top of the upright piano looking for scraps while she cooked. When one of the daughters, Rosie, emigrated to America in 1957 the entire street turned out to bid her bon voyage. Even my mam, who loved young Rosie but who rarely mixed with the neighbours, had tears streaming down her face. That was it for Rosie – off to the United States to start a new life, never to be seen in Eccles Place again. Shamie was the youngest of the five sons and the street's wide boy. Every Saturday night, he would go dancing at the National Ballroom in Parnell Square. Many a Saturday night he would stick his head out the bedroom window, half-naked, his face covered in foam, and shout at me, 'Here, Egan, get me a packet of Gillette razor blades and ten Woodbine.' He'd throw me a two-shilling coin. 'And you can keep the change,' which might be as much as sixpence. Twenty minutes later, Shamie would stroll down the street looking for all the world like Clark Gable with two tiny pieces of newspaper on either side of his chin where he had cut himself shaving.

But back to Dr Singer. Three hours later, having missed my dinner and feeling like I was starving to death, I was still sitting beside the tailfin, having told my mam I couldn't leave it until the Arab returned. 'I'm not running a guest house!' she'd screamed at me. 'Get in here now or there won't be any stew left.' Ugh! I hated stew, gristly lumps of fat mutton and hard carrots – I wasn't missing anything, I thought. As it was starting to get dark, the Arab returned with Flash Hughie McLaughlin to show off his stunning Bristol tailfin. 'Good lad,' he said as his massive hand reached into mine with half a crown. 'Do a good job, get well paid, that's the secret,' he said to me, as I stared in disbelief at the shining half crown. A single and a smoked cod was my first thought. 'You can stuff your fat mutton stew, ma. I won't be having any,' I said to myself as I ran excitedly in the direction of Johnny Ray's chipper on the corner of Temple Street.

It was the first of many half crowns that Dr. Paul Singer gave me over the period of a year or more. I minded his tailfin, collected his cigars or his laundry, picked up packages from the Gresham Hotel in O'Connell Street, and brought adverts to the *Evening Mail* offices in Lord Edward Street. But the most exciting thing was the trip to Dún Laoghaire – in the tailfin Cadillac, no less! – to unload boxes of catalogues at Shanahan's, the stamp auction showrooms. Dún Laoghaire was the furthest I had ever been from Eccles Street since travelling on the train to Killiney with my aunt Theresa for a seaside picnic as a child. Little did I know at the age of thirteen, however, that the Arab – in fact an émigré from Slovakia – was to be unmasked as one of the biggest fraudsters in the early history of the Irish state. Singer spent forty days in the High Court, conducting his own defence. He was accused of setting up a stamp auction Ponzi scheme (selling rare stamps so that he did not have to pay off earlier investors). He finally walked free from the Irish courts, the prosecution failing to prove its case beyond a reasonable doubt. This made me happy, but when I asked my mother what he did wrong she just said he was a chancer, burning the candle at both ends. 'Like a gangster, Mam?' I asked, failing to get a response.

You may well ask what the gangster doctor was doing in a back lane at Eccles Place meeting up with the likes of Flash Hughie. The explanation was simple. In order to get people to invest in his dodgy stamps scheme, he had to have *Stamps for Sale* catalogues printed every few weeks. While

11

I was minding the Bristol 404 tailfin, the good doctor was overseeing the printing of the next edition of his stamp auction investment brochure in the Fleet printing works. I often wondered in later years if minding the gleaming Bristol 404 tailfin and running errands on so many occasions while the Arab printed his dodgy catalogues made me an accessory to his crimes.

In the 50s, No. 8 Sherard Street was the home of St Francis Xavier's Boys Club. It was a three-storey over-basement building facing the side entrance of the Jesuit Church of St Francis Xavier on Gardiner Street. The club was founded by a group of young men in their twenties, keen to offer young lads and teenagers from the north inner city somewhere to meet and hang out other than on street corners. The club had three levels of membership – juniors, seniors and brothers. If you stayed long enough, you graduated to become a brother (aka youth leader). My mother's brother Christy Cox was a youth leader and also one of the founding members of the club. She insisted I join – 'It will keep you off the street at night,' she told me. Some of the other great brothers and seniors who had a big influence on me and how I approached my future were Eddie Power, Joe O'Connor, Danny Fitzpatrick and Lesley Brooks. Not having a father at home, I looked up to these guys as role models, especially Eddie Power, who was the first positive role model in my life. He took time out to help me believe that I had something to offer. He gave me the responsibility of being the club's table tennis team captain. He told me before every match, 'You can win this, just stay calm and seek out your opponent's weakness.' It seems now like such a little thing, but when you're twelve it means everything and more to have someone believe in you. I met Eddie again when I was 60, and I told him how his guidance and belief had never left me.

It is difficult to put into context how influential and guiding the club and the older members were, in relation to how my later life came together. I tried hard to embrace the values taught at the club and to pass on my good fortune when it came my way in later life. In 1956, at the age of ten, it was a refuge for me. It made an enormous difference and opened a whole new world of exciting activities, including boxing, billiards, table tennis and football. It even had its own library. At twelve, I won the club's junior table tennis championship. It was the first time in my life I had ever competed and won at anything. I kept the silver trophy on our window ledge for a whole year. To cap it all off, at the end of every evening, following a guidance chat from the head brother, you got tea and a jam doughnut. I made new and loyal friends, some for an entire lifetime, and to say I looked forward to the three nights a week I spent there would be a gross understatement. Truly the happiest days of my young life were played out at this wonderful place in Sherrard Street. I was for the first time experiencing a togetherness and a sense of belonging unknown to me at home or at school.

When I was twelve, the club brought me on my first ever holiday. Fifty of us went by bus, for a week, to a Jesuit retreat house in Sallins, County Kildare. I can still see the open fire with two huge frying pans filled with dozens of brown crispy sausages and fried potatoes, which were served most mornings for breakfast. At home, if my mam had the money we got one sausage and a fried egg with fried bread every Sunday morning. It was in Sallins that weekend that I heard my first ever pop song performed live. It was 'Blackboard of My Heart' and it was played by a group of the senior lads on guitars and washboard as we sat by a campfire close to the River Liffey. I have been all over the world on great holidays, but if I could, just once more, step into the twilight zone and relive that week in Sallins in 1958 I would forego any further sunshine trips without hesitation.

Maybe it was being part of a team or just the independence of being my own person, out from under my mother's apron, but whatever it was, St Francis Xavier's Boys' Club was the making of me. I learned from the brothers that the pathway of life was best navigated through respect, truth, generosity and hard work. The club's motto, repeated at every event by head brother Mick Proctor, was 'Remember, boys, in life you reap what you sow. If you do bad things, bad things will happen to you, but if you do good things you will always have a better life.' They are words that are written in chalk on the blackboard of my heart.

My mother had blind faith in God and the Roman Catholic Church. She accepted her faith without question and bore until her dying day the shroud of guilt for ever imposed on her as a single deserted mother with four children in the Ireland of the 1940s. It was her cross and burden and she would carry it to her grave. As a single mother, she believed that only God and his Divine Mother could, and would, forgive her the sins of a failed relationship. An attractive woman in her mid-30s, she hid away from any kind of social contact. Her world was built around her four fatherless children and immediate family. For years, she knew she was the target of the local gossipmongers, and rather than give them fuel for the fire she became semi-reclusive, only leaving the house for early mass and work. As the youngest child, I escaped the torment of her guilt. Despite her loving, caring nature, she radiated her inner sense of unfairness, anger and rejection onto my eldest sister, Carmel, and brother, Jim. It was as if they were somehow responsible for the breakdown of her marriage and the loss of my father, and so she ruled our little house with a severe hand. My younger sister, Margaret, would be grounded often for disobeying her rules, and in later life, she never spoke to my mother. My sisters, in their late teens, even with regular boyfriends, faced strict curfews and had to be in before 10 p.m. 'Don't make our mother out to be a saint when you're writing your story,' said my brother, Jim. 'Maybe she was to you because you were the youngest, but to the girls and me she was as hard as nails.'

My mother had no doubt that since she was a married woman, albeit a 'deserted' one, she was forbidden to seek any kind of new intimate or romantic relationships. It just didn't happen. No man would go near her, a woman on her own with four kids. Had she even dared to smile at a single man in 1950 she would have been excommunicated and dismissed as a slut. Such was the stigma borne by a single woman in Holy Ireland of the 40s and 50s (and beyond).

Yet here she was, a young woman married for life to a man who to all intents and purposes no longer existed and whom she still desperately loved. She looked out for the postman every day for a letter or card that never arrived. She must have been so afraid and probably cried herself to sleep every night. How on earth would she manage without him? The era was still mired in post-wartime limitations – there wasn't enough food to go around and ration books were the norm. I can't begin to under-stand her situation, her despair, her loneliness and her isolation. With four children under the age of ten, her situation was almost without hope. It's no wonder the Artane Boys' Home and the Sacred Heart Home for Girls loomed large in her daily vision of survival. It's too late now to thank my grandmother, my grandfather and my mother's younger brothers and sisters for what they did for us throughout the war years and well into the 50s. If I ever wanted words to define the togetherness of home and family there is no greater example than my grandparents, Margaret Rita and Christopher Cox of 22 Leo Street, their sons, Paddy, Seanie, Michael, Seamus, Christopher Junior, and the girls, Rita, Theresa, and, of course, my mother, Mary. I should have expressed my thanks and gratitude when they were all still alive.

None of them spoke of my mother's early life, and my father's name was never mentioned. In their minds, he no longer existed. Questions repeatedly asked of my grandparents and my mother about my dad's whereabouts were politely shunned. 'Some other time,' Mam would answer, sadness etched into her face but still embracing me with a hug. Right up until the time she was informed of James Egan's death in 1987 (nine years after his passing) by the UK Ministry of Defence, where we discovered he had been working as a clerk, my mother never mentioned him again. Incidentally, there was no significant other person in my father's life either. He died in 1978, having lived single and alone for more than 32 years after leaving my mam. For all those years, he had the same room in a lodging house in Southend, England. The landlady informed us that no lady friends, or any friends for that matter, ever called to the guest house to see him. Hearing of his death, my mother's thoughts must have flashed back to that August night in 1945, when she spent her last night of passion in his arms. From that date until her death in April 2002 she would never again feel the embrace she craved. She lived for ever in hope that my father would return, but he did not and she never saw him again.

She would sit behind the curtains in our tiny house in Eccles Place and watch the neighbours go about their daily lives. She knew them all by name but rarely had more than a few words of greeting, if any, to exchange. She would attend mass almost every morning at the Jesuit church of St Francis Xavier on Gardiner Street. As always happened during the month of May every year, at 7 p.m. every evening I would be dragged in off the streets in the middle of a football match or game to recite the rosary while kneeling on the stone floor in our kitchen. ('No, you can't use a cushion! St. Bernadette or the saints never had cushions.') Sunday afternoon walks would regularly take us to Glasnevin Cemetery, where my mam would say a decade of the rosary at the grave of her grand-mother, and later her mother, who died in 1958. She insisted my brother and sisters and I went to 8 a.m. mass every morning during Lent and that we got confession once a month. She did everything she could to guide us in what she believed was the path of goodness and respect. Nobody, espe-cially under the circumstances she faced in 1945 and after the war, could have done more. She died in April 2002 at the age of 87, and her faith and belief in the Church and the power of the Lord never once waned. To me, she will for ever be a saint.

One of the very last things I did with mam before she died was to bring her back to that magnificent house overlooking Palmerston Park, the very same house that fifty years earlier she had cleaned for that kind lady, Mrs McMahon. In one of life's wonderful serendipitous moments, myself and my then partner, Caroline, had purchased it for £1 million. It was Christmas 2001, just four months before Mam died. She was weak and wheelchair-bound, and while I don't think she understood the significance of it, for me it was her victory – a victory for her and all the years she had worked every hour God sent to give my brother, sisters and me a better life. She had, against all the odds, overcome numerous challenges as a single mother in Ireland of the 1950s and managed to raise four children on her own. It was a remarkable achievement and one of which I am immensely proud. From the first day I went out to work and brought home my very first wage packet of £1. 17s, she would give me back a half crown for weekend spending. She would tell me, 'Don't be afraid to work hard, listen and learn and take it all in; the boss will always notice a hard worker.' Like my mother had done every day of her working life, I followed that advice. I believed her words and discovered my appetite for hard work was the ingredient I possessed and thrived on more than any other.

Living in a grand house on Palmerston Park, Dublin 6, one of the finest roads in the city, alongside Supreme Court judges and ambassadors was a world away from the tenements of Eccles Street in the 50s. It was one of many impossible dreams I was to chase and achieve during my fifty years in the entertainment business. As for the old days and my childhood haunts, it's true to say that my north inner-city childhood streets were once paved with a rich tarmacadam of history, but not anymore. The Mater Hospital has grown out of all proportion and it now takes up over 70 per cent of Eccles Street, Eccles Place and the back gardens of Leo Street, not to mention a large section of the North Circular Road. Dorset Street and Synnott Place have fallen into deep neglect. The buzz is gone and the area is almost forgotten. My home in Eccles Place is gone, as is that of Leopold Bloom and Shamie 'Two Horses' Woods, and Harry Clarke's workshops. Leopold and Harry Clarke will for ever be a part of north side Dublin's starring cast, but the likes of myself and Shamie are just leaves adrift in life's blustery winds.

2: 'YOU HAVE TOO MUCH TO FUCKING SAY'

One afternoon in May 1991 I received a telephone call from Brendan O'Carroll. 'Meet me in the Horse Show House. I want to talk business.'

Out of the blue, he offered me the job of managing what was then called *The Outrageous Comedy Show*. And there began the most incredible journey of my fifty years in showbiz. Admittedly, it was short-lived, just over two years, but I would not change a second, despite being dumped after doing what I considered to be a good job. I kept things together in what was the most chaotic of operations. There had been little or no pre-planning or financial accountability. 'Just do the fucking thing, Pat, and stop moaning,' Brendan would constantly tell me. This was Brendan's style. Ideas and instant solutions just flew out of the top of his seemingly ever-awake brain. His well-publicised PMA (positive mental attitude) brought immediate answers to every imaginable problem. In fact, his PMA was the driving force behind everything he did.

During our first six or nine months together, I could do no wrong. I organised a proper accounting system and put both a short-term and a long-term business plan in place. I attempted to bring in a more professional approach to dealing with venues. Brendan wrote to me twice during this period, thanking me for a job well done, and telling me I had become more than a manager to him – I was also a friend. To him, I had become a brother, like Gerry Browne, who was Brendan's sidekick, his closest friend and the leader of his comedy showband. That kind of appreciation drove me on to do the very best job I could possibly do for Brendan and his *Outrageous Comedy Show*.

Brendan wanted to move out of playing pubs, gain further exposure via television on the likes of *The Late Late Show*, play big venues and take over the world. I like to think that in some small way I kickstarted getting him noticed. I moved him out of the pubs and started booking theatre shows. On our first attempt at this, we sold out five nights at the Olympia Theatre. We jammed the Basketball Arena in Tallaght, played the Lyric in London's West End. We even beat U2 to the top of the charts with Brendan's one-camera video shoot *Live at the Tivoli*. The video sold 20,000 copies and cost a mere £5,000 to film. Brendan was brilliant, but the production quality was so awful it was an embarrassment. Yet we got away with it, and it was Brendan's first number 1 in any medium.

When no one else wanted to know, I got Michael O'Brien at O'Brien Press to take a gamble on the first of Brendan's *Mammy* books. 'There's no fucking money in this book lark, Pat,' Brendan would shout at me. 'Publishers appear to be as tight as a donkey's arse! And besides, this is taking up far too much of my time.' Sinead Troy (my assistant at the time and now a successful senior music business executive) was 100 per cent responsible for getting the final draft to print. I am not exaggerating – Sinead lived in Brendan's pocket for a week, day and night, trying to get him to finish the book and meet the print deadline. On this occasion Brendan's tardiness was due to a lack of interest (because O'Brien Press refused to pay a big advance), but throughout my time with Brendan he seldom, if ever, met deadlines. Minutes before going on air with Gareth O'Callaghan on his 2FM radio show, it would be panic stations all around. Little pieces of notepaper with lines scribbled on them would be hurriedly passed around his bunch of ham actors, which at the time included me. Brendan presented me with a gold plaque to celebrate my three appearances on the radio show *Mrs Brown's Boys*. It's still proudly on my home office wall alongside Brendan's Platinum Awards for *Live at the Tivoli* and *How's Your Wobbly Bits?*

Another of his great ideas, which never came to fruition, was a monthly comic. He had some wonderful original ideas for it, but as his workload increased the project faded into the background. A pity – I was to have my own cartoon page, 'Egan's Dilemma', and was chuffed when Brendan presented me with a copy of the original drawings. As for the books, Michael O'Brien's gamble paid off and *The Mammy* became the first of three number 1 bestsellers. Brendan thanked me in the credits of the first book for my work on getting it out: 'To Pat Egan, a true friend but a grumpy fucker.' Trust me, someone had to be grumpy, because Brendan's 'fly by the seat of your pants' approach of doing things really knew no limits. Brendan never stopped working, and he might call with some new job or idea for me to follow up on at any time from seven in the morning to midnight.

Similarly, his attitude towards money and his generosity with it was endless. Whatever else might be said about Brendan, one thing I know to be true is that he's the most giving of people. 'I hear Twink is having a mortgage problem, I'll send her five thousand ... I'm starting a painting business with Mick, who lives near me in Ashbourne. I told him to drop by the office to pick up a cheque because he needs to buy a van and paint stock – give him nine thousand ... Oh, and give a thousand to the local football club in Tallaght from our Basketball Arena show.' And on and on it went. Every Monday morning, I'd meet with Brendan and Gerry Browne at the Coolquay Lodge on the Ashbourne Road. We'd have breakfast together and divvy up the weekend gig takings. When it came to sharing the fruits of his success, Brendan never overlooked or forgot anybody, no matter how small their role. At times he'd even leave himself short of cash. His generosity was a lesson in sharing that I have come to appreciate greatly. 'Pat, here's an extra two grand for you on top of your twenty per cent; you did a great job on promoting the shows. Same for you, Gerry.' When I suggested he should invest some of this in a pension fund for himself and Gerry, he said, 'Fuck that. There's plenty more where that came from.' I did eventually get them both to take out good long-term pensions, but they stopped paying into them after I left, when finances got tighter. (Twenty years later, I got a call from Gerry after his split from Brendan asking if there was anything left in that pension fund!)

I was not around when Gerry and Brendan parted ways. The breakup came around the time of the *Sparrow's Trap* movie calamity. Having borrowed funds from some questionable sources to finance the project, they had got themselves up to their necks in debt. Gerry approached me for a loan of £75,000 to help complete the project, but I refused as I could see no way the movie would ever get finished. It never was finished and will go down as one of Brendan's only major misjudgements. He always believed, thanks to his PMA, that he never needed other professionals. He was the tea boy, the sound man, the lighting man, the producer, the scriptwriter, the director, the promoter and the star of every show and, as we have seen, so it has proved to be.

As for Gerry, a larger than life, rough around the edges guy, with a caring and happy personality, he was Brendan's best lifelong pal. Both from Finglas, North Dublin, and both from large families, they had been through some tough times together. Gerry had given Brendan his first stage break with his band at the Rathmines Inn, where Brendan did a 'blue' version of a *Mr and Mrs* stage show routine. Out of this partnership grew the *Outrageous Comedy Show*, for which Gerry, who was a good songwriter in his own right, opened the show with his three-piece band. Brendan would then come storming on stage with his off-the-wall, highly risqué comedy stand-up routine. Gerry was one of the real good guys, the kind of person Brendan needed by his side if a fight broke out, which it often did in some of the dodgy venues that the *Outrageous Comedy Show* gigged in. Dedicated and loyal beyond question, he was always 100 per cent behind his best friend. Whatever Brendan wanted done, Gerry was the man to do it.

It was truly a crying shame that Gerry never benefited from Brendan's later international success. Next to Brendan, no one – and I mean no one – did as much to help put *Mrs Brown's Boys* on the international map as Browner. Like Brendan, Gerry had many brothers and sisters, and of course, Mrs Browne was their mother. While Brendan might not admit it, it's widely believed that the *Mammy* books (and subsequent related work) are based on Gerry's mother and her sons. Brendan spent many years visiting the Browne household and by all accounts Mrs Browne treated him as very much one of the family. Brendan's eagle eye for a good comedy plot would not have missed the swings and roundabouts of a real larger-than-life Finglas family and their hard-working, dedicated mother.

O'Carroll's huge international success with *Mrs Brown's Boys* may have surprised some people, but the one person who always knew it was going to happen was Brendan O'Carroll. Blind faith and a relentless self-belief that anything he touched would turn to gold drove Brendan from project to project. Nothing was unachievable or too big to contemplate. Whether it was starting his own domestic airline or buying the

• •

'I am going to pull this fucking gig and you will end up with egg all over your face.' – John Reid, Elton John's manager, to me.

• •

Umbro sports franchise in Belgium for £250,000, Brendan believed in it. 'Brendan, I don't know a feckin' thing about sportswear,' I told him when he asked me to be involved in the Umbro deal. 'Just go over to Brussels and buy it!' he shouted. 'Stop fucking moaning and just do it.' Much to my relief, the franchise idea never happened. Neither did his 'All Aboard For Castlebar' local airline plan, which he launched off the top of his head on an RTÉ radio show.

There were no small incidents in Brendan's life. Every story was a headliner, from the partner who robbed him of his share in the Finglas Castle cabaret bar to how Brendan Grace once gave him a brand new car as a present but took the keys back when he fired him from the job as his tour manager. Ironic in the end that O'Carroll would become the international comedy superstar that Grace always wanted to be.

After just two years, I had run my course as Brendan's flavour of the month. That's how it was with him: one day you were the greatest thing since sliced bread, the next you were given the deaf and dead treatment. Anyone outside the inner family circle who got too close, or who had an opinion, sooner or later got the chop. The list was endless. Brendan liked to surround himself with people who'd say the things he liked to hear. Making any kind of a critical comment was frowned upon big time and if you so much as uttered one you would be blanked for days on end.

I heard from Gerry that I was to be replaced by Brendan's new 'flavour of the month' – multi-millionaire ex-showband performer, Tommy Swarbrigg. I couldn't believe it. 'You're replacing me with fucking Tommy Swarbrigg? Are you fucking joking me? Swarbrigg is getting *my* job?' It should be said that Tommy is a very nice man and a good promoter, but from my experience back then he had a reputation for being very tight with his fortune – the polar opposite of Brendan's philosophy of (and I quote) 'Give everybody an extra thousand pounds, Pat.'

Brendan called a breakfast meeting and gave me the bad news straight to my face. 'You're out, you're fired. You have too much to fucking say.' In fairness, his final words to me were 'How much do I owe you?' And then I was gone. I was no longer a director of 4 Cute Hoors, Brendan's slang name for our company Four Q Tours Limited, and I had to hand back my Honorary Membership of the Pig Wankers Club (another of Brendan's in-house secret societies). I had, in all honesty, lost a job that I loved. No two days in the life of Brendan O'Carroll were ever the same. It was mayhem and magic and I loved every minute of it. Like Gerry Browne, all

I ever wanted was to watch Brendan's back. To make sure I took care of business on his behalf so that he could get on with doing what he does best – making people laugh. Yes, I was hurt, not in a begrudging way, but because I had lost someone I believed at the time to be a friend for life. My ex-partner Caroline and Brendan's ex-wife, Doreen, were good pals. We had all gone on holidays together, and Brendan is my daughter Layla's godfather. None of this mattered to him; loyalty was never very high on his agenda. As his star rose in the sky he would soon be in a position to surround himself with all the yes men money could buy.

Just like a lot of others much closer to Brendan than I had ever been, I had passed my sell-by date. Unlike Gerry, I was lucky in that I had a career as a concert promoter and my own poster company to fall back on. Having an opinion was my downfall. A co-director in one of my companies, Anne Gara, who could read Brendan well, always told me to 'keep your big fucking mouth shut, let him do things his way and just keep taking the money'.

3: 'PAT, WE'RE IN REAL TROUBLE'

*T*he late Frank Mullen, a former Garda Inspector, President of Dalkey United and a mentor to Paul McGrath throughout his career, had approached me about securing ongoing corporate work for the sportsman after his playing days were over. Paul was hot property and undoubtedly the most popular personality ever in the history of Irish sport. He could do no wrong as far as the Irish public was concerned and despite his demons, thousands of fans and many businesses wanted to be associated with the great man.

One of Paul's biggest drawbacks was that he was so nice to everyone he just didn't know how to say no. He was so sympathetic and obliging. Sales of works, garden fêtes, bonny baby competitions, fundraisers, jumble sales, charity matches – you name it, Paul did it. No one, however, was paying him a penny. Paul was saying yes to stuff that he couldn't remember the next day. He made promises and then forgot to turn up. He got pressurised by friends and former teammates to turn up for gigs they had arranged. I will for ever remember the day we were at a meeting with Champion Sports when Paul took a phone call from Kevin Moran. 'Where are you, Paul?' I could hear Kevin shouting. 'You're supposed to be in fucking Waterford. You've bloody well let me down and you better get down here fast.'

Together with Frank and Paul's wife, Caroline, we put a business plan in place whereby he agreed to put all engagement requests and offers of work through my office. It worked brilliantly for close to eighteen months, probably the longest period Paul had ever been off the drink. We were at that meeting with Champion Sports because I had secured a £150,000 branding contract with them for Paul. Because of his name and personality, there were offers coming from everywhere. In his first year with our office, he was on target to earn over £350,000. I had secured short- and long-term sponsorship from a wide range of companies. As well as Champion Sports and a £40,000 World Cup contract from the BBC's *Match of the Day*, there were Slattery Travel, The Department of Health, Rehab Scratch Cards, Independent Newspapers UK, Advance Cosmetic Surgery, Moneypenny Finance Ltd, Gresham Hotel Group, GE Capital, Europa Mazda Centre, Manchester United Corporate Division, Cuisine de France, Guinness Italia 90 Reunion, Irish Poster Advertising, Spar. We were turning away dozens of personal appearance requests. Offers came in from the UK of £10,000–£20,000 for TV quiz games and store openings. He even launched the Euro in Ireland! The opportunities were multiples of tenfold. If he could stay sober he was made for life.

I set up Paul McGrath's Legends of Sport enterprises and sporting dinners. We sold out over a hundred tables at the Burlington for dinners at £2,000 a table with the likes of George Best, Liverpool manager Gérard Houllier, and legends of rugby Sean Fitzpatrick, David Campese, Will Carling and Tony Ward. We also sold out lunches, all branded in Paul's name, for refereeing legend Pierluigi Collina, Lester Piggott, and Liverpool greats Kenny Dalglish, Tommy Smith and Phil Thompson. In terms of an after-football career, Paul was simply gold dust. The highly respected *Sunday Times* columnist Paul Kimmage, a close friend of Paul's, marvelled at the transformation in his personality. In one of his columns, he wrote that he couldn't believe Paul had finally embraced a no-alcohol life and was a reformed character.

Paul McGrath's Superstars was another successful project he fronted for corporate clients. The idea had actually come from Brendan O'Carroll as part of his own team-building strategy. Starting with a big fry-up breakfast, the full day of activities included nine holes of golf, quad bike races, archery, horse riding, clay pigeon shooting and bowling. The day concluded with dinner and a table quiz at Stillorgan Park Hotel. The first event was sponsored by IIB Bank (rebranded to KBC Bank in 2008), with the then-unknown Keith Barry doing table tricks. It was a brilliant day out for everyone, and the sponsor was so satisfied with it they agreed to sponsor Paul for a twelve-month period for a fee of €35,000. There was no indication at this time of what was to come.

I had four or five Superstars bookings in the bag when the wheels started to come off the rollercoaster that was Paul McGrath Sporting

Enterprises. I first noticed a change in him at a dinner in the Burlington Hotel. He kept slipping out during dinner and on the way to the gents would grab a quick short at the bar. He then started to pick up other people's drinks at our table and knock them back. He had also been taking some sort of tablets that affected his personality. The following week he was to appear at a big event in Newcastle alongside Alan Shearer, the Premiership's goal-scoring legend. The fee for Paul's appearance was £10,000. He never turned up at the lunch event, but instead went on a bender.

I knew for certain we were in trouble the day before the launch of the Euro in Ireland, when Paul's wife, Caroline, called me from Manchester, in tears and panicking. 'Oh, Pat, we're in real trouble. When I came home from town this evening I found Paul lying in the entrance hall. He is so out of it I can't revive him. What are we going to do? He will never make it to Dublin for the launch of the Euro!' That evening, Frank Mullen took a flight to Manchester. I don't know how he and Caroline managed it, but somehow, the following afternoon they arrived in Dublin with Paul. He did the Euro launch photoshoot that evening. By the time the photos appeared on the front pages the next morning, Paul was already resident in the Rutland Clinic.

Paul made a great recovery after his stay in the Rutland, and things started to look up as 2001 came to a close. But the final breaking point for Paul and his after-football career was the 2002 World Cup. The deal I had secured with BBC's *Match of the Day* had been signed. Paul was to feature as a touchline analyst on a number of games, including Ireland's matches. It was a deal that would have secured his long-term financial future. I was so proud that I had managed to secure such a lucrative deal, and Caroline was over the moon with his ongoing recovery. Not only Caroline – everyone across the entire country wanted Paul to do well. No personality from Irish sport, showbiz, music or movies had ever had so many fans rooting for them. Along with the BBC World Cup job, Paul was to host the jumbo jet flight from Dublin to Tokyo for Slattery Travel. When he arrived in Tokyo, he was to be met on arrival by the *Match of the Day* team to begin his TV broadcasting career.

Paul caught the first flight from Manchester to Dublin, and arrived smiling, chatty and in great shape. I had gone to the airport to wish him well before introducing him to the Slattery Travel personnel, who briefed him on what his flight hosting responsibilities were – meet and greets, handshaking and so on. What happened on that flight has been well documented. Paul started drinking and had words with some of the female passengers. He was in a severely intoxicated state when the flight arrived in Tokyo. The *Match of the Day* welcoming party were shocked, to say the least. I got a call from London telling me in no uncertain terms how disappointed they were, that Paul was in no fit state to work and was being sent home to Manchester on the very next plane. Slattery Travel also pulled the plug. Inevitably, Paul lost other press and radio World Cup deals. Caroline phoned me, distraught and in tears. My farewell to him at Dublin airport was the very last I heard from Paul. I had a lot of explaining to do to all his clients, who also felt let down and disappointed, but not surprised by the bad press. What could and should have been a glittering after-football career lay in ruins.

In 2009, I received a call from a friend of Paul's, a lovely woman by the name of Juanita, whom I had met previously, with Paul. She asked if I would look over a book contract he had been offered. I agreed, and she sent the contract to me by courier. I asked for a small percentage in return for my advice. It was a fair request, as I felt I had lost a sizeable amount of money on my previous association with Paul. I never heard back from her. The book contract was for €450,000.

4: 'ARE YOU PAT EGAN? YOU WENT OUT WITH MY MOTHER'

*B*ecause my mother was out working two jobs a day, I spent most of my school years and early teens living at Grandma Cox's house at 22 Leo Street. I loved her home cooking, steamed jam puddings, apple tarts and corned beef and cabbage, but most of all I loved her house because she had a radio. Not everyone had a radio in the 50s. My grandma's favourite programme was a lunchtime family drama, *The Kennedys of Castleross*, sponsored by Cadbury. The rest of the sponsored shows were music-driven, and depending on who the presenter was you might, with a bit of luck, hear Elvis or Al Martino. There was no such thing as a DJ at Radio Éireann until the late 60s. If the presenter was Jimmy McGee or Liam Devally, you got a stomach full of Joe Lynch, Brendan O'Dowd, or the Emerald Girls Pipe Band. In today's terms, their musical tastes were equivalent to being sentenced to a lifetime of listening to wee Daniel O'Donnell. On the other hand, if the presenter was Ken Stewart, you got a splash of Bill Haley, Fats Domino, Bobby Darin, Elvis, Ella Fitzgerald and even the occasional Nina Simone track. At that time, Ken lived in a very different world from anyone else in Irish radio. The Americans were making the greatest music ever heard and the only people at Radio Éireann who knew anything about it were Ken Stewart (and in later years the great Larry Gogan and BP Fallon).

I can remember to this day the first time in 1960 that I heard Ken play The Drifters' song 'Save the Last Dance for Me'. It was simply spellbinding, sending a frozen arrow down my spine. It was the sexiest song any fourteen-year-old had ever heard:

You can dance every dance with the guy
Who gives you the eye, let him hold you tight.
You can smile every smile for the man
Who held your hand 'neath the pale moonlight.
But don't forget who's takin' you home
And in whose arms you're gonna be.
So darlin', save the last dance for me.

I relived the song over and over in my mind. I could see the beautiful blonde Lana Turner on the dance floor. I was at the Home Farm football club Saturday night hop in Whitehall and had burst through the doors just in time for the last dance, and I could see Lana on the floor, desperately seeking me out over some guy's shoulder. I brushed him aside just in time to hold her passionately for the last dance of the night. I was in teenage heaven. I can still hear the burning passion in the voice of the Drifters' lead singer Ben E. King, pleading 'darlin', save the last dance for me'. That song, more than any other in my teen years, was responsible for driving my love of pop music.

I only discovered in recent times that the story behind that song is dramatic and romantic beyond words. Paralysed by polio from birth, Doc Pomus, the writer of the song – who also wrote dozens of other 60s hits, including a bunch of songs for Elvis Presley – said that the inspiration for it came to him at his wedding reception when, confined to a wheelchair, he watched his brother dancing with his new wife while he himself was forced to sit it out and watch as she danced and smiled. He remembered that day writing the lyrics on the back of his own wedding invitation. 'I had a moment of jealousy, which is evident in the song's second verse, as I watched my new wife enjoying herself. I just wanted her to know she could dance her heart away, but not to forget to save the last dance for me and in whose arms she was going to be.'

Much to my mother's annoyance, from the time I became a teenager Saturdays and Sundays were spent in one of three local cinemas. There was the Drumcondra Grand, directly across the road from my school, St Pats, on the main road to Dublin airport; the State, and the Bohemian, which were both in Phibsborough, just up the road from my home in

Eccles Place. I always tried to see the main movie twice. I would arrive a few minutes after it started and make a point of ensuring that the head usher saw me hanging around the lobby in advance of buying my ticket. Eight pence, one shilling, or one shilling and sixpence were the prices. When I could, I bought the one shilling ticket because it made me feel I was a more serious movie buff. The only time I went to the eightpenny flea seats was Sunday afternoon at the Drummer so I could sit next to some young wan I fancied in the hope of getting a kiss and cuddle, which in 60s slang was called a 'ware'. Don't ask, because I have no idea how or why the word 'ware' was related to kissing. Sunday movies tended to be crappy Randolph Scott, Audie Murphy cowboys'n'Injuns stuff, yet no one cared or noticed what was showing. It was all about parading around the aisles showing off your hip new threads and ensuring you scored that 'ware' from the coolest girl so that you could brag to your mates that you hit it off with the lovely Susan Moore in the back row at the Drummer.

For my more serious movie viewing, I always went to the State. It was so much more modern and fancier than the Drummer or the Bohemian. Once in the door, slipping into the blackness, I lived in a dream world somewhere beyond Hollywood's twilight zone, where I fought great World War II battles with John Wayne, rode side by side with Zorro, and lived in a jungle tent with Tarzan. But what I loved most of all was falling in love with Jayne Mansfield. I had never seen a woman with such curves. Why I wondered, did the girls I knew not have curves like Jayne? After seeing the exquisite Lana Turner in *Madame X*, the stunningly beautiful Ava Gardner in *55 Days at Peking*, and the sexy Gina Lollobrigida in *Trapeze*, I decided that there was no point falling in love with just one woman when I could fall in love with them all. And so began a never-ending romance with all things related to entertainment, movies, music, stage musicals and beautiful women (not all of them, of course, but more than fourteen-year-old me could, perhaps, have ever imagined). Every pleasure, of course, has its price and mine was a clattering from my mother across the back of the head and legs with a wooden spoon for spending two hours longer at the same movie than my sisters had.

I left school at thirteen with my Primary Certificate under my arm. Even now, I still wonder how the hell I ever managed that. I spent a few wasted months at Denmark Street Technical College before starting work as a messenger boy for hardware firm Thomas Corry in Smithfield Square, Dublin 7. I hated the bike's big wicker basket on the front and the flat

29

metal plate under the crossbar with the words 'Thomas Corry and Sons' painted between my legs. I knew it wasn't cool to be a messenger boy and I didn't want any of the girls I fancied in the Dominican Convent in Eccles Street to know I had a rubbish job. When I could, I used my own bike to deliver parcels all over the city from hardware shops in Drumcondra to Thomas Street. I took bank lodgements to the National Bank on College Green every morning. Corry's had a big wholesale warehouse and stylish showrooms, stocking everything from hammers and nails to fancy Swiss watches. Fifteen guys worked in the big storeroom, another four on the showroom floor. In the first floor offices, much to my delight, there were ten young female typists, and four men, working in different departments: Accounts, Stock Control, Imports, Advertising. Thomas Corry, the boss, had a private office on the same floor, as did the general manager, Patrick Stapleton. I knew if I worked hard I could get a promotion to the showrooms or stock control departments and so I made it my business to impress Thomas Corry with my work ethic and punctuality. I would be sitting outside the office door every morning when he drove up to help him with his briefcase and files. He drank a lot of water, and I had to fill six large bottles every morning and place them on a table by his desk. I'd keep an eye on them during the day and make sure to refill them. He would ask me about my home life, how my mam was and what my dad did. I think when I told him my dad had died in the war (which was, of course, a lie) he felt sympathy for me. He promoted me to the stock control department, and gave me a pay rise from £1 17s 6d a week to £2 2s. (I always told people my dad died in the war because I knew no better. As far as I knew he was dead. Later, my brother Jim told me that Dad, who was a mechanic, got a job fixing Spitfires during the final years of the war and that he had suffered shell shock at an RAF airbase that had been attacked by the Germans during the Battle of Britain. This part, I believe, was true.)

The stock control department was incredibly boring. Every incoming delivery and sales docket had to be recorded. My department boss was Tommy White, who lived in Francis Street. I liked Tommy, who was a very promising middle-distance runner and a big Jim Reeves fan. I looked up to him a lot because of his success as a runner, but he didn't like me getting any credit from Thomas Corry for a job well done. Neither did he like Cliff Richard, which upset me greatly as Cliff was my early teen idol. In the early 60s, Cliff Richard and the Shadows were the hottest act in pop music. Cliff's first hits a few years earlier – the likes of 'Move It', 'High Class Baby', 'Living Doll' – were, as John Lennon later said, the only decent British rock'n'roll songs of the late 50s. I liked Cliff so much that I started the Irish branch of the Cliff Richard Fan Club, along with Pam Hojes (a sister of my pal Jon Hojes, who died tragically young, at just nineteen, from leukaemia) from South Circular Road. The year before he arrived in Dublin for a concert in 1962 had been the pinnacle of his career. *The Young Ones* movie had been a monster success and the Dublin Adelphi shows were sold out months in advance. He was the first major star I met. As head of the fan club I went to Dublin airport to greet him and the Shadows. It was a real big buzz to shake hands with one of the world's greatest teen idols. He invited me to come to the Gresham Hotel but with hundreds of screaming girls jammed up against the hotel front doors, I was turned away, feeling greatly disappointed. The concert was amazing and even today, despite him having turned into a bit of a rich man's Daniel O'Donnell, I still play his early hits. 'He's a queer,' Tommy White would say to me, but in 1962, I had no idea what being 'queer' was about. To me, Cliff was just the coolest cat around, so none of that mattered to me. Tommy would taunt me in front of the younger office girls and I hated him for it. 'He's a queer and a jessie and you're just like him, Egan – a right sissy!' Betty 'Beehive' Whelan, one of the young typists and the office sex symbol would stand up for me. Aah, Betty! I can still see her miming to 'Bobby's Girl', the Susan Maughan hit, and looking for all the world like Alma Cogan with her beehive hairstyle and her black mascaraed eyes flashing as she waved her big boobs towards my blushing face. Betty had class and was a very tough cookie. None of the store lads would risk flirting with her or giving her a gentle smack on the bottom, even in 1962. Betty stood her ground as a woman – the guys could admire but God help those who dared to touch.

After three years at Corry's I got another promotion. I was now on the sales team and on £4 a week. I liked the sales job a lot – meeting customers face to face was more interesting. Our new boss, Thomas Corry Junior, had taken over following his father's sudden death at the age of 59. Not even all that daily intake of water could save him. I'd really liked old man Corry. He had been good to me as a kid and was a proper old-fashioned boss. He didn't have to, but he shared the company's success with his staff. He brought us all to his fine house in Rathgar at Christmas for an annual party and everyone got a gift. I remember the joy of receiving a wallet with a ten-shilling note inside. It was another lesson for me in the art of sharing. I have discovered in my life that the joy of giving far outweighs any other gesture of kindness. Thomas Corry Junior was a very cool guy. Then in his late thirties, he had worked at Pinewood Studios making films like Cliff's *The Young Ones*, the *Carry On* series and the early James Bond films. What a comedown, surely, even if he was the new boss. Moving from the glamour of the movies to the nuts and bolts hardware business – how boring for him, I thought.

As I approached my eighteenth birthday I felt the time had come to move on. From my desk in the stock control office, I had watched from the office window the set for the Richard Burton movie *The Spy Who Came in from the Cold* being built in Smithfield Square. After work, I'd hang around watching the lighting technicians prepare for a shoot. I saw Claire Bloom have her make-up enhanced just before the director shouted his instructions to roll the cameras. It all seemed so much more mysterious and exciting than the daily grind over a bunch of stock control ledgers. I knew in my heart that I had bigger fish to fry and chasing the showbusiness dream was one of them. I had enjoyed almost four years at Thomas Corry and Sons. It was a great company with great people who had taught me the value of hard work and honest endeavour, but it was time for me to say goodbye (just like James Darren, whose 'Goodbye Cruel World, I'm Off to Join the Circus', was number 3 in the American Top Ten in 1961).

From the age of fourteen to eighteen, Billy Fury, Dusty Springfield, Del Shannon, Gene Pitney and Roy Orbison were my other great influences. I have never lost my love for any of their classic hits. Even today, when I hear a great 60s track, I feel the pangs of nostalgia grabbing hold of my senses. I regret never getting to see Roy Orbison on one of his many Irish tours back then. He was, alongside Elvis, one of the truly great stars of popular music. In recent years, I toured a brilliant Australian Roy Orbison tribute act starring Dean Bourne. When I say that listening to Dean is like stepping back in time I'm not lying. He has perfected Roy's brilliance like no other. There is nowhere to hide when you're imitating Roy's singing – you either have it or you don't, and very, very few do have it. Every night

'It's wonderful to get this rehearsal done before we start our UK tour.' – Neil Sedaka at the Point in Dublin. Cue an audience in uproar having paid £45 a ticket.

on his Irish tour when Dean stepped up to the microphone to sing 'Only the Lonely' you could hear an audible gasp of 'Oh, my God, he sounds just like Roy.' I can vouch for that, not just on one song but throughout his entire performance.

Later in life, I was privileged to be Gene Pitney's tour promoter and friend. He would email and phone me regularly to chat about business and touring. He loved Irish audiences and would always say that he wished the UK ones were as good. In 1988 he released, with Marc Almond, a duet version of his 1967 UK number 1 hit single, 'Something's Gotten Hold of My Heart'. He had tried for several years to come up with another duet of one of his previous hit songs and came upon the idea of doing 'Backstage', his 1966 smash, with the Irish boyband Westlife. Louis Walsh was the Westlife's manager as well as a big fan of Gene. They always met up in Gene's dressing room before his gigs. Like a real fan, Louis would always arrive with a bunch of Gene's old albums under his arm for signing. Louis agreed that it was a great idea, but Westlife said no. Gene was bitterly disappointed. It was a great song and would have worked a treat. Gene was a brilliant songwriter – he had written 'Hello Mary Lou' for Rick Nelson and 'He's a Rebel' for the Crystals and had recorded with Phil Spector – and he was not used to younger acts refusing his help. I tried to console him by saying that the Westlife guys were too young to appreciate his work. 'They just don't know their pop history,' I told him. Gene died on 5 April 2006, alone in his hotel room after a performance in Cardiff, after a heart attack. That alone was a shock – clean living, slim, in great shape and always careful about his diet, he was the last guy you would think would be a risk of a heart attack. He worked out regularly and drank only red wine. As a promoter, I had lost not only one of my favourite artists but also a good friend. I presented a tribute concert, *24 Hours from Tulsa*, in Gene's honour at the National Concert Hall in 2015. The place was jammed to the roof. MD Eugene McCarthy put a brilliant band together and the great Tommy Carey was spellbinding as he recreated Gene's voice and sang his hits. The show went on to play a ten-date UK tour to great acclaim.

Billy Fury's *Play it Cool* was another movie I saw at least half a dozen times. I played the *Sound of Fury* album non-stop. It was great rock'n'roll but, as with Cliff, his record company steered him away from the wild rock image and into becoming a middle of the road pop act. *Play it Cool* also featured Helen Shapiro, another favourite of mine from the 60s. I loved her big hit 'You Don't Know'. The lyrics said everything I was feeling in my teen years – oh, why did I have to be a teenager in love? Billy Fury never lost that really cool rock'n'roll touch, and when I first heard 'Halfway to Paradise' it seemed to mirror every pain I was going through as a very shy teenager. I was always a sucker for 'teen loser' love songs. I saw myself time and time again as the guy who always lost in love, the guy who never got to kiss the best-looking girl. Songs like 'Why Must I Be a Teenager in Love', 'Earth Angel', 'Crying', 'In Dreams', 'Backstage', 'Tell Laura I Love Her', 'You Don't Know' and 'Halfway to Paradise' were my daily diet of tearjerkers and heartbreakers. I would retreat to my tiny bedroom and play the same songs over and over to console my cracked heart – broken in pieces because Yvonne Cooper, another gorgeous Sandra Dee lookalike attending the Dominican Convent next door, had refused to smile at me!

Those tear-jerking songs were the soundtrack of my teenage years. I was a Billy Fury clone, trying always to look moody as hell in my sister's fancy silver blouse, collar tipped up at the back of my neck and my black hair slicked over in a DA – duck's arse – style with the help of half a bottle of Brylcreem. I would stand in front of the mirror with my mam's hair-brush in my hand and replicate Billy's sexiest shapes while I mimed to his great hits 'Jealousy' and 'A Thousand Stars'. I would fall to my knees on the last line of 'Halfway to Paradise' and plead to my dream school-girl Mary Maguire, 'So near yet so far away … Don't leave me halfway to paradise.' These regular dramas happened as I listened on my £7 portable 45 rpm record player that I'd bought on the never-never when I started working. I had seen it in the window of Telefusion in Henry Street for three shillings a week over 36 weeks. I must have gone down to gaze at it ten times before eventually buying it. At fifteen, this was the biggest purchase of my short life. 'You're going to make every payment yourself, and if I catch you playing that sinful and unholy 'St Therese of the Roses' on it I will dump you and your record yoke out the front door,' said my mother. Mario Lanza could sing 'Ava Maria' in our house till the cows came home, but she hated the Malcolm Vaughan's hit about Saint Therese and would turn off the radio the moment it came on.

Of all my favourite 60s star singers, one stood head and shoulders above all the others – I adored Dusty Springfield. Dusty's real name was Mary Isobel Catherine Bernadette O'Brien. She had a strong Irish back-ground and was 'one of us', I thought, which brought her even closer to my heart. From the first day I saw her on a tiny ten-inch black and white television screen, singing 'Island of Dreams', she was my pop teen queen. I loved her style and dress sense, and I followed her career right up until she died from breast cancer in 1999. Seldom a day goes by that I don't play at least one of her hits. She made my teenage heart ache. No one could sing a tear-jerking ballad like Dusty. Her pleading voice was mesmerising. When I read her biography years later I realised that she lived her tragic and tormented life through every line of those soul-destroying songs. I could feel her heartbreak and pain in every word. The really great thing about Dusty was that when I played her songs I felt she was singing only to me. 'All I See Is You', 'Losing You', 'I Close My Eyes and Count to Ten', 'How Can I Be Sure', 'Take Another Little Piece of My Heart', 'Goin' Back', 'I Just Don't Know What to Do with Myself' – with her teased beehive hairdo and her deep black mascaraed eyes, Dusty could look inside my soul like no other singer. She understood my teenage desperation and anguish, my tears, my shyness and the sorrow of my rejection. In recent times, I was sent a quote, something that Dusty had said in later life about her time as a teen idol. 'A lot of my life has no real clarity. I look at those old TV clips and I remember the circumstances very clearly. Was I happy or not happy? If I don't identify with the person it's because I invented her in the first place. She was an invention but my own invention. I was my own Svengali.'

As you can tell, my early teenage years were full of short-term but intense crushes. I fell in love on a monthly basis with every good-looking girl I met, even girls I had never even spoken to. Elvis used to sing, 'Wise men say, only fools rush in.' Well, I can assure you, I was the biggest sixteen-year-old fool in town. If it wasn't the stylish Patsy O'Connor it was the beautiful Susan Moore or the lovely Breda Quigley ... These days, when I am running gigs at the National Concert Hall or Bord Gáis Energy Theatre, I often get approached by young women in their 30s or 40s who say, 'Are you Pat Egan? You went out with my mother. Do you remember her?' 'Yes, of course,' I always answer. 'I remember her well, she was a beautiful girl.'

My favourite teen queen, Mary Maguire, was a Dominican schoolgirl who lived in Gardiner Street across the road from St Francis Xavier's Church. An Audrey Hepburn lookalike, she was just the most beautiful young lady I had ever seen. I definitely wanted to marry her. Mary's brother, Pharaoh, was a good pal, and one of the few teenagers back then who had a car - a Hillman. Pharaoh was a big guy for seventeen and when he discovered that Mary and I had a thing going on, he wasn't happy at all. 'Tell Egan I will kill him,' was the word on the street from the big brother. When my mam was at work, Mary would come to my house every evening after school to hear the latest hits coupled with an inevitable kiss and cuddle. One afternoon, Pharaoh drove up behind me on Dorset Street, jumped out of the car and dragged me across the bonnet threatening to knock my head off. 'Stay away from my sister, do you hear me? You're too old for her!' he shouted before dumping me on the ground. Mary was fifteen and I hadn't yet celebrated my seventeeth birthday.

Now you know why I was forever singing Dion and the Belmont's hit '(Why must I be) A Teenager in Love'.

5: 'PAT, THERE IS £7,500 IN THAT BAG'

*O*ver the years, I have promoted some great comedians and some very weird and wonderful ones too. They include Freddie Starr, Jasper Carrott, Phil Cool, Kevin Bloody Wilson, Bill Bailey, Lee Evans, Eddie Izzard and, the most famous of them all, Billy Connolly. I have no hesitation in saying that I liked Freddie Starr and got to know him well on and off stage. I should add, though, that the time spent with any touring act, is, at the most, ten days (Billy Connolly was the exception, as he often stayed in Ireland for up to six weeks at a time). Most acts, however, are here and gone in a few days. The person you meet is wearing the celebrity mask and you don't get close enough to get to know them. In my case, getting close was never the objective – their managers were much more interesting. With the talent, it was more a case of 'Hello, I'm Pat, the promoter. Welcome to Dublin,' and then it was goodbye the following day. With Freddie Starr, the scenario was very different. He liked you to be close by all the time, at breakfast, dinner and after the show. He would call me at 5 a.m. to come to his room and have tea and toast. Freddie had a thing about toast. It was never four pieces on a plate but fifty slices on a tray with a monster pot of jam. He would fire six or eight at me and tell me to get stuck in!

'Now,' he would begin. 'Tell me about the deal you made with my manager, Leon. How much are you paying me? Tell me the truth now, Pat.' Leon Fisk was Freddie's longest-serving manager. He was a former member of the Dallas Boys, who in the 1950s were Britain's first-ever boy band. I liked dealing with Leon, he was fair and straight, and I would always say that to Freddie. At the same time as asking me about what his deal was for the Irish dates, Freddie would then reach under his bed, pull out an envelope and say, 'There's five thousand [or seven thousand five hundred, whatever it might be] cash in there. I want you to put it on such and such a horse in the two-thirty at Newmarket.' I did this on at least three occasions during the tour, and Freddie picked a winner each time.

'Oh, and by the way, Pat, I want a masseur in the room at around four p.m.'

'No problem,' I assured him. 'The hotel will sort one for you.'

'No, Pat, you big softie. I don't want one of 'those' massages, I want a bit of action.'

He ended up arranging for a hooker, and she spent the rest of the night with him.

Years later, in 1994, I had to laugh out loud when I heard the news story about Freddie's gardener being charged with the alleged theft of £40,000 worth of his jewellery. When questioned by the police the gardener claimed the jewellery had been given to him by Freddie as a reward for oral sex over a period of five years. However, the gardener was discredited in court when he was unable to state whether or not Freddie's penis was circumcised. The gardener was found guilty and sentenced to 15 months in jail. Knowing Freddie as I did, I wouldn't be surprised if he and the gardener had something going on, because nothing about Freddie would surprise me.

When I told Freddie's manager, Leon, that he'd asked about our deal, he said his client trusted no one, especially not managers and promoters. 'Do you know that he once emptied a briefcase with close to twenty thousand pounds in it into a fire at the home of a UK promoter?' Seemingly, Freddie got wind the promoter was trying to shaft him. Leon, who was there at the time, recalled Freddie in a rage shouting at the promoter at the top of his voice. 'See this fucking money? You think I need this shit? Nobody screws Freddie Starr!' And he dumped the promoter's money into the blazing fire.

Freddie was totally off the wall. A hellraiser, eccentric, outrageously rude and totally unpredictable. Everything he did was extreme – there was no middle ground. His routine was sexist and sometimes racist, and like his contemporaries Benny Hill and Jim Davidson, he ended up being left far behind in the late 80s when a new generation of alternative stand-up comics like Billy Connolly, Lenny Henry and Ben Elton rose to prominence. During the 70s and 80s, however, Starr was out on his own. He was a brilliant impressionist and singer who had few equals in the business at that time. In the early 80s he was the UK's highest-paid entertainer, earning over ten million per year. He had fabulous homes in England and Spain, Rolls-Royces, speedboats and racehorses.

From my experiences of touring with him, I was aware that sex and Freddie went hand in hand. When he was on tour in Ireland (and, presumably, elsewhere), it was evident that he had an insatiable appetite for women. It seemed as if he had his own shuttle service from Dublin and Belfast airports, collecting and dropping off a variety of showgirls, housewives, prostitutes. All were mature women and certainly not teenagers. A lot of the time he was more to be pitied than laughed at. My own assessment of him as a person is that he was desperately alone, without a true friend in the entire world and never truly loved by anyone for himself. 'No one would give me the time of day, Pat, if I wasn't Freddie Starr. No one wanted to know me when I was plain old Frederick Fowell' (that was his real name). He looked at me with a pitiful face. 'Would you?' Like his hero Elvis Presley, Freddie's twin brother died at birth. At six years old, Freddie stopped speaking and was taken into care after suffering physical abuse at the hands of his drunken father. As a little boy, his father had asked him to jump off a table. 'I'll catch you,' his father promised. Freddie jumped, but his father took his arms away and he crashed to the floor, breaking both legs. His father picked him up, stroked his hair and said, 'Never trust anyone in your life. Not even your own father.'

The most bizarre event in my time with Freddie took place at the Olympia Theatre in the late 80s. Freddie's stage set was worked out with split-second timing. He could have done it in his sleep. In fact, after three years with him even I could have nearly done it. (This was another reason for the decline in his popularity – he never altered his stage routine in twenty years. Unlike a Billy Connolly gig, if you saw Freddie's show once you never needed to see it a second time.) On the night in question, Freddie was not happy with his band's performance and he cut his set short by five or more minutes. Walking off stage he called me aside. 'Those fucking guys have played out of tune all fucking night. I'm disgusted with them. Make sure you don't let them leave the dressing room until I have a go at them.' I could hear him from the hallway shouting orders at the guys. Twenty minutes later he came out and said, 'Fuck them, they can stew now.' Almost two hours later they were still in the dressing room while Freddie and I waited outside the door.

'Now, Pat,' said Freddie. 'This all came about because you gave the guys a gift.' I couldn't deny it. Along with giving the visiting acts personal embroidered towels, one of the things I like to do is present band members, purely as a 'Welcome to Ireland' gesture, with a small gift of miniature Irish whiskeys. Deadly serious, Freddie asked me not to give them any more gifts. 'You're spoiling them!' To emphasise his point, the following night Freddie played an end-of-run midnight sold-out show. He had an after-show steak dinner delivered to his dressing room just before heading to Dublin airport, where a private jet was on standby to fly him directly to London. It was long after midnight when we arrived at the airport, and as we passed through an almost deserted departure lounge, I spotted two of Freddie's band members preparing to settle down for a few hours' kip on a lounge bench. In my experience, in the 60s and 70s touring bands rarely received hotel or travel fees. They were paid a straight gig rate and had to sort their own digs and transport. The two musicians were clearly saving a few bob by kipping at the airport and getting the first flight out next morning. I knew Freddie quite well at this stage and didn't think twice. 'Freddie, there's two of your lads settling down for the night, would you not give them a lift back to London?' He looked at me and said very sharply, 'Pat, did I not tell you the other night that they played out of tune? Fuck them!'

Freddie wanted more than anything else to crack America. He did two tours opening for the UK crooner Engelbert Humperdinck, and despite doing reasonably well he couldn't understand that in the USA he was as close to an entertainment nobody as you could get. Used to getting VIP treatment wherever he went in the UK, stateside he was ignored. 'I had to queue for dinner tables in shitty restaurants,' he told me. 'When I went to TV stations for interviews I'd be left waiting in reception for ages and then I'd discover the presenters had no idea who the fuck I was.' In the late 90s, he came back to Dublin, with another promoter, for his last ever Irish show at Vicar Street. It did poor business. He called me on his way to Dublin asking me what hotel he was staying at and could I get his favourite chauffeur (Michael Devine) to pick him up. 'Freddie', I said, 'you're not working with me this time, you're with someone else.' I tried to explain that I wasn't promoting the show, but he wasn't listening. 'Ah, Pat, why is that? Do you not love me anymore?'

Looking back now I suppose I should have seen it was all going to end in tears. Starr's career was already well past its peak in the early

2000s, but there is no denying that the accusations of a link to Jimmy Savile and the 2012 Operation Yewtree investigation into allegations of historical sexual abuse were the final nails in his performing career. One thing I know for sure is that in our ten-year relationship, Freddie may have talked about sex from breakfast to bedtime, but he never uttered a word or even a hint about liking young or underage girls. While suffering a great injustice by being held on bail for almost two years during Operation Yewtree, his work dried up. In the end, due to insufficient evidence, he was never charged in connection with the investigations, but it was far too late; the damage had been done. Counterclaims by Freddie against his accusers failed, and he was left with a £1m legal bill. From being Britain's wealthiest entertainer in the 80s, with a reputed fortune of over £12 million, he died penniless in the Spanish town of Mijas in 2019.

6: 'MR MORRISON HAS CHANGED HIS MIND'

A few weeks after leaving Thomas Corry and Sons, I heard on the grapevine that a new club, the Five in Harcourt Street, was looking for a resident DJ. It was paying £6 a week for four nights spinning the latest hits. Money for jam to my ears.

Brothers Tony and Brendan O'Brien were the owners. Brendan, who was in his late twenties, drove a Jaguar, and his girlfriend, a hairdresser, was a real Judy Geeson (the star of *To Sir, with Love*) lookalike. I thought he had it all. *Now that's living*, I said to myself. The Judy Geeson looka-like was an ex-girlfriend of movie maker Noel Pearson – another guy who had it all and seemed to be always one step ahead of the pack. At that time he was managing The Chessmen, one of Ireland's better and more progressive showbands (the group featured Robert Ballagh on bass – the very same bass guitar that Phil Lynott would conquer the world with in the 80s. Bobby Ballagh, meanwhile, would achieve justified international acclaim and status with his original artworks and paintings). I was a big fan of the original Chessmen, fronted by Alan Dee, and saw them play regularly at the Matt Talbot Hall in Granby Row. Next to The Freshmen, The Chessmen would rank as one of Ireland's better showbands. Strongly influenced by The Hollies, they had real stage presence and style – maybe be too much for the bland and musically restricted ballroom market.

The older of the O'Brien brothers, Tony, was the businessman at the Five Club. He called the shots and gave me the job because I had the best collection of 45s (vinyl singles). At the interview, he liked the fact that I knew who had written every hit he mentioned and that I would be spending half my wages on new releases. That part was easy for me. The difficult part? I suffered from panic attacks and stage fright, and while I knew every singer, songwriter and record producer on the planet, I really should never have been let near a stage. I had a confidence problem and would blush like a rose anytime I met new people or was the focus of attention. I hated it and overcoming it took years. In fact, I never really have overcome it, and it was only because I could give real informed introductions to the records I played that I survived my early years as a DJ. At one time, I was so stage-shy I would hide behind the band's big Marshall guitar speakers so that no one in the audience could see me. As time passed, I gained more confidence, and while I was never comfortable on stage I did lots of live appearances across the country for *New Spotlight* magazine. Jim Aiken was good to me and I compèred various shows he promoted, including The Hollies, The Who, Fleetwood Mac, Gary Glitter, and the *New Spotlight* Award shows at the National Stadium. I have no doubt that lack of confidence held me back big time, both in my early career and later as a businessman. Maybe it was an education thing, but it hurt me inside to know that I was as good or better at my job than most of the competition but I didn't always get the results I deserved.

When I told my mother that the Five Club would pay three pounds a week more than I was getting in my Thomas Corry job, she smiled and said, 'Maybe you're not such a dunce after all.' Of all the 60s beat clubs, the Five was unique. There was something wild and adventurous about being a member – the exclusivity of having your own membership card gave you a genuine sense of belonging to an elite band of swinging 60s ravers. It was almost like a secret sect, a community of working-class Dublin teenagers who had discovered a musical nirvana. Songs first heard at the Five would remain for ever in my memory. 'What Becomes of the Broken Hearted', 'Reach Out (I'll Be There)', 'Midnight Hour', 'Don't Let Me Be Misunderstood', 'You Keep Me Hangin' On', 'Light My Fire', Hey Joe', 'Keep on Running', 'Out of Time', 'Don't Worry Baby', 'Jumpin' Jack Flash', 'River Deep, Mountain High', 'I Heard it Through the Grapevine', 'When a Man Loves a Woman', 'Be My Baby' ... Friendships built around those great music sessions have, for many, lasted an entire lifetime. To my mind, no generation of teenagers ever had it so good.

The Five had competition from the Go-Go and Apartment clubs on Abbey Street and the Scene, Parnell Square, but they weren't in the same league in terms of hipness or class. The O'Brien brothers ran a tight ship and kept the Five exclusive to regulars and guests only. New members had to have a friend or family member already enrolled to gain a membership card. As the club's resident DJ, I had VIP status, which included having my name and image painted on the wall of the entrance hall. I was also allowed twelve free Club Orange drinks a week and I could bring in one girl-friend a night free of charge. The club had its own Mod brigade (including Eammon Purdy, Pete Thompson, Tony McGowan, Charlie Gaughran, Liam McGuinness, John May, Jim Langan, Dan Healy, Mike O'Brien, John Hojes, Eamonn Dignam, Pat and Gerry Keys, Tom Canavan, Ben Appleby and Kevin Fennell) as well as the coolest 'chicks' in town (including Margie Purdy, Anita Gioconda, Theresa Ryan, Bernie Ennis, Christine Wall, the Hill sisters, Maureen Higgins, Margaret Canavan, Dodo McGovern, Emma Sutcliffe). Of the three hundred or more kids who went there every week, I would have been on first name terms with 90 per cent of them. Even today, fifty years on, I still meet dozens of old members via Facebook. In the late 90s the club's old doorman, Matt Sheffi, organised a reunion that was a genuine blast from the past. The first impression when you have not seen someone for thirty years is 'How the hell did we all get so old so fast?' I am planning to hold a fiftieth celebration reunion in early 2022.

In my three years spinning discs at the Five, I don't recall ever seeing a fight, but then there was no alcohol sold in clubs or dance halls in the 60s, and not surprisingly no one missed what they never had. Tony Johnston was my fellow DJ at the Five. He filled in on my nights off and built up a great following by playing super-hot sounds from the Stax, Chess and Atlantic labels. Most of the music Tony and I played at the Five hadn't been heard anywhere else in Ireland. No one on Irish radio was playing Motown in 1967. We imported our own sounds from the US and the UK, and Tara Records (Tara Street), Murrays (Ormond Quay) and Dolphin (Capel Street) were the only record shops in Dublin worth visiting. Another younger stand-in DJ at the Five who had the potential to break

• •

'You turned on the fucking house lights while I was still on stage. You're finished! It's your last gig for me!' – A raging Paul Brady to me at the National Stadium, April 1986, when the bouncers turned on the lights while Paul was doing his encore. It was nearing 11 p.m. and the bouncers did not want to miss last orders at the nearby pub.

• •

into the big time was Pat Arnold, who went on to front one of the popular Dublin pirate stations, but with only Radio Éireann to choose from all the club DJs had limited options for progressing their careers.

I went to Radio Caroline North, an offshore radio station, in the mid-60s. Britain had introduced the Marine Offences Act, which was intended to prevent pirate radio stations broadcasting in the UK, and in response the station was giving two fingers to the establishment. I went for an interview with the station's founder, Ronan O'Rahilly, at his office in Grafton Street. 'I hear you're popular in Dublin,' he said. 'How would you like to join us on Caroline?' The wages were £15 a week and as many cigarettes as you could smoke. The roster was three weeks on, one week off. The ship was the MV *Caroline*, anchored in Ramsey Bay, off the Isle of Man. I sailed out in a strong gale on a small fishing boat from Greenore, near Dundalk. I had to make three attempts to get off the fishing boat and climb up a rope ladder dangling from the *Caroline*. It was, let me tell you, a hairy experience. It got worse. Before my first time on air, my nerves started to go. My anxiety levels increased and I had a panic attack. The fact that everyone was so unfriendly made it worse. The station head, 'Daffy' Don Allen, had little time to teach me the ropes. I made only two broadcasts at the 6 a.m. news slot before really cracking up. I came home with my tail firmly locked between my legs. But I didn't hang around. Not wanting to face my friends at the Five, I went straight to London, where I stayed with my then-girlfriend Maureen Higgins, whose dad owned a pub on Ladbrook Grove. I stayed in London for almost a month before returning to work at the Five Club.

Visually, the Five had a lot in common with Liverpool's famous Cavern Club: two small parallel tunnels, each about twenty foot wide and maybe 150 long, with a small stage at the far end. The resident band was the Liverpudlian-influenced Creatures, led by Liam McKenna, with Frank Boylan, Ray McDonald and Brian Harris. They had one single, 'Turn Out the Light', which got a US release, but international fame never followed. Keith Emerson and The Nice were the biggest 'name' act ever to play the venue. I can still recall the crew and bouncers trying to engineer Emerson's gigantic Hammond organ down the narrow stairs and on to the tiny stage.

We didn't know it at the time, but the Five and its members were at the forefront of a major sea change in cultural Ireland. The mid-60s marked the beginning of the end for the showband generation. The power of Church and State over Irish family life was for the first time being openly questioned. Teenagers were no longer buying the Catholic prop- aganda agenda – they were setting their own. The writing was not only on the wall, it was scrawled in big bold letters. Our Beatles-influenced generation would no longer be suppressed and censored to death. The beginning of the decline in teenagers going to mass can be traced back to this time. Clubs like the Five, the Moulin Rouge, the Go-Go and the Scene were the footprints of a new, more diverse, more open society. The Five Club was featured in the acclaimed, if controversial, 1967 documentary *The Rocky Road to Dublin*, which argued that Ireland was dominated by cultural isolationism and religious discipline but that the winds of change were evident in Dublin's nightlife, and nowhere more so than in the beat clubs of Dublin. If I could have one wish it would be to step back to the 60s and a wild Saturday night at the Five. It really was the mecca of Irish beat clubs.

I had only been working at the club for six months when John Coughlan, the managing editor and publisher of *New Spotlight* magazine (which at this time was selling over 50,000 copies a week) offered me the job of beat group columnist as well as being the magazine's roving reporter around the nightclubs. He agreed to pay me £4 a week. John was a special guy; young, dynamic and a trailblazer in the magazine business of the 60s. He was always good to me and I admired his style, and his beautiful girlfriend Margaret. Here I was, barely able to write more than a few sentences, moonlighting around the best nightspots and flashiest joints in town as a columnist and writer. Without Liz McHugh, *Spotlight*'s advertising manager, and the great Jim Flanagan (a former RTÉ news editor working there part-time, who subbed all my stuff) I'd never have got anything into print. The then editor of *Spotlight*, Michael Hand, one of the legendary Drogheda twins, would shout across the office at the top of his voice, 'Get in here fast, Egan! You're fucking illiterate!', and would tear strips off my journalistic endeavours. Michael didn't like me. Luckily, his identical twin, Jim (a pioneering promoter and future manager of the Dubliners, Paddy Reilly and Brendan Grace), was the complete opposite. Jim could not have been more helpful to me, always offering tips and support. I liked Jim a lot, but he had a reputation as a rabble-rouser and troublemaker in the business. He thought nothing of calling people out who he regarded as posers and spoofers. There was no grey area with Jim.

He either liked you or he didn't, and I was grateful many times that he saw some good in me.

Incidentally, Jim's son Brian came to work with me twice over a twenty-year period. His contribution to the success of Pat Egan Management was immense. Brian, one of the most likeable guys working in the business, was highly respected by all the acts that his father managed, but none more so than The Dubliners. Brian brought the Dubs into our stable of acts and we did dozens of shows with them over the years, including one of my proudest moments as a concert promoter – the 50th Anniversary concert at the Royal Albert Hall. I had previously promoted shows in the UK, but had always wanted to see my name on a poster outside the famous London venue, and thanks to The Dubliners I achieved that in 2017. All the boys in The Dubliners, but especially John Sheahan, Ronnie Drew and Barney McKenna, held Brian in great esteem. It was also thanks to Brian that I became a close pal of Jim McCann. Jim had the most beautiful voice, which was so evident in his classic hit song 'Grace'. Sadly, following a diagnosis of serious throat cancer, Jim lost his ability to sing and had to live a very restricted life. He was also a highly talented photographer and graphic artist and became our concert artwork designer. During the last three years of his life, I would spend two enjoyable afternoons every week at his home, which he shared with his beautiful wife, Phil (who sadly died just a short time after Jim), discussing our new show artworks. I just loved his company. Jim could be the funniest, sharpest man. Billy Connolly once told me he regarded Jim as one of the greatest storytellers he had ever met.

Just how highly Brian Hand was regarded by The Dubliners was illustrated when Barney McKenna died. Eamonn Campbell, Seán Cannon and sometime Dubliner Gerry O'Connor wanted to continue playing as The Dubliners, but the group's leader, John Sheahan, was against them using the name. John felt that after Barney's death and fifty years on the road, it was time for the final curtain call. He did not want any Dubliners tribute bands touring, yet the demand for The Dubliners and their music was still out there across Europe. Eamonn and Seán, who had been part of the group for over 25 years, took serious offence at being called a tribute band. They were highly upset with John but determined to continue playing. It was Brian Hand who stepped in and muted the anger when he suggested that Eamonn and Seán continue playing, but as 'The Dublin Legends'. John Sheahan reluctantly accepted the compromise. The Dublin Legends (minus the very popular and likeable Eamonn, who died in 2018, but with other ex-Dubliners, including Seán Cannon and Gerry O'Connor) continue to tour, spreading the gospel of The Dubliners and their music far and wide. The same production touring team (led by Pat, Tom and Gary O'Brien) who for fifty years drove hundreds of thousands of miles across Europe with Ireland's most legendary folk heroes, are also still on the road with The Dublin Legends. As Barney famously said at the group's 50th Anniversary show at the Royal Albert Hall, 'It's too late to stop now, lads.'

Spotlight magazine's office was originally in Grafton Street, on the top floor of a building right next to the offices of the Royal Showband. The lovely Carol Hanna, later to become Louis Walsh's mentor and the doyenne of Irish showbiz agents, was secretary to TJ Byrne, the trail-blazing manager of the Royal Showband. Carol would feed me the very latest titbits of showbiz gossip for my behind-the-scenes weekly column 'Where It's At'. She would give me the lowdown about who was with whom, and who was doing what with so and so, and did I know Red Hurley was dating the fashion model Grace whatever-her-name-is? Her final words to me after our catch-up chats were always, 'Now remember, Pat Egan, I never told you that.'

Spotlight was selling so well that John Coughlan and the entire team moved to the Creation building at the fabulous old John Player factory on Botanic Road. There were five or six offices allocated to *Spotlight* and the rest were for *Woman's Way* and other Creation magazines. In a bizarre coincidence, one of the co-owners of the Creation group was none other than 'Flash' Hughie McLaughlin, friend and printer to my old pal, the notorious Dr Paul Singer. Flash Hughie's co-owner at the stunning new building was his old mate Gerry McGuinness, the dapper boyfriend of the very beautiful Eurovision star Alma Carroll. Hadn't the two boys, like myself, come a long way in ten years? From a shitty tin shed printing works in a back lane behind Eccles Street, where they printed the swindler Paul Singer's stamp auction brochures, to owning this historical John Player building on Botanic Road? You had to hand it to them. Two guys well ahead of the game. (In 1973, McLaughlin and McGuinness would launch the *Sunday World*, Ireland's most successful ever tabloid newspaper.)

Heather Parsons was eighteen when I first met her. With bewitching dark sultry eyes and a mod Mary Quant hair style, she was a junior writer with *Woman's Way*. We dated a couple of times and later we became good friends. A brilliant journalist, Heather was the outdoor type. She enjoyed wild and adventurous hobbies like parachuting and river kayaking while I preferred to stand on dry land and watch her daredevil stunts. In later life, she was the editor of the *RTÉ Guide* and the *Sunday Tribune* magazine. In 1985, she went to Medjugorje, where the mother of God had allegedly been appearing to six young people over a four-year period. Heather went not as a pilgrim but as a sceptical Protestant journalist. What Heather witnessed in Medjugorje in 1985 changed her life for ever. She had gone there expecting to find Marian propaganda, but what she found instead was a life-changing gospel. Three and a half years after she first travelled to Medjugorje with the intention of exposing fraud, she was received into the Catholic Church. Heather later published a best-selling book, *A Light Between the Hills*, which is still in print. If you are ever feeling lost, alone or in a dark place, Heather's experience at Medjugorje will give you a reason to question and believe. I know it did for me.

The first office in the *New Spotlight* headquarters was occupied by the blustering accounts head, Jim Slye. Jim, a really nice fella but as tight as a duck's arse, would, with his unique stutter, try to bluff his way out of paying me my £4 4s a week until the end of every month – or longer if he could get away with it. 'Pat, Pat, later, later – I'm just sorting out last month's sales figures. I will have that for you on Monday.' Of course, Jim always failed to say which Monday. As can be viewed from the attached 1966 hand-scribbled note, Jim kept a very detailed bookkeeping account of payments of all the contributors, not in a wages ledger but on the back of a scrap of notepaper. The total wage sum for all of us was £27 6s a week. To be honest, I would have worked there for nothing. It had to be one of the best jobs any teenager could have wished for. It was a unique and pioneering time in Irish show business, never to be repeated. It might not have had the street cred of *Rolling Stone* or *New Musical Express*, but as far as the Irish scene was concerned *New Spotlight* was the last word, the bible of Irish showbiz.

The rest of the new offices were split between Liz McHugh (advertising) and Jim Carew (design and art). In later life Liz founded CSL event management, which handled all the corporate business for Leinster rugby, Irish Horse Racing and the FAI. The large newsroom functioned on a come and go basis – there was myself, the late Shay Healy, Donal Corvin, the legendary Sammy Smyth, Jim Flanagan and future media whizz kid James Morrissey. Editor Michael Hand and managing editor John Coughlan shared the remaining offices. Star writers BP Fallon and Larry Gogan seldom came to the office. Exactly what Michael Hand did as editor I still have no idea whatsoever. He was forever out at lunch or on a touring freebie to America or Killarney with one showband or another – the Capitol, the Royal, the Dixies or Dermot O'Brien's band. When he did come to work, he and John Coughlan would hold court with a right bunch of redneck hill-billy showband managers who included Peter Dempsey, Charlie McBrien, Jim Hand, Connie Lynch and, occasionally, Oliver Barry and Seamus Casey. They would always be joined by Sam Smyth and Donal Corvin. I was allowed to deliver the coffee tray but never allowed to stay. 'Leave it, Egan, and get out. You're too feckin' nosy to be in here!' Michael Hand would bark. Within minutes, roars of laughter would fill the office corridors as one story after another about life in the showband fast lane were unloaded.

Spotlight gave me an in with lots of the cool dudes of the day. I got into all the clubs in town for free and every group was keen to get on my right side in the hope of receiving positive coverage and improved ratings in my monthly *New Spotlight* popularity polls. The best bands of the early years, 1963–66, included The Four Keys, The Greenbeats, The Chosen Few, Peter Adler and the Action, The Creatures, The People, The Next In Line, The Method, Sam Mahood, Soul Foundation, Them, The Strangers, Vampires, The Gentry, and Taste. I got to know a lot of the guys well, but some would get the hump if I made any critical remarks in my column. On one of my regular nights in Club Arthur, when I was doing my DJ spot before the band came on stage, the manager of Some People, Jackie Johnston, had a go at me, knocking my turntables off the stage and boxing me about the head, before a bouncer jumped in to drag him away. Jackie later became Dickie Rock's manager and we became pals. By then we were able to laugh about the old times when what I wrote in my column was the be-all and end-all for groups trying to make it big.

The bands making the biggest international waves in those early days were Bluesville, with Ian Whitcomb, who amazingly got to the American Billboard Top Ten with 'You Turn Me On'. Belfast's Them had UK hits with 'Baby Please Don't Go' and 'Here Comes the Night'. Taste were starting to break big on the UK progressive scene. Moses K and the Prophets, another Belfast band featuring former members of Them, also entered the UK Top 50. In 1967, The People, featuring the great guitarist and gentleman Henry McCullough, were signed to Track Records by Chas Chandler, the manager of guitar legend Jimi Hendrix. Chandler changed the group's name to Eire Apparent, and Hendrix produced their only album, 1969's *Sunrise*.

In 1960, a few years before I got involved in the business and when I was still playing in the streets around Leo Street and the North Circular Road, flash cars were a real rarity – it was even rarer to see one being driven by a guy in his teens. I watched every day with admiration a silver sports saloon that would tear at speed across the North Circular Road from Innisfallen Parade into Leo Street and then on towards downtown O'Connell Street. The guy drove like Steve McQueen and looked like the American teen star Bobby Darin. He was always dressed in fancy Ivy League jackets and he had style written all over him. His name was Michael Ryan. A drummer with The Four Keys, one of Ireland's first rock groups, he was to me a star. At that time, I had no idea who the dude was, but I knew I wanted some of what he had and that, somehow, I was going to get it. Years later, when I met Michael, we laughed about his silver sports car. He told me the car was in bits back then, and that when he drove around sharp bends the passenger door would fly open and the passenger seat, which wasn't properly fixed to the floor, would take off into the distance. A total gentleman, Michael played a major role in the development of the club scene in Ireland. He opened one of Dublin's most popular clubs, Sloopy's, towards the end of the 60s, and later a number of hotels. In 2020, he was featured on an RTÉ *Nationwide* special showcasing his spectacular gardens and home in Killiney. I knew back in 1960 when I first set eyes on the guy that he had it all. I was right.

I was constantly writing in *Spotlight* about Van Morrison complaining about the lack of attention he and Rory Gallagher were getting from the Irish media and RTÉ Radio. So much so that I once received a letter from Van's mother in Belfast with up-to-date news on what Van was up to in the USA, where he had headed to after quitting Them. She thanked me for keeping Van's name alive and said that he appreciated it very much. I was delighted because I had always believed, even in 1965, that Van was Ireland's greatest ever rock star. In the early summer of 1967, an airmail parcel landed on my desk at *Spotlight*. It contained two copies of a song called 'Brown Eyed Girl' and a letter from Van thanking me for all the coverage I was giving him in *Spotlight*. I believe that these were the very first copies of the song anywhere in Europe. I played the track hundreds of times at my Five Club sessions long before it was ever heard on Irish radio. You can imagine my excitement when a year or more later I got a phone call from Van at the *Spotlight* office. At first, I was sure it was a hoax call from Sam Smyth and Donal Corvin, both of whom were always winding up people. But no, this really was Van himself calling.

Because he tends to grunt, it was hard to make out what he was saying, so I had to ask him to repeat himself. He said he was staying at a rented house near Navan and would I like to drop down for dinner. Would I *what*? Finally, I thought, I'm going to meet my rock hero. I had been wanting to meet him for years. How great was this? Dinner with Van Morrison! The house was a country estate with a long driveway. I was welcomed at the door by Van's housekeeper, who invited me to wait in the drawing-room and told me, 'Mr Morrison will be with you shortly.' Twenty minutes later and there was still no sign of Van. Eventually, the nice lady returned. 'I am so sorry', she said, 'but Mr Morrison has changed his mind and he won't be dining this evening.' I recall walking back to my car in disbelief and disappointment. I did eventually meet the great man twice in later years when he played concerts for me at Cork City Hall and the National Stadium. I suffered his rudeness and his abrasive manner when he blanked me, first while we were travelling in the same car on a completely silent three-and-a-half-hour journey between Dublin and Cork; and again when we met at the Shelbourne Hotel, when he merely grunted at me and walked away. I never took it personally because I knew that was his style. Just working for the man was enough for me. The contracts for Van's Irish gigs in the 1970s came from my one-time pal, Paul Charles at Asgard. The deal was 90/10 of the net box office in favour of Van. Deals of 90 per cent in favour of the artist were unprecedented in Ireland at that time. They had only been introduced in the USA by Peter Grant, the notorious manager of Led Zeppelin. Yes, Paul Charles and Van 'The Man' were right on top of their game.

I got to know Rory Gallagher and his brother Donal in the 70s. I had travelled up and down to Cork with them a couple of times and they came in to visit our new store, Rainbow Records, in Patrick Street, Cork, soon after we opened. They invited me to meet their mother at her home in Douglas, and I recall Rory demonstrating a brand-new VHS player, which had just come on the market. It was the first one I had ever seen. I was about to get married at that time and Rory sent me a wedding gift that took pride of place in my new home. If Van was rude and obnoxious, Rory was the other extreme. He made time to chat to everyone and his manner was a bit like that of the young Phil Lynott: soft, shy, courteous, always welcoming and friendly. Because he worked mainly in the UK in the late

60s, with Taste, we didn't see much of Rory on the Dublin club scene. He played one of his very few club dates at the Scene in June 1967. He had come to meet me for an interview and to visit the Five Club on the evening his Stratocaster was stolen. The well-circulated photo of me with Phil and Rory was taken outside the Five. I'd told Phil I was doing an interview with Rory for *Spotlight* and he asked if he could come along as he was very keen to meet him. At this stage Taste were starting to break big in the UK, but Phil had not yet joined Skid Row. It was the first meeting of two guys who would go on to become, alongside Van Morrison, the biggest names in Irish rock history. Both would die too young, when they were in the prime of life. I was fortunate to have known both of them and I cherish the memories of having seen both of them perform on stage many times.

My DJ business was boosted big time by the *New Spotlight* job. I was now resident DJ at both the Five and the Moulin Rouge. In addition, I had afternoon hops at the Crystal Ballroom and the TV Club. I had my own lunchtime disco stand in Switzer's Store in Grafton Street, where I'd interview stars like Keith West (*A Teenage Opera*) and Steve Howe (Yes). The former owner of Shelbourne FC, Ollie Byrne, paid me £20 for my Saturday night spot at his Countdown Club. I liked Ollie a lot. He was generous and had a really good heart, but it was hidden behind a wild and volatile temper that you just didn't want to be on the receiving end of. Ollie deserves to be remembered not for the few times he strayed off the highway, but as the pioneering, hardworking entrepreneur that he was, even if he did have an unorthodox way of doing business. His achievements in Irish soccer are colossal and for me, he will always be a larger than life, loveable rogue.

Ollie's sidekick in many of his early club projects and promotions was young Terry O'Neill from Phibsborough, who went on to manage the original Thin Lizzy and later ran McGonagle's, the rock club in South Anne Street, for millionaire Bill Fuller. The couple might well have been the original template for the television series *Minder* in reverse. Ollie certainly had a touch of Arthur Daley about him but, unlike Arthur, he was well able to handle himself. Terry, on the other hand, was a brilliant ideas man but seemed to be forever chasing the shadows of Ollie's misadventures.

For *New Spotlight* in the 60s and early 70s, I interviewed some big names of the era –American rock'n'roll legend Gene Vincent, the brilliant Del Shannon, Julie Grant, David Garrick, Cliff Richard, and Twinkle – who all had Top 20 hits in the UK and the USA. In June 1967, I met one of my early teen idols, and yet another tragic figure, Del Shannon. Del was a true original with his unique falsetto trademark vocals, and in the mid-60s he had massive hits in the USA and Europe with some of the best self-written written singles of the day – 'Runaway', 'Hats off to Larry', 'Swiss Maid', 'Little Town Flirt'. Shannon was also well loved in Ireland for the showband hits he wrote for Joe Dolan ('The Answer to Everything') and Tony Keeling and the Graduates ('Kelly'). He was also the first American artist to cover a Beatles song (his version of 'From Me To You' was a US hit). I caught up with him when he was late finishing a television spot at RTÉ and he asked me to jump in the car with him and do the interview on the way to the airport. What I remember most about the short trip from Donnybrook was his reaction to the news that came on the car radio that Israel had invaded Egypt and the Six-Day War had begun. 'Oh, my God,' he said. 'That is a war that will never end.' And how true his words have turned out to be. Suffering from severe depression, Shannon shot himself on 8th February 1990. Like Roy Orbison, Shannon made a huge impression on many of his younger contemporaries. The Traveling Wilburys honoured him by recording 'Runaway' and Jeff Lynne produced his posthumous 1991 album *Rock On*. He was inducted into the Rock and Roll Hall of Fame in 1999.

Another teen idol, Gene Vincent, came to Ireland in 1971, very close to the end of his career. Ollie Byrne booked him into the Countdown Club for what turned out to be one of Vincent's last ever shows. I did one of my first big interviews with him for *New Spotlight* and I can still visualise him as if it were yesterday. Dressed entirely in black leather, he was seated in a worn-out armchair in Ollie Byrne's office, with a bottle of Jack Daniels in one hand and a guitar in the other. At the height of his fame, Vincent had been a genuine 50s rock'n'roll superstar. He was favourably compared with Elvis Presley in 1956, when his 'Be-Bop-a-Lula' was a significant US hit. He had appeared with my one-time crush Jane Mansfield in the movie *The Girl Can't Help It*, appeared on the Ed Sullivan Show and even had his own star on Hollywood's Walk of Fame. In Australia, Vincent had topped the bill with Little Richard in front of a crowd of 72,000 fans in a Sydney football stadium. Yet here he was, in what could only be described as a nightclub dump on a Dublin back street, playing to fewer than 150 people. In 1960, while on tour in the UK, Vincent and Eddie Cochran (of 'Summertime Blues' fame) were involved in a high-speed car crash. Cochran was killed. Vincent broke his ribs and collarbone and further damaged an already weak right leg, which resulted in him having to drag it behind him as he walked. The line I recall most clearly from our interview was, 'You know, I should have been bigger than Elvis.' Indeed ... It was sad and pitiful to watch him drag himself across the Countdown floor to the stage. He died a few months later, another victim of fame's fleeting embers.

Along with my *Spotlight* 'Beat' and 'Where it's At' columns, I also wrote a regular 'Rave Girl' section. Myself and photographer Martin Nolan would go around the clubs talking to the trendiest mini-skirted teenagers about their favourite fashions, showbands, groups and movie stars. I met a lot of the swinging 60s 'rave girls' in Sloopy's, Zhivago and Moulin Rouge. Stunning young ladies like Pam Conway, Irene Greeley, Carol Dickson, Marie Allen, Gay Flavin, Wendy Hutchinson, Breda Joyce, Martina Kelly, Ann Newman, Tina Doyle and Pauline Carolan, a lot of whom went on to successful modelling or media jobs. I was also hanging out with the coolest dudes in town, guys like Brush Shiels, Phil Lynott, Pat Quigley, Mike O'Brien, John Farrell, Cahir O'Doherty, Henry McCullough, Danny Hughes, Tom Canavan, Eamonn Purdy, BP Fallon, John Hojes, Derry Glenn, Tony Bradfield, Deejay Lee, Terry O'Neill, Robbie Brennan, Jimmy Fanning, Tony Johnston, and Steve and Smiley Bolger.

Was I having a ball and a blast and everything in between? In the terminology of the day, you bet your sweet ass I was. By the late 60s I was the busiest DJ on the club scene, and I was making big money, well over £150 cash a week. What I was doing with my newfound riches is best summed up in the words of George Best: 'I spent all my cash on birds and drink and the rest I just squandered.'

Boy. It's Larry Mullen

My lifelong pal Adrienne Foley was looking after the Tape Shop in Duke Street in 1978. I generally just dropped by at lunchtime to pick up messages, drop off stock and have a sandwich in Graham O'Sullivan's across the street. I always had a real soft spot for Duke Street – there was a great cosmopolitan buzz about the place. You had three definitively Dublin bars within yards of each other – The Bailey, Davy Byrne's and Kehoe's. The Jean Machine, Brown Thomas, It's a Beautiful Day, Sullivan's Deli, fashion designer Pat Crowley and Golden Discs were at one end and I was at the other. It was a real advantage to have a shop in such a trendy street. I would work the shop some lunchtimes, and on Adrienne's day off

55

I never ceased to be amazed at the string of beautiful woman who passed by my front door. It was just non-stop. I had a short-distance imaginary visual love affair with all the regular ones although I spoke only to a few. Some were very famous elegant, sophisticated and very highbrow, like the Guinness heiress Miranda Guinness, Countess of Iveagh; she was a regular customer, as were writer Edna O'Brien, singers Alma Carroll and Sandie Jones, fashion queens Judy Hill, Lorna Townsend, Karla Elliott, Alison Doody and, well, the list goes on and on. The few women I did get up the courage to speak to – Margaret Stenvall, a Pan Am air hostess, and Philomena Prescott, a woman ten years my senior who ran the Fáilte Ireland office in Dawson Street – soon gave me the bum's rush when they discovered I had a girlfriend. You can't blame a guy for trying I suppose, and as my mam used to say, 'the cat can look at the king'. During my thirteen years on Duke Street, I certainly did look at the beauty queens of Grafton Street as they glided daily like models on a catwalk past my shop window.

All that has nothing whatsoever to do with U2, but it was on Duke Street in 1978 that a good-looking blonde kid named Larry first came to my notice. One lunchtime, Adrienne said that a lad had dropped in that morning looking for me and that his band, U2, wanted to play support to The Stranglers at a gig I was promoting at the Top Hat, Dún Laoghaire. I didn't know if The Stranglers had their own support act – sometimes visiting acts do and sometimes they don't. A few days later, Larry dropped in again but missed me. In the meantime, I had discovered that I did need a support act for The Stranglers gig, and so when Larry came in the following day I finally met him face to face. I recall him being polite and mannerly, saying that they would really appreciate getting the gig as The Stranglers' audience was perfect for them. I told him that £50 was all I had to pay the support and if he was happy with that the gig was his. He was happy and U2 opened the show at the Top Hat in front of 2,000-plus punk fans. I don't remember a lot about the show or their performance, but I do recall having lots of grief at the front door from fans who had no

* *
'Christy will see you now, Pat.' – Michael Devine, Christy Moore's driver, as he ushered me into the back of Christy's transit van for an audience in his mobile dressing room, which came with armchairs and all mod cons.
* *

tickets. The other thing that stands out in my memory was being called backstage to the dressing rooms just as The Stranglers were about to go on. I found their tour manager ranting:

'That fucking bass player from the support band lifted two bottles of wine out of our dressing room.'

'Listen,' I said. 'I'll get you two more, no problem at all.'

As the band made their way to the stage, lead singer Hugh Cornwell shouted, 'Tell those fuckers they will never open for The Stranglers again!' Little did he know that before too long U2 would never again be looking for a leg-up from any band.

To give The Stranglers full credit, their career has spanned five decades and while never touching the heights of their support act that fateful day in 1978, they have outlived almost every other band of that era. Other punk groups I promoted in those years included Buzzcocks, Eddie and the Hot Rods, Stiff Little Fingers, The Undertones and New Model Army. I recall the SLF gig like few others. The venue was the Mansion House on Dawson Street, and from the minute we opened the doors there was blood on the floor. It was total mayhem. The bouncers had just stopped one fight when another and then another broke out. I was never so pleased to see a gig end. The fighting went on throughout the entire 75 minutes the band were on stage and when it was over it continued out into Dawson Street. Running battles continued into Grafton Street and was still going on half an hour after the gig ended.

To be fair to Larry Mullen Jr, he never forgot I gave U2 that spot at the Top Hat. I have bumped into him a few times over the years at airports and at awards ceremonies, and he always makes it his business to shake hands and say hello. He remains modest and soft-spoken, friendly and approachable. At the time, giving them the gig meant very little to me, but over the years, as their fame grew and record sale went through the proverbial roof, I was continually asked did I really pay just £50 to U2 for that gig? I was chuffed in 1985 to receive from the band a special personal engraved platinum award for *The Unforgettable Fire* album in recognition of 300,000 sales that our poster company contributed to the marketing and advertising success of the album. It hangs proudly on my home office wall next to my Brendan O'Carroll, Eric Clapton and Billy Connolly awards collection.

During my days running the Waterfront Rock Café, I was for ever trying to come up with ideas to promote the place and increase its profile.

Lucy Gaffney, who in her early marketing days before she became Denis O'Brien's right-hand assistant, worked at the *Irish Press* and later 98fm. Despite her elevation to the very top of Ireland's female business rankings, Lucy, the most classy and elegant of ladies, has remained exactly the same bubbly, attractive, charming woman I first met at the *Irish Press* offices in Parnell Square some thirty-five years ago. Way back in March 1992, I received a call from Lucy, who was then at 98fm. She told me that the radio station and U2 were auctioning something special for a combination of Alone, the Simon Community, and the Dublin Aids Alliance. The 'something special' was actually quite unique: the boys had signed one of the Trabant cars that had been used during their *Achtung Baby/Zooropa* world tours, and that I should bid for it on the live-on-air 98fm auction and put it on show at the Waterfront. The car's number plate was U298FM. The Trabant was an East German motor car, if you could call it that. It looked like a large lawnmower with a roof. One of the doors was damaged, and it appeared to be made of very light plastic cardboard, which I was informed was made from cotton waste and phenol resins from the Soviet Union. It had no fuel gauge, no indicators or turn signals, no seat belts, no external fuel door, and it ran on a mixture of gasoline and oil. It had been painted a mix of psychedelic pink with bright blue squares all over and signed in big block capital letters by the band members. Lucy's idea seemed like a good one, so after someone put in an opening bid for £5,000 and the bidding rose rapidly to £12,500, I put in my first shot at £13,500, at which point my office phone rang. It was Harry Crosbie on the line asking me did I want this yoke as he had been beefing up the bidding, which was now at £16,000. I said I did. 'Well, then, go for it,' he said. 'I'm pulling out of it now.' I made the final bid of £17,500 and within no time the motor vehicle – the pride of East Germany – was mine. What the fuck I was going to do with it, however, I really had no idea.

I have always enjoyed my few dealings with Harry Crosbie. Whether it's hiring poster sites or renting the Point for a gig, he is always 100 per cent upfront, no bullshitting. What you see is what you get. I've known the charming and beautiful Rita, his wife, since she danced in the 60s clubs and, like her husband, she has no airs and graces. A really very special lady. As for the Trabant, after just one weekend outside the Waterfront I had to move it to prevent it being wrecked by enthusiastic fans who were constantly climbing all over it. Then I had it under covers outside my house in Palmerston Park for over a year. Sometime later, I sold it to my long-time pal Vivian O'Rourke from Polygram Records for a few grand. The Trabant was featured in a 1994 Millers pop and rock memorabilia hard-covered book by Stephen Maycock, who was at that time Britain's foremost expert on rock'n'roll memorabilia.

7: 'ERIC WANTS WHAT?!'

*I*t was the night of 16 March 1979. Myself and Roger Forrester, Eric Clapton's manager, arrived back at the Shelbourne Hotel after a gig that Eric had just done for (believe it or not) the Irish Army at Collins Barracks.

'He wants a football table brought to his suite,' said Roger. 'You know, those big hand-played football game things where two players swing the little players around and smash the ball?'

'Roger, are you joking me? It's eleven o'clock at night. Where the fuck am I going to get one of those?'

'Would I joke with you, Pat?'

Over the years, I had become accustomed to being on the receiving end of all kinds of demands from acts. They would ask for weird and wonderful things, which often had nothing to do with the show or performances. I had been asked for artificial legs, hookers, fishing rods, white powder, sex videos, rare American whiskey, even a jet and a helicopter at short notice, but a twelve-stone or more football table at almost midnight beat them all. And then it came to me. There was an all-night snooker hall and slot machine joint at the far corner of St Stephen's Green, just at the end of Harcourt Street, which was a good ten-minute walk from the hotel. I made a telephone call, as I knew it would be open at that time of night. Much to my relief, they had a football table. I explained who I was and who was looking for it.

'Eric Clapton wants to play our football table?' said the manager. 'That's bloody great. Bring him up – we'll look after him.'

I had to explain the situation. 'No, he wants to play it in his hotel bedroom.'

St. Francis Xavier's Boys Club 1958 – I'm in the back row, second left. The greatest learning curve of my young life.

Front left: my grandmother Margaret Rita Cox – a tough woman who saved us all from the clutches of the Church and the institutions. Back left: my grandfather.

James Egan – the father I never met.

Mam, aged 80, with me and David, 1997.

My mam – second right. My Granda Cox directly behind me. Grandma Cox on the left. Aunt Teresa's wedding, 1957.

My son Graham and I in happier days.

My daughter Layla and son David recently.

My daughter Deborah and her partner, Matt, with my grandchildren Farrah, Fiona and Beau.

All dressed up with my beautiful wife, Helena.

AUGUST

HITSVILLE '68
top beat club and group magazine
6ᴰ

P a t   E g a n

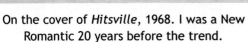

Alan Keen, 'When we were Your

RORY GALLAGHER collected a special award international achievement

Presenting Rory Gallagher with his *New Spotlight* Award sometime in 1969 at the National Boxing Stadium.

On the cover of *Hitsville*, 1968. I was a New Romantic 20 years before the trend.

Myself and close pals Mike O'Brien, Jon Hodges and Phil Lynott with the rest of the boys on Stephen's Green, 1968. Chasing the great freedom dream.

With legends Phil Lynott and Rory Gallagher circa 1969.

CONTRIBUTORS. No. 52

Larry Sogan   3. 3. 0
                   2. 2. 0
Pat Egan   4 - 4 - 0
N Dillon   5 - 5 - 0
Shay Healy   5 - 5 - 0.
Ken Stewart   4 - 4 - 0
T. V. Eakie   3. 3. 0
                   ─────────
                   27) 6 . 0

B.P. Fallon

Premier Promotions

Festivals
Carnivals
a Speciality

Tipperary

BEST FOR DANCES, SHOWBANDS, BALLAD GROUPS

Official Confirmation on behalf of the Ballroom

THIS IS TO CONFIRM MY BOOKING OF THE Thin Lizzy

IN THE Marian Hall, Tipperary Town

ON Tuesday 25th August, 1970

THE AGREED FEE IS £ 33

MEAL FOR THE BAND CAN BE HAD AT Mrs. Halligan's, Galbally Rd.,
                                                    Tipperary.
HOURS OF DANCING 8 P.m. sharp to 11 p.m.

REMARKS

Signed _____
On behalf of the Ballroom

The *New Spotlight* wages bill – £27. 6s. for an all-star line-up. BP Fallon was the big star writer on £10 a week but we weren't supposed to know that.

Thin Lizzy in the big time. A premier ballroom gig in 1970 for a fee of just £33.

Star-Club
8A SOUTH KING STREET

Date. 15th June. 1970........

CONFIRMATION

This is to confirm our booking of TIN LIZZIE on Sunday, 5th July 1970
at a fee of £25 plus.

Signed ....
Vincent Mooney.

The Star Club 1970 gig. A confirmation of 'Tin' Lizzy for a fee of just £25.

Having a few pints with Rory.

There was silence on the other end of the phone line, and then: 'How the fuck is he going to that?' the manager asked, quite reasonably.

'You're going to sell it to me. And you're going to get four or five of your guys to carry it across the Green to the Shelbourne Hotel.'

Another few seconds of silence. 'Are you serious?! That table cost me over a thousand pounds, it weighs a ton, and who's going to pay the lads for the heavy lifting?'

'Eric Clapton will,' I said.

It was after midnight when five big guys carried the football table down Stephen's Green and turned right past the top of Grafton Street towards the Shelbourne Hotel. Somehow, the lads had been able to manoeuvre the table into the lobby without doing any noticeable damage. 'What have we got here?' asked the night porter, who clearly wasn't happy. 'You can't bring that in here, no way.' In my best authoritarian voice, I told him it was for Mr Eric Clapton. 'He's in the Princess Grace Suite and it's a special request.' At this point, the lads just let it down slowly on the marble floor and fucked off – there was no way they were going up three flights of stairs with a 12-stone football yoke for anyone, let alone Eric Clapton. Delighted I had delivered what Eric had wanted, I rang his manager Roger in his room to tell him the table had arrived. 'Pat, I think he's fallen asleep. Get them to leave it downstairs, he can play it tomorrow.' It cost over £1,000 to get Eric his football table, plus the cash for the heavy lifters. After the tour finished, I sold it back to the same guy who gave it to us for £350. Did Eric ever play it? Never.

From 1977 to 1991, I was Eric Clapton's Irish tour promoter. The early years with Eric came after he had kicked his well-chronicled heavy drug use and entered into a self-destructive drinking orgy that lasted a long number of years. Sometime in the mid-70s, Roger Forrester took over Eric's management of Eric from Robert Stigwood, at that time best known for managing Cream, Clapton, and the Bee Gees. I used to go to Stigwood's London office to hound Roger about including Ireland on Eric's next tour of Europe. 'Go see Harvey Goldsmith in Oxford Street, ' advised Roger. 'Harvey's promoting the tour. I'll give him a call and he'll look after you.' And Harvey did. It was the beginning of a relationship as Eric's Irish promoter that lasted fourteen years. Harvey Goldsmith was always good to me; he gave me acts such as Wham, Nik Kershaw, Shirley Bassey, Queen and Clapton to promote in Ireland. Unlike a lot of other big-time managers and promoters, Harvey loved the limelight. In those early days, he was, to me, as big a star as the acts he promoted. Honoured by the Queen with a CBE, Harvey was the promoter behind the Live Aid London and JFK Philadelphia concerts in 1985. I was chuffed when he included my name on the list of credits for the Live Aid promotion – I had sold 700 tickets for the event in Ireland. Thanks to Harvey, that one-line mention on the Live Aid events credits, having only played a tiny part in the biggest rock event in history – it reached an audience of 1.9 billion people – is a highlight of which I am very proud.

Clapton toured Ireland five times between 1977 and 1991. Mostly it was just one-off Dublin and Cork shows. His first shows in Ireland were in June 1977 at the National Boxing Stadium. It was just after the recording of his *Slowhand* album, and Irish fans were treated to classics like 'Wonderful Tonight', 'I Shot the Sheriff', 'Cocaine' and 'Layla'. The band Eric used on his first Irish trip was George Terry on guitar, Jamie Oldaker on drums, Dick Sims on keyboards, Carl Radle on bass, and Marcy Levy and Yvonne Elliman on backing vocals. Although he was drinking heavily during the tour, it did not seem to affect his ability to deliver standout performances.

Eric returned in 1979 and played an eight-day tour that is still remembered over forty years later for the peculiarity of the venues chosen. When Roger asked me to put a tour together he said, 'Eric wants to play to the people, so pick out the best street cred venues you can find. And, Pat, he also wants to play a show for the Irish Army.' Unless I'm mistaken, this was the first (and possibly only) time a rock superstar had specifically requested to play a gig for the army. The list of venues I drew up for Roger included the Golden Grill, Letterkenny; St John's CYMS, Tralee; the Savoy Cinema, Limerick; Strandhill Ballroom, Sligo; the Downtown Club, Dundalk; and the mess hall in Collins Barracks; as well as his regular Dublin National Stadium and Cork City Hall shows. Roger looked over the gig schedule. 'I can't have Eric playing in a place called the Golden Grill,' he said. 'It will look like he's hit skid row.' Much to the disappointment of the Golden Grill management the date never happened and a second Dublin date was added instead.

During this tour, Eric was going through a very serious drinking period, and in some performances, it was clearly affecting his playing. The lead guitar solos were left up to his ace sidekick, Albert Lee, to cover up the cracks, which he did brilliantly. Eric would start drinking at 11 a.m. with a few pints and a couple of brandies in the hotel bar. He would often be accompanied by PR man Terry O'Neill, who at that time was managing the tour support act, the Freddie White Band, featuring the late guitar wild man Philip Donnelly. Eric would miss the early evening soundchecks because Roger would want him to sleep off the effects of the day's drinking before he went on stage that night. It did not always work out that way, however. Sometimes Eric didn't get to sleep it off and would be almost legless twenty minutes before showtime. When that happened, he'd be carried out to the side of the stage by his long-time minder Alfie O'Leary, a sixteen-stone former associate of the notorious Kray twins. (Eric had, in his early days, actually played a gig for the Krays in a London pub – just Eric and three mates on stage playing for them.) An oxygen tank and mask were set up at the side of the stage, and Eric would sit there for fifteen minutes with the mask on before the announcement was made – 'Ladies and gentlemen, please welcome Eric Clapton!' Somehow or other, he got through the Irish tour, but unless he stopped drinking he was headed for Boothill Cemetery.

Having already kicked a heroin addiction, Eric started seven years of heavy drinking in 1974. His huge consumption of alcohol finally caught up with him when he collapsed after coming off stage in Wisconsin in March 1981. The daily consumption of a bottle of brandy and painkillers had resulted in serious ulcers, including one the size of a golf ball that was about to burst. The doctors told him, 'Another twenty-four hours and you'd have been a dead man.' Eric recovered well, but went back on the drink again for a time, eventually kicking the habit for good in 1983. Anyway, during the 1979 Irish tour, the definite highlight was the show he played for the Irish army at Collins Barracks. The army went out of their way to show appreciation by hosting a lavish after-party for Eric, his band and crew. The show had been a great success and by the time the encore of 'Layla' had finished, eight hundred soldiers were on their feet and dancing in the aisles. The following day, St Patrick's Day, Eric played at the National Stadium, and despite being under the influence managed to deliver another brilliant performance.

Eric returned again in January 1981, when he played the RDS Simmon-scourt Arena. It was only the second such arena gig in Dublin. I had promoted the first one at the venue in 1979 with Queen, which at the time was a ground-breaking promotion. We sold 11,000 standing tickets for Eric's show, but unlike Queen, the production used was not in keeping with the size of the venue. We got away with it, but the performance and show could have been better. On that tour, Eric was still drinking

63

heavily. We also played Cork City Hall, Leisureland Galway and Carlow Youth Centre. Two nights later, Eric was back at the Rainbow in London. In 1983, Eric played two shows at the National Stadium as part of the Money and Cigarettes tour. He was finally off the drink, having completed four weeks of intensive rehabilitation in Minneapolis. Eric joined Alcoholics Anonymous and devoted much of his time to attending their meetings during his 1982 US tour. He had come very close to the edge many times in his life as a heroin user and an unstable alcoholic. Yet somehow, when all appeared lost, he made a remarkable recovery.

It was eight years before he came back to Ireland, but the guy who played The Point (now the 3Arena) in 1991 bore no resemblance to the Eric Clapton who had previously toured the country. His drinking days were now history, he looked super-fit and healthy, and he was immaculately dressed in the finest Versace suits. He genuinely looked like a new man. Roger Forrester had hired The Point for two weeks of rehearsal prior to Eric's record-breaking 24-night run at the Royal Albert Hall. Although all the musicians who were to feature at the RAH Hall gig came to Dublin for the rehearsals (including Ray Cooper, Steve Ferrone, Phil Palmer, Alan Clark, singers Katie Kissoon and Tessa Niles), the band who played the Irish shows comprised only four players – Eric, keyboard player Greg Phillinganes (who would go on to be Michael Jackson's music director), bass player Nathan East (of Stevie Wonder's band) and Eric's good friend, drummer Phil Collins. Roger tells the story that at the end of the RAH shows, a Japanese promoter offered £12,000,000 to bring the show to Tokyo for a few days. Roger told him Eric was about to go on holidays, so maybe some other time! (Eric did eventually go to Tokyo and played a number of shows with George Harrison.)

Sir Peter Blake, best known for creating the sleeve artwork for The Beatles' *Sgt. Pepper* album was also in town to work on a book for the high-end book publishers Genesis. Celebrating Eric's record run at the Royal Albert Hall, the 3,000 limited edition book *24 Nights* was personally signed by Eric and George Harrison and sold at £250 a copy. Sir Peter spent the time during the Dublin rehearsal sessions sketching Clapton while he prepared for the show during the day, as well as sound checking and performing on stage. The result was a collection of artworks offering a fascinating portrait of how this historical musical feat happened. I was over the moon to have replicas of our local Pat Egan backstage passes and dressing room signs printed and featuring strongly in *24 Nights*. The owner of Genesis, Brian Roylance, was also in Dublin to have discussions with Eric. I'm a huge admirer of Brian's great work producing the most magnificent handcrafted music books, and I'm proud to possess some of the editions signed by The Beatles. Speaking of books, during that week Roger gave me an envelope containing £7,000 with instructions to pick up a rare edition at Cathach Books in Duke Street. The book was number 19 of the Bodley Head's limited edition of James Joyce's *Ulysses* and had been signed by the author. It was a gift from Eric to his friend Brian Roylance; no better man to value its greatness.

Another very famous visitor to Dublin that week was Derek Taylor, a legend in pop journalism, and best known as The Beatles' press officer and close friend to all the Fab Four. In showbiz circles he was sometimes referred to as the fifth Beatle, but, for me, only one man can rightfully claim that title and that's Sir George Martin. Derek wrote a brilliant commentary about his week in Dublin that is also included in *24 Nights*. Derek was born in Liverpool and worked as a reporter with the *Daily Express* before joining Brian Epstein and The Beatles as their press officer. He had also spent a lot of time in California working the media for the Beach Boys, the Byrds and the Mamas and Papas. It was a real pleasure to meet him at the Point rehearsals. Michael Kamen also came to Dublin – he was a big name in film music; he had composed the *Royal Albert Hall Concerto for Eric Clapton*, and also conducted the hundred-piece orchestra and huge choir at the RAH. Michael told a wonderful story about Mafia life at the after-show wrap party – I have always loved stories about criminal characters. When Michael and his wife moved to New York they met any number of weird and wonderful people. One was a man with serious mob connections, who talked about a rich woman he admired who had incredible paintings all over her apartment – 'a Rembrandt on one wall and a Chopin over the fireplace!' On another occasion, when someone accused him of having no friends, he replied, 'You have to be fuckin' kidding me – I've got friends I haven't even used yet!'

The two pre-RAH shows in Dublin, which took place on 31 January and 1 February 1991, were the last shows I promoted for Eric. It was the end of a wonderful experience working for the brilliant guitar legend. I often get asked what kind of guy he was and I always answer, 'Just an ordinary guy who loves playing his guitar, supporting West Bromwich Albion and enjoying himself.' Yes, he was a star, but for him, stardom was merely a consequence of his brilliance as a guitarist. Being on stage playing the blues was when he was happiest; playing the guitar was how he best expressed himself. Eric and Roger split in the mid-90s over differences relating to the setting up of the guitarist's Crossroads addiction centre on the Caribbean island of Antigua, but I still keep in touch with Roger. He told me that after splitting with Eric he received offers to take on some very big names but turned them all down. I think Roger had been like a father to Eric for over twenty years and it broke his heart when the relationship fell apart. Roger had nursed him through the long years of drugs and alcoholism, and overseen his renaissance, but Eric felt he was now able to stand on his own two feet and no longer needed a close personal manager. For me, Roger was the kindest and most accommodating manager of any of the superstars I promoted, and I am immensely proud that I can still call him my friend

Marianne Faithfull and Pattie Boyd were two of the most recognisable and iconic faces of the swinging 60s. There wasn't a guy I knew at that time who didn't fancy one or the other – or both! I had met Pattie Boyd, the former wife of Beatle George Harrison and later Eric Clapton, a number of times when she came to Ireland with Eric in the late 70s and early 80s. She had danced a high-kicking Irish jig alongside her sister on stage with Eric's band at the National Stadium on St Patrick's night 1979. I was totally in awe of meeting her in person – what a thrill. This was the woman who had inspired three of the greatest songs in popular music history: 'Wonderful Tonight', 'Something' and the rock classic 'Layla'. (In 1993 I named my own daughter Layla after her.)

In 1979, Eric and his manager had become the owners of the Barberstown country house hotel, a thirteenth-century castle in Straffan, County Kildare. They had come over for a week's fishing on the Liffey and had stayed at the castle. Eric was so smitten with the place that they bought it – as you do if you're a multi-millionaire rock star. It is the most beautiful building, with pretty gardens and walks close along the Liffey, but it soon became clear that they had no idea what they were going to do with it. A couple of years later, my phone rang. It was Roger on the line. 'Eric is tired of the castle,' he said. 'Do you know anyone with four hundred thousand or thereabouts who might be interested in buying it?' I knew no one in the 80s with that sort of money. It might as well have been £4 million! It was eventually sold in the mid-80s to Ken Healy, who turned it into one of the most stunning country house hotels in Ireland. Ken is still operating it to this very day. I have been back there a number of times to reminisce and relive the memories of some of the best late music sessions of my entire life. Not only is Barberstown steeped in history, it's also unique in hosting so many great jam sessions featuring the world's best session musicians and stars. The venue's baby grand piano truly rocked when Procol Harum's Gary Brooker rattled the keys, supported by Albert Lee, Donald 'Duck' Dunn, Chris Stainton, Carl Radle, George Terry, Dick Sims, Yvonne Elliman, Phil Collins and Eric Clapton. Other regular visitors during Eric's ownership included Mick Jagger and Ronnie Wood.

Fast forward to January 2014. I got a call at my office. 'There's a Pattie Boyd on the line for you,' said Michelle King, my long-time and favourite assistant. I stopped in my tracks for a moment. Was there another Pattie Boyd who I wasn't aware of? No, it was her. She was calling to seek my help in tracking down some lost or mislaid film footage of a unique event. The Straffan House estate (now the K Club) was just down the road from Barberstown Castle. In the 70s, the estate was owned by Kevin McClory, the James Bond film producer, and my good pal Danny Hughes was the resident DJ. According to Danny, once a month Kevin ran the best fun-filled, most outrageous parties, attended by his high society and film star friends. The most famous of these wild nights was 14 September 1975, when McClory hired Duffy's Circus's big top for a spectacular one-off charity concert event. Billed as the 'Best Loved Clowns in the World', the show was a circus fantasy featuring renowned Hollywood movie director John Huston as the ringmaster, decked out in shiny knee-high black boots, braided red jacket and a top hat. He was supported by none other than James Bond himself, Sean Connery. Next up was a Hollywood beauty, the only female member of Sinatra's Rat Pack, Shirley MacLaine, supported by Burgess Meredith (best known at that time as the Penguin in the 1960s cartoonish *Batman* TV series, and future star of the early Rocky movies). The guest list also included Eric Clapton, of course, *To Sir, with Love*'s Judy Geeson, Abbey Theatre legend Siobhán McKenna, Milo O'Shea, Danny Cummins, Niall Buggy, and the Chieftains. At the after-party was the band The Others, featuring Ronan Collins on drums. DJ was Danny Hughes, and lest we forget, all Duffy's Circus performers and animals were there. Admission to the Big Top extravaganza was £20, which was a huge ticket price back in 1975.

After a life in rock'n'roll, Pattie Boyd had moved on to become a top-rate photographer and TV documentary maker. She wanted me to help her track down a film of that exclusive Big Top concert. Almost forty years later, I had no idea where to start. Dozens of phone calls and a few days' work later, I was about drop it when I came up with the name of Norman Fulham, Kevin McClory's solicitor. Norman told me he had spent many years sorting out McClory's estate, which was, he said, in an unholy mess. Was I in luck? Did he know anything about the missing film? Seemingly there were reels and reels of film left in McClory's basement, and 'Yes,' said Norman. 'I do recall a Duffy's Circus one.' I got back to Pattie with the good news. 'Utterly brilliant, Pat! Well done!' she said. 'I was just about to give up. Thank you so very much, you've made my day.' I spoke to Ronan Collins about the Big Top event, and he told me that because it was so different from the usual run of gigs The Others played, he remembered it well. 'It was one of those super gigs a young band will never forget,' he said. He recalled that while they were setting up their gear in near-darkness, two scruffy-looking hippy-type guys walked over to the stage and started to mess with their guitars and Ronan's drums. 'Ah, come on lads, will ya feck off!' Ronan said to them. 'We're trying to set up here for the gig.' The guys just laughed and went away. Half an hour later, when the band started playing their set, Ronan saw the two guys on the dance floor. It was only then that he realised who he had told to feck off: Mick Jagger and Eric Clapton.

Of course, whenever Jagger's name is mentioned another name is almost always in the conversation – Marianne Faithfull. I first met Marianne in 1986 when she called the office and asked if I had time for a coffee. Had I what? Someone had told her I was the best guy to put together a short Irish tour for her. I was delighted, and meeting the lady was another highlight to add to the long list of famous names from the swinging 60s I had been lucky enough to meet and work with. No woman in rock'n'roll was a greater survivor than Marianne. Her drug history and fall into homelessness has been well documented, yet she lived to reinvent herself time and time again. Her song 'Dreamin' my Dreams' had been a number 1 in Ireland and a huge seller for her in 1975. In 1979, she made a dramatic comeback with the hugely acclaimed bestselling album *Broken English*, which received a Grammy nomination and is regarded by many as her finest work. A song from the album, 'The Ballad of Lucy Jordan', was also a major hit.

Marianne and I had a couple of meetings. We got on well together, and out of the blue she asked me to be her European tour agent. Having always been a home bird, I had no real experience of the European tour market, but I pretended I did and said yes. She invited me and my then partner Caroline to dinner at her home on the Carton House estate. This was another one-off fabulous experience – the most exquisite dinner setting of my entire life. Shell Cottage, where Marianne lived for some years, was built in 1750 for Emily Mary FitzGerald, the great-granddaughter of King Charles II and one of his mistresses. Nothing on the outside of the house hints at the incredible interior. Emily had decorated the cottage with marine life from all over the world, and whenever her friends sailed abroad they would return with sea urchins, birds' eggs, shells, crystals – anything from the sea. She would then attach the items to the furniture, walls and windows, giving an astounding kaleidoscopic visual display. The centrepiece of the house is a beautiful dome lined with thousands of tropical shells of every size. Visitors to the cottage had included Queen Victoria and Princess Grace Kelly of Monaco. Emily had 23 children, one of whom was Lord Edward FitzGerald, leader of the 1798 rebellion. Here I was once again, a Dorset Street corner boy stepping into the history of true aristocrats, and having dinner with Marianne Faithfull under a shell dome built for the great-granddaughter of a king.

I put some Irish dates together for Marianne, yet they sold with limited success. Three nights at the Tivoli in Dublin did very good business but the out-of-town dates didn't sell as well. However, Marianne was happy with a job well done and invited Caroline and me to New York on an all-expenses-paid trip. She was recording and filming a live album, *Blazing Away*, for Island Records, at St Ann's Cathedral in Brooklyn. The band that night featured top-notch players such as Garth Hudson from the Band, the great Dr. John and guitarist Barry Reynolds. Marianne, always gracious and kind, introduced me to everyone in the band as her new agent from Ireland. I had asked her to confirm to me in writing that I had the rights to book her dates across Europe, which she did. When I got back from New York and with the help of a UK contact I immediately started to book dates in Holland and Germany. Despite coming up with a number of good bookings, the tour, much to my disappointment, never came together. Marianne had taken US dates in preference and I never heard from her again.

* * *

In 1979, Elton John was the first act I ever promoted to demand three bottles of Cristal champagne in his dressing room – and to increase it to six if his manager John Reid was in attendance.

* * *

8: 'ELTON WILL BE FURIOUS'

*E*lton John gave the nod to his tour manager that he wanted a certain young guy in the hugely excited audience brought backstage after the show. Elton, the tour manager told me, just wanted to say hello to him: 'Give that lad a backstage pass and tell him Elton wants to meet him.' By the time the show ended, myself and Harry McKeown, the venue's head bouncer, had had to fight our way into the audience and bring six guys backstage who Elton fancied talking to. Elton was in Dublin's National Boxing Stadium on the South Circular Road for a sell-out show of his Single Man tour, on which he was joined on stage by multi-talented percussionist Ray Cooper. The year was 1977, and tickets were just £5.

It was the first time as a promoter I had encountered the notorious John Reid, the flamboyant gay manager of Queen and Elton John. Reid would go on to manage Billy Connolly, and some years later would be chosen by Michael Flatley to handle his career after *Riverdance*, but was then quickly fired. I had known that John had a fearsome reputation for creating havoc. The problem, however, with the National Boxing Stadium (built for approximately £12,000 in 1939 as a purpose-built boxing stadium) is that it was never intended to stage concert events. It was just what it said on the tin – a boxing ring, no more, no less.

A lot of the early events I saw there, such as the *New Spotlight* Awards, The Who and The Hollies, were presented from the ring in the centre of the 2,200-seat space. This was in the days before sound and lighting systems were 'flown' from the roof, out of view of the audience. In later years, the stage was shifted to another point in the room, which although better was still too small for rock gigs and still had serious sight-line problems. Elton John's road crew stacked the sound system far too high on the corners of the stage, and in doing so blocked the view of at least five hundred of the capacity crowd. This had been a major problem at every gig at this particular venue, but Elton John's crew refused point-blank to drop the height of the sound system. I kicked up a stink with the tour manager and told him that unless he did something we would have a riot on our hands. I was terrified, frankly, because so many people would not be able to see Elton perform. Fifteen minutes before showtime, I could already see some members of the audience starting to complain to the bouncers. One thing the venue security didn't have was charm. They were mostly former boxers with little or no awareness of politeness and courtesy. 'Nothing to do with me, sham, see the promoter.'

'Pat, for fuck's sake, you better get it sorted fast,' said Harry McKeown. Another ex-boxer, at least Harry still had a brain that functioned. 'If not we're in real trouble.' At that very second, I felt a hand on my shoulder grabbing my jacket. The person who owned the hand swung me around and pushed me against the wall. I was face to face with the infamous John Reid.

'Who the fuck do you think you are, interfering with the production? Nobody tells Elton John's crew anything but me. I'm going to pull this show right now.' John stormed off into the small backstage area to discuss it with Elton. I was halfway to shitting myself. Would he really do such a thing fifteen minutes before the show with 2,200 people already in the venue? As I was thinking this, the tour manager came rushing backstage to tell Reid that the crew had sorted the problem. To my great relief, they were working on dropping the height of the PA bins. The show finally went up thirty minutes late. I had survived once again by the skin of my teeth (which, to be honest, was a regular occurrence in my forty-plus years as a promoter).

Later, when I'd started a lengthy spell as Billy Connolly's promoter, I met John again. This time we got on really well. If he knew that John was coming to one of his Irish shows, Billy would say, 'There are only three people safe in the house tonight, Pat. You, me and the tour manager.' What Billy meant by this was that John was always liable to get involved in some kind of skirmish or other. Which he did on one occasion – at the Shelbourne Hotel. After one of Billy's shows, he had dinner with him and said it was too early for bed and they should go out on the town. Billy declined, saying he was having an early night. Billy rarely went anywhere after the shows other than for an Indian meal. So John turned to me. 'Let's go, Pat! Show me the bright lights of Dublin town.'

We started out in Bad Bobs in Temple Bar. The joint was jumping and jammed right up to the door. John loved the band, Hank Halfhead and the Rambling Turkeys, and asked me to get their number – he was planning a summer jamboree at his country house outside London. Just before closing time, we moved on to one of the city's few gay-friendly pubs, Bartley Dunne's. (Regarded as Dublin's most famous and oldest gay pub, it was demolished in 1990 and replaced with the pub/nightclub Break for the Border. It was repurposed in 2019 as Bartley's.) I'd told John that the likes of Richard Burton, Elizabeth Taylor, Laurence Harvey and Kim Novak had been regular customers there when they were filming in Dublin in the 1960s. With its weighty scarlet drapes, hidden alcoves, wine bottle candle holders, old-school jazz/soul music and a huge collection of multi-coloured liqueurs twinkling behind the bar counter, Bartley Dunne's was much more to John's liking. The barman was calling last drinks, and John vowed to come back as he loved its cosmopolitan ambience. The next stop was a gay club on Ely Place. This is where John said to me, 'Pat, I think you should leave me here alone. Go on, go home to your beautiful wife.' Leave him I did, but it wasn't too long before I met up with him again. At 4 a.m. my phone rang …

'I'm outside the Shelbourne Hotel, on the street,' John said. 'I've been thrown out of the hotel. Can you pick me up?' *What the hell?*, I thought, still half asleep. *Never a dull moment.* There he was, sitting with his bags on the steps of the Georgian house next door to the Shelbourne. I had a quick word with the Shelbourne night porter, who told me that John had brought three men back to his suite. A fight had ensued, resulting in broken bottles and overturned furniture, before continuing in the hotel corridors. A number of guests had complained about a boxing match and loud shouting. 'Where to now, John?' I asked, as he told me that he had lost a very valuable diamond Cartier cufflink, which had been a present from Elton. John told me he had to find it, otherwise Elton would be furious. 'It's not the value of it, Pat,' he said quietly, 'it's only twenty grand. It's the sentimental value.'

Despite a thorough search around the various venues, the Cartier cufflink never turned up.

9: AVOIDING A POTENTIAL DISASTER

*F*or their debut Irish visit, Queen arrived in Dublin in November 1979 to play the RDS Simmonscourt Arena. I remember the gig more than most because it was the first time I had come close to a potentially really serious incident that might have ended my promoting career before it had got off the ground. No other Irish promoter had used the arena to stage a rock gig, and there was a reason for that – the venue was little more than a huge cowshed. And yet it was the only venue in Dublin that could cater for Queen's vast stage and lighting show and an expected crowd of twelve thousand fans. I knew I was taking a big financial risk, but with Oliver Barry on board as my co-promoter, I felt confident that I was breaking new ground in my career. The show would be by far the biggest ever indoor concert staged in Ireland at that time. As Liam Collins wrote in the *Evening Herald* on 23 November, 'At 5 a.m. the Simmonscourt was smelling of bulls and horse shit but all that was about to change.' The load-in time for the 45-person crew (44 men and one woman) was 6 a.m. The number was increased by twenty local humpers I employed to unload the five juggernaut trucks and two vans. Queen was the first UK group to bring in such heavyweight transport to Dublin. Another first was the use of over six hundred colour lights, including four hundred overhead lamps that weighed almost four tonnes. No one from Dublin working on the gig had ever seen a lighting rig like it. I remember the stage costing something in the region of £3,000 to build and the overall bill for everything – excluding the band's fee – was close to £25,000. Queen's fee was £10,000 plus all extras, but with 12,000 tickets at a fiver each, we knew we were on to a winner.

Fans had started to arrive from 10 a.m., eight hours before showtime. I had no security on duty that early in the day and many fans who had travelled long distances started to come into the venue, much to the annoyance of the tour manager, Gerry Stickles. 'Get these fucking people out of here fast!' he shouted at me. As the venue had never previously staged a concert, no set systems were in place about how best to operate the simple attention-to-detail elements that are so important when dealing with large crowds. To avoid fans coming on site I had the main entrance gates to Simmonscourt closed, but I had not anticipated the build-up of fans outside the gates so early in the evening. By 5 p.m., with no crash barriers or queuing system in place, upwards of two thousand fans were now crammed up against the steel gates and there was no way we could open them without people at the front falling forward and getting injured. My long-time pal Harry McKeown was in charge of security and was concerned that we might have a disaster on our hands. The only way we could relieve pressure from the gates was to get at least ten bouncers into the crowd near the front of the crush and try to push back while at the same time getting people at the back to stop pushing forward. I was at my wits' end - I could see that the pressure on the gates was starting to affect the brick pillars that were holding the gates in place. In a panic, I watched the cement falling away from between the bricks in the pillars, and I knew there was a serious accident just waiting to happen. I was praying that Harry's men were getting into the crowd. Just seconds before the gates were about to collapse, I made the call to open them and try to slowly filter through some of those being crushed. With security holding one side of the gates closed and Harry's men relieving the pressure out front we managed to avoid a total disaster. Crowd control barriers as used at today's major gigs had not even been invented back in 1979, so many of the crowd control problems, accidents and even deaths were still to materialise in later years. That day, I learned a lesson in crowd control that I have never forgotten, and it really was such a simple one. I never ran a gig again where I did not have security and police barriers in place from at least midday to ensure an orderly build-up of fans. It was an approach that avoided any more Simmonscourt-type near-disasters. I count myself very lucky that I never had any serious accidents in those early years of pioneering rock gigs, but sometimes it really was touch and go.

We had been instructed by Queen's management to supply four limos, one each for Freddie, John, Roger and Brian. It was the first time

I had ever received such a request. The show featured all the big Queen hits of the period, but it was received with mixed reviews. 'While the band performance and lighting show got five stars, it was the cavernous size of Simmonscourt that failed to excite. Even the massive sound rig seemed inadequate in such a vast space. Which is a pity because the fact that a rock group of Queen's stature has now appeared in Dublin, it has opened up even greater possibilities that we might now see acts such as The Eagles, Rolling Stones or Rod Stewart crossing the Irish sea to gig in Dublin,' wrote Mike Clare in his *Evening Herald* review.

What do I remember of Freddie Mercury that day in 1979? I met him at the airport and he was talkative and friendly on the ride into town. He asked about how the Troubles in the North had affected my gigs and told me he had some friends in Dublin he wanted to make sure were on the guest list for the gig. The band invited me and my close staff, Liz and Adrienne, back to the Gresham Hotel for an after-show dinner that Rory Cowan (the future *Mrs Brown's Boys* actor, then press officer at EMI) was hosting for the band. So I had dinner with a true rock'n'roll superstar who, to me, seemed just like a very ordinary guy. Much to my disappointment, I missed out on Queen's next visit to Ireland by a cat's whisker when Jim Aiken presented them at Slane in 1986. However, I had plenty of other successes to console myself with between 1979 and 1984 – during those years I promoted more outdoor gigs than any other Irish promoter.

1979, Dalymount Park: Status Quo, Judas Priest, Rockpile, The Undertones, Bogey Boys

1979, RDS Simmonscourt: Queen, Eric Clapton, Elkie Brooks, Joan Armatrading

1980, Dalymount Park: Bob Marley, Ronnie Lane's Slim Chance, Bagatelle

1981, Dalymount Park: The Selector, The Beat, Tokyo Olympics (The Specials pulled out just before the gig when 'Ghost Town' went to number 1 in the UK)

1982, Dalymount Park: Meat Loaf, Shakatak, Budgie, Tokyo Olympics

1983, Dalymount Park: Black Sabbath, Motörhead, Twisted Sister, Anvil, Mama's Boys

10: LAST TANGO WITH PHIL

*T*never knew Phil Lynott the rock star. The guy I knew and became friends with was not the all-conquering alpha male sex symbol – he was just a sixteen-year-old kid, soft-spoken, very shy and always courteous.

Phil, John Hojes, John Farrell, Mike O'Brien, Tony Bradfield, the Hud's manager, and me, all hung out together in our early career days. Phil, at that time, was still in the Black Eagles. Mike O'Brien was the singer with the Hud's and later the Real McCoy. John Farrell, my best mate from Cabra, was lead singer with The Movement, later The Dreams. John, Phil's best pal in those early days, was a DJ at the Scene club in Parnell Square. Because of my late nights working at the Five Club, I rarely got to bed before 2 a.m. and wouldn't be up until midday the following day. 'Get up! Get up!' Mam would shake me and say, 'that black boy Philip is downstairs waiting in the parlour for you.' She always called him Philip, the black boy. Phil would sit in the front room having tea and a fig roll while I got my act together. Mam often remarked how gently spoken, mannerly and polite Phil was, 'a lovely lad'.

At sixteen, Phil had a quiet way about him, and although he was shy he was not afraid to make his views known. I was appearing as a pop news-reader on Danny Hughes's RTÉ TV show *Like Now*, which was filmed at the Top Hat Ballroom, Dún Laoghaire. I was plagued by stage fright, barely making it to the end of my spot without falling apart. I knew I should have done better. I imagined the camera guys and the next act on were all looking at me in disbelief or sympathy. The first person across the floor to me was Phil, who put his arm around my shoulder and said, 'You were great, man, well done.'

'No, Phil,' I said. 'I fucked up. Everyone thinks I lost it.'

'Just listen,' he said. 'You were great, so don't mind anyone else. What do they know?'

My old pal Danny Hughes was a guy I was in awe of at the time. He compèred and presented effortlessly. He had style and charisma and it was a shame he never pursued a career in TV and radio. Danny bowed out in 1981 after being caught up in the horrible Stardust fire disaster; he was the DJ on the St Valentine's night when 48 young lives were lost. Danny had a terrific personality, a strong comedy streak and was a brilliant mimic. He would have made a great talk show host, but the experience of Stardust halted something within him, never to be restarted.

Phil and I and the others used to hang out together around Grafton Street, the Coffee Inn, Synnott Place, Dorset Street Wimpy Bar, and the clubs. There was nothing out of the ordinary happening, we were just a bunch of young guys out looking for a good time. All our conversations revolved around hit bands, music, the latest new threads, and girls. Most of this took place during Phil's time between the Black Eagles and joining Skid Row. In early '68, Phil and I did about five or six disco appearances for *New Spotlight* magazine. We also judged a couple of beauty events and, as always with Phil, he picked out the best-looking girl for himself. We judged Miss Mod '67 and Miss Kildare '68. *Spotlight*'s editor, John Coughlan, would give me £20, and after paying for my petrol, I would split the balance with Phil. As usual, Phil would always pick the winner, leaving me to console the runners-up. In later years, if I am not mistaken, Phil was a judge in front of a twenty million TV audience on Miss World 1978. Not in some dodgy marquee in Naas, but in the Royal Albert Hall, no less! I always wondered if he scored with the winner, Miss Argentina, just like he did with Miss Kildare 1968. Phil always believed he was going to make it, but in '68 he was desperately searching for direction and leadership, two things he found the day he met Brush Sheils.

Even in those early days, Phil had a way with words, and he was a great romantic. I had a big crush on a beautiful girl from Cushendall, County Antrim. A student at Queen's University, Belfast, she was a big fan of the Gentry, one of the top Northern groups, which was fronted by the charismatic Cahir O'Doherty. She would travel down for their gigs in Dublin and stay over with friends for the weekend. Phil was aware I was smitten but too shy to make my move. 'Look,' he said to me on one of the weekends. 'I wrote this for you last night. It's a poem. I'll pass it on to her at the gig tonight from you and then you can ask her to dance.' The girl in question believed I had written the romantic words myself. I never had the courage to tell her the truth.

In 1968, along with writing for *New Spotlight*, I also worked on my lifelong friend Tony Bradfield's short-lived magazine *Hitsville*. The new Skid Row, with guitarist Benny Cheevers and Phil Lynott, were on the cover of the first issue. It was a brilliantly produced monthly magazine, mainly about Dublin bands and clubs. I wrote a regular column called 'The One who Speaks His Mind', and I was also featured on the cover in August '68. The Five Club beauty Ruth Gill, was Miss Hitsville in August '68. John Hojes did record reviews, and my DJ pals Derry Glenn, Stevie Bolger, Danny Hughes and DJ Lee, were also writing regular columns. The death that year of Phil's best pal, John Hojes, at just twenty, of leukaemia, had an enormous effect on Phil. He took it very badly, and for a few days after the funeral went on the booze. Terry O'Neill, later Thin Lizzy's manager, remembers it as being the first time he had ever seen Phil legless; 'He was just totally out of it with grief.' It was also the first time I heard Phil use the phrase 'only the good die young'. Any time after that when John's name came up Phil would always say that John was just like James Dean – only the good die young. The September 68 edition of *Hitsville* had Granny's Intentions on the cover and ran a full-page tribute to John Hojes, who had died that month.

Phil hung around Synnott Place with another close pal of mine, the bass player Pat Quigley, a member of The Movement and Orphanage. The basement in Pat's big tenement house was used as a rehearsal place for a number of groups. Synnott Place and Pat Quigley's basement played a pivotal part in the genesis of Irish rock. The Movement, the Orphanage and Skid Row all rehearsed there, and the roots of Thin Lizzy can be traced to the area. I went regularly to hear the bands and would find Phil chatting up Pat's young sister, Breda. Those rehearsals were my very first experience of seeing live bands rehearse and create new songs, and even though I had no musical talent I got a great buzz from just hanging out with musicians. One audition still alive in my memory involved a singer from Cabra, an albino guy with a big mound of snow-white hair worn in an afro style. He refused to sing unless all the lights were turned off because he would blush if anyone looked at him performing. It was a feeling I knew all too well.

It was at one of those rehearsals I first met the illustrious Brendan 'Brush' Shiels. Ben, as we called him, was the man to know in the 60s. He was the first guy I ever saw with a Beatles album, and although only a year or two older than the rest of us he came across as having already done it all. There was a touch of Eamon Dunphy about him. When he spoke about music and bands, everyone listened. Brush was a charismatic stage performer, and the progressive hard rock version of Skid Row that he fronted with Gary Moore and Noel Bridgeman was to my mind the most exciting live band ever produced on the Irish scene. At their peak they were both mind-blowing and breath-taking. How they missed out on fame and fell through the cracks in the pyramid of stardom is hard to explain because no other Irish band deserved it more. Although Brush was never in Thin Lizzy, the shadow of his influence was ever present. He was the master, plain and simple, to both Gary Moore, Philo, and Noel Bridgeman, and they served his legacy well. Over the years I got to know Noel Bridgeman well – he was such a lovely soft likeable guy. During his time with Mary Black I tried endlessly to get him to record the song 'Across the Universe', a John Lennon original. Noel did an amazing vocal on the song, backed by Mary and her band. It was a show stopper and by far the best version of one of Lennon's less acclaimed great songs. We lost Noel in 2021, a great voice and brilliant drummer. While Noel wasn't young, like Phil and Rory, I still like to use the phrase 'only the good die young' for all the musicians who have passed away during my lifetime. Maybe it's because music people never really grow old. With music in your blood and in your heart, you really are forever young.

As the 70s approached, Phil became busier and more involved in music, first with Skid Row and then with Thin Lizzy. Our careers were moving in different directions, but we stayed in touch. I wrote about him every week in my *Spotlight* column and he regularly topped my popularity poll of Irish rock stars. He often dropped in to my newly opened record store, the Sound Cellar. He was my very first customer and bought the album *The Freewheelin' Bob Dylan*. He used the Sound Cellar for two different photoshoots with the excellent photographer Roy Esmonde. Although we no longer hung out together, we were still good pals, but Phil was moving in a different social circle. His pals were now from dope-smoking, hippy, progressive rock and folk acts like Mellow Candle and Dr Strangely Strange. When he invited me to a party in his new flat in Clontarf I expected booze and blondes but instead found everyone sitting on the floor in a large circle, passing around joints and listening to the Incredible String Band. Not being a dope smoker, I couldn't see the fun in it, so I left.

Like everyone else on the Dublin rock scene, I was blown away to see Thin Lizzy on *Top of the Pops*. Musically, 'Whiskey in the Jar' was a bad song choice for a rock band, but it served its purpose and gave them that elusive breakthrough in Britain. With the help of Kid Jensen at Radio Luxembourg and John Peel at the BBC, they had cracked it. The road to rock greatness lay ahead. I was delighted when Kid Jensen referenced me in an interview as the person who brought Thin Lizzy to his attention. 'I never missed Pat Egan's *Spotlight* column,' he said. The follow up to 'Whiskey' was one of Philip's originals, 'Randolph's Tango'. It was a good song, but not one that I felt was going to make the charts and I said so in my *New Spotlight* review. Even though I was right – the song bombed and disappeared without a trace – Philip took offence. He rang me at *Spotlight* and said, 'What's this shit you're laying on me, man? I thought you were my friend.' I tried to say I was helping him by telling the truth – that someone at Decca, the record company, had called it wrong and the important second hit never happened. Phil hung up and never spoke to me again. In 1986, when I heard he had died, my first thoughts were his own words on the day his best pal John Hojes passed away – only the good die young.

> *There's an old photo of Dan, I wish you could have seen*
> *Of him and the boys posed, standing in St Stephen's Green*
> *You see they were part of the great freedom dream.*
>
> (© Phil Lynott, 'Shades of a Blue Orphanage', 1972)

At 23, knowing that my club DJ-ing days were numbered and that I was never going to make it on radio, having missed my chance on Radio Caroline, I started looking out for new ways to progress my career in the music business. I had spent the previous couple of years living it up.

• •

The trademark raggy denim jeans worn on stage by Status Quo were not their normal day wear – they were specially ironed, stitched and returned to wardrobe immediately after they came off stage.

• •

Partying my life away. I had been drinking way more than my share of scotch and coke, and suffering the most horrendous hangovers. I drank scotch and coke because it was George Harrison's drink of choice and if it was good enough for a Beatle it was good enough for me. (In later years, I fell in love with the blonde in the black dress – a pint of Guinness. Of course, in 1969 I thought Guinness was only for old men.) I was never much of a drinker compared to my mates – I simply couldn't hold my booze. I was falling out of pubs at closing time with no idea where I was going. After a club or party night, I would wake up next to a girl whose name I didn't know, unable even to remember how we'd met. I was also driving around at night way over the limit. I can still recall to this day being stopped late one night – I was so inebriated I had forgotten to put on the car lights – on Butt Bridge by a big country Garda sergeant. 'You're drunk, young fella,' he said. 'Put the lights on now and go home to bed and sleep it off.' When I was drinking I regularly made a total asshole of myself, talking complete bullshit and just pouring my money into the gutter, and myself along with it.

Because I worked weekends DJ-ing, the big drinking night of the week for me was Monday, which was also the *New Spotlight* night out. It always started at around nine o'clock in the Zodiac (now Bruxelles) in Harry Street. Then I'd head off to the weekly *Spotlight* bash at the TV Club in Harcourt Street in my very best threads. The small Zodiac bar was always jammed with showband and group heads, as well as some to-die-for women. Holding up the bar, and not just on Mondays, were the resident league of serious drinkers led by Tony Bradfield, Mike O'Brien, Michael Hutchinson, Noel 'The Tec' Glynn and his brother Shay. They were regularly joined by other notorious rednecks like Dan McGrattan, Aiden Hand, Ollie Byrne, Jock McDonald, Billy Brown, Tiger Taylor, Ray Elliott and Phil Lynott. Terry O'Neill was barely sixteen at the time, yet was regularly to be found sneaking into the Zodiac just before closing time. 'Pat, will you get me a Celebration?' he'd ask. 'That feckin' barman won't serve me.'

Little did we know then that forty years later, a bronze life-sized statue of one of our pals would be placed right outside the door of the former Zodiac. Not in memory of our drinking club, but in celebration of one Philip Parris Lynott 1949-1986.

It was at the TV Club one Monday night that Cork man Oliver Barry, who managed The Freshmen, The Hoedowners and The Wolfe Tones, saved my life (in retrospect, quite literally) by offering me £500 to start my own business. It was the break I needed to get out of the clubs and drinking holes, and I grabbed it with both hands.

Oliver was the best and most creative young manager of the entire showband era. At a time when the majority of band managers just took dates in a little black diary or over the phone, Oliver was way ahead of the curve. Without question, The Freshmen were the most musically talented showband. Had he been born ten years later, Billy Brown, The Freshmen's multi-talented leader, would have been right up there with the very best rock acts of the day. A brilliant musician and vocalist, Billy's talent was wasted playing the ballroom circuit. He deserved a better platform to display and develop his many skills. Like a handful of other showband musicians of that time, he was simply too good for the rest of them. The Freshmen's 1970 *Peace on Earth* concept album, which included linked narration by acclaimed theatre actor Micheál MacLiammóir, still stands today as the only credible original work ever produced by any showband.

Olivier Barry was always up for trying something new. At a time when major international touring acts were bypassing Ireland, Oliver jumped on a plane and went stateside to chase the very biggest acts in popular music history. Of the world's top four acts, Frank Sinatra, Elvis Presley, Michael Jackson and The Beatles, Oliver managed to sign up two of them for a one-off Irish appearance. This was simply unheard of at that time. He also had an ill-fated crack at a gig by the Rolling Stones, but ticket sales bombed because the date clashed with Italia 90. Still, Oliver walked away smiling because they pulled their world tour and compensated him generously.

His Siamsa Cois Lee was one of the pioneering outdoor festival events. Stars such as John Denver, Kris Kristofferson and Glen Campbell flew in especially from the USA to headline the event. Unlike other promoters, Oliver liked to gamble on one-off events. He thought nothing of offering $500,000 to Michael Jackson for his first Irish shows. Oliver also managed the rebel song group the Wolfe Tones, whose songs became the musical voice of the IRA's propaganda movement. Under Oliver's shrewd management during the 70s, the Wolfe Tones set up their own record label, Triskel, which resulted in them selling vast numbers of between 50,000 and 80,000 copies of each of their albums. As Oliver said to me, 'Pat, the Wolfe Tones walked into my offices as pure socialists and walked out as capitalists.'

Oliver was a regular at the weekly *New Spotlight* Monday nights showband party at the TV Club. Monday was a night off for most bands, and their managers would get together for a chinwag and assessment of who was and wasn't doing business. The manager of the TV Club, Sean Sharkey, who always wore a dress suit and bow tie, stood at the front door with his bouncers, and John Coughlan, the *Spotlight* editor, would greet the various showband stars and managers. Sean, always a good guy to me, booked me as a DJ for the TV Club's teenage hops. He would always drag me to one side on a Monday night and warn me not to arrive next week in a drunken state or he would not let me in. 'And you will lose your gig here as well.' I never did.

Oliver, along with Jim Hand, Jim's brother Michael, and the *Spotlight* management gang (John Coughlan, Liz McHugh, Yvonne Dean, Donal Corvin, Sammy Smyth, Jim Slye, Shay Healy and James Morrissey) along with a bunch of good old boys, hillbilly showband managers, were regularly in attendance at the bar, which, believe it or not, sold hardly any alcohol (a glass of Blue Nun was the only alcohol available). However, most of the guys would arrive well tanked up, as like myself they'd have spent the previous few hours knocking them back in the Bailey, Bartley Dunne's or the Zodiac.

Anyway, I had an idea to open a record store, and even though I was earning £150 a week playing records, I had no money. One Monday night at the TV Club, I got into conversation with Oliver, and told him about my idea for the progressive rock music store. I didn't want to sell showbands, or Jim Reeves, Tom Jones or any other middle-of-the-road music. It would specialise in progressive rock and underground music only. 'Go for it,' said Oliver. 'Do you have a shop in mind?' I told him there was a basement available at 47 Nassau Street, right on the corner of Grafton Street. 'Brilliant location,' he said. 'Meet me at the Bank of Ireland in O'Connell Street at ten tomorrow morning, and I'll sort out a five hundred pound loan so you can get started.' As partners, we opened the Sound Cellar in December 1969, the first of six stores. We had to close the shop almost immediately when the basement got flooded, but we reopened in February 1970. In 1972, Oliver and I formed a company, Pat Egan Sound Ltd, which celebrates its fiftieth anniversary in 2022. We went on to promote ground-breaking gigs together, including Queen at RDS Simmonscourt, and Bob Marley, Black Sabbath, Status Quo and Meat Loaf at Dalymount Park. Fifty years later, Pat Egan Sound Ltd continues to run (except during the pandemic interruption) almost 250 shows a year, from small arts theatres to the 3Arena. I can never thank Oliver Barry enough for the loan of that £500 – it really did save my life in many ways.

'The rent for the basement will be £3 a week and I will give you the electric light for free.' So said Maureen Higgins, the elderly lady who ran the Cathedral Touring Agency, which was on the ground floor of 47 Nassau Street. Can you believe it? On the corner of Grafton Street, a sizeable space to open my great idea, for just £144 a year rent and free electricity! Even by 70s standards, it was a giveaway. To get the Sound Cellar looking different with the right visual style and ambience I installed about twenty coloured lamps to replace the one single light bulb that was there on the day I first rented the place. The coloured spot lamps were used to light up the album displays. I also put over a hundred old singles on the ceiling to make the Cellar look cool and trendy, which it most certainly was in 1971.

About ten years later, when the building was taken over by Neenan Travel, I received a solicitor's letter from one of the other tenants, Dublin Theatre Festival (which ran two offices on the first floor) to say that they had been paying my ESB bill for ten years and that I had been unlawfully using their power supply. They wanted me to pay up or they would take legal action. Luckily for me, I had a series of rent books dating back to when Maureen Higgins had written 'Rent £3 pounds a week with free light'. In double-quick time, new ESB meters were installed and my rent was increased to £25 a week.

In 2020, my best old pal Tommy Tighe, who bought the lease from me in the early 80s, celebrated 50 years of the Sound Cellar as Ireland's most iconic record store. Tommy was a close boyhood friend from Parnell Street who, like myself, had limited education but great street sense and quick-fire cop on. A brilliant worker, who knows every album and band that has existed since 1970, he is, like me, proof that given the opportunity, hard work and in-depth knowledge of your chosen path can bring its just rewards.

Oliver Barry continued to be a very special person throughout my early business years. He had contacts everywhere and he never hesitated to use them in our interest. From dealings with banks to his many associates in the entertainment business, asking Oliver to be my business partner was my best ever decision.

In his 2010 autobiography, *The Thing Is* …, Dave Fanning, a regular Sound Cellar customer and RTÉ's most credible DJ, devoted two full pages to the importance of the Sound Cellar to the developing Irish music scene in the early 70s and into the 80s. It meant a great deal to me that such a knowledgeable music man and broadcaster gave such high praise to the Sound Cellar as the only shop In Ireland where you could get the hip sounds of the day within a week after their UK release. Sound Cellar had become a very trendy joint to buy your albums and to hang out or be seen, and so I decided to build its profile by highlighting one major release every week and discounting it in the way that Virgin was doing in the UK. Rory Gallagher's self-titled debut solo album (released in May 1971) was my first pick. I dropped the price from £2 2s 6d to £1.99. It was the very first time the price of any album had been dropped below the recommended retail figure and there were raised eyebrows in the record companies.

Jack Fitzgerald was the main man in record retailing in Ireland in the 70s and 80s. His Golden Discs group had twenty or so shops across the country in main streets and shopping centres; he was also Jim Aiken's main concert ticket agent. At 9 a.m. on the very first morning of the Rory Gallagher discount offer, there was a queue of about thirty fans waiting for me to open to get Rory's new album for £1.99. Standing at the back of the queue, looking for all the world like the big shot businessman, was the dapper Mr Fitzgerald. Jack, a man on top of his game, had come to see the reaction to my big discount offer. When the first rush of fans had been sorted, Jack came up to the counter and in a very softly spoken tone, but with an underlying menace, said 'Young man, a word please. Just a little piece of advice as you're only starting off in the business and you need to learn how things operate. This discount lark is not a good idea and my advice to you is to drop it.'

Continuing with the discounts contributed greatly to the success of the Sound Cellar. The problem with new album releases in the 70s was that it could take up to two months for the local companies to release them here. I had an ongoing battle with the local labels, but EMI in Dominick Street were by far the worst offenders. The first Tír na nÓg album (self-ti-tled, released in May 1971) was in huge demand but took about three months to reach Dublin. The whole importation thing was a shambles. So much so that I approached Donal and Rory Gallagher about starting up their own label and distribution operations. I went further than that and had meetings in London with Island Records MD David Betteridge (who had taken over from Chris Blackwell) and George McManus at Polydor to complain about the delays in getting albums released in Ireland at the same time as the UK. I managed to get around it by flying to England once a fortnight to purchase up to 250 advance copies of new releases at a time and have them shipped to Dublin.

John Woods at Pye (and later Polydor) was the pioneering Irish record company boss of his day. An absolute gentleman, John was responsible for the early development of the record business in Ireland. At the height of the showband boom, acts on his Pye label were outselling all the other local releases by four to one. John was an easy man to talk to and even though I had no standing in the business in 1964, he would still invite me to his office in Parnell Square for a coffee and to chat about the developing beat scene. In 1969 I compiled a group compilation album for him with the still puzzling title of *Paddy Is Dead and the Kids Know It*. I had come up with the name as a way of telling the kids that the showband paddy-wackery attitude was on its last legs, and that a new generation of young Irish musicians was about to take over. The album, which sold a few thousand copies, was released on Pye Golden Guinea (so-called because the budget label sold albums at one guinea – one pound and one shilling) and featured acts such as The Bye-Laws, Purple Pussycat, Mitch Mahon and the Editions, the Pan Pipers, Some People, and Taxi. John had a great team at Pye, including Vivian O'Rourke, Freddie Blake, Jackie Ayres, Jimmy Morrisey and Pat Kennedy.

One piece of advice Oliver Barry offered, but which I did not take, was that if I started promoting concerts, Jim Aiken wouldn't be happy and would pull his ticket agency from us. Jim was a genuinely nice man who had time for everyone – you did not have to be a big player to get his attention. He was approachable, friendly and a great listener. Himself and Mickey Connolly would come to collect ticket money from our store, and Jim always wanted to know how business was, what was selling, and what did I think of this act and that band, and so on. He would spend up to fifteen minutes picking your brain about developing trends, but he also always showed respect, making you feel you were part of his success by looking after his ticket sales. But it came to pass, as Oliver had predicted, that when I promoted my first gigs at the National Boxing Stadium, Jim pulled his tickets from us and gave the lot to Golden Discs. This move upset Oliver because of the loss of revenue; it didn't damage our relationship, but Oliver had been right, it was premature on my part. Trying to establish myself as a promoter needed a lot more money in the bank than I had. I quickly realised I should have listened to the sensible advice of my more experienced business partner. Many times in my younger years, I dived into things like buying a house or car, agreeing to deals without doing the groundwork and research. 'Always look at the bigger picture,' counselled Oliver. 'Take your time because there will always be another opportunity, so don't go jumping in.'

Jim Aiken may have been referred to as 'Gentleman Jim' in the business, but when the chips were down, or when he perceived they were sliding that way, he had a ruthless side that I was on the receiving end of on occasion. I had promoted the first Irish gig for Queen at the RDS Simmonscourt, and when the band became available for another Irish show I approached the RDS only to discover that Jim had blocked the date I had requested. In simple terms, I had Queen, but he had the date I wanted and would not release it to me. Jim cut me stone dead: 'You're wasting your time. I have the act sorted so you can forget it – you won't be promoting Queen ever again.' Unknown to me, Jim had made a much bigger offer to Queen to play Slane. Despite going back and forward to London to chase the UK agent Harvey Goldsmith and the group's management I was not able to deliver. Lord Henry Mountcharles had also told me, 'If you have the act you have Slane,' but it wasn't to be. Slane was the one gig I would have loved to have promoted – it was by far Ireland's biggest and most prestigious live showcase event.

There's a great story relating to the ticket sales set-up we had with Jim Aiken for many years. On a sunny Saturday afternoon in the mid-70s I was at my Tape Shop at 13 Duke Street. We had that morning sold out our allocation of 400-plus tickets for a Rory Gallagher show. Jim was Rory's long-time promoter and I had sold tickets for every tour, including all those ground-breaking nights that Rory played at Cork City Hall, which was jammed with over two thousand kids who had just discovered Rory. As Ireland's pioneering guitarist and bluesman, Rory delivered some of the most electrifying nights ever witnessed in Irish rock history. At the height of his popularity, he had no equal in terms of live performances – he was simply explosive.

We had taken around £3,000 on that Saturday morning at the Tape Shop and I had placed it safely under the very bottom of the counter. Jim would always drop in himself just before closing to collect the cash and pay me our 5 per cent commission, which was big money in the 70s. At around 4 p.m., I heard a commotion in the street outside – tyres screeching, car doors banging, voices shouting. *What the hell's happening?* I wondered.

An armed raid was taking place two doors up from me at No. 11. Two armed raiders had held up the cake shop and got away with £200. I knew instantly they had hit the wrong premises. They were confused and failed to check the location properly. The cake shop at No. 11 Duke Street had had £200 in its till, while the Tape Shop at No. 13 had over £3,000! When Jim arrived that evening to pick up his loot, I had a box of buns, which I gave him when he entered our shop. 'Sorry, Jim, the cash is gone. We were robbed, but the thieves left you this as a present!' We laughed our heads off. We could just see the headlines, 'Cake shop robbery thieves get away with £200 and a box of doughnuts in mistaken store hold up' on the front page of the *Sunday Press*.

Having two successful music stores in downtown Dublin was not enough for me. I wanted to take on the big boys – Golden Discs, Dolphin, Murray Brothers. My problem was that Dublin was overrun with record shops. Oliver Barry suggested we focus on Cork city, which had no real contemporary record stores. Cork in 1974 was to be an entirely new experience for me. My life was turned on its head on both a personal and a business level. Oliver Barry had purchased 120 Patrick Street, a terrific four-storey premises for Rainbow Records. From day one, business was booming. There was little competition in Cork – the only other store worth talking about was Ursula's in Oliver Plunkett Street, but it looked tired and dated compared with our spanking new Rainbow Records, which boasted its own listening booths and personal headphones. Rainbow Records was the first of four stores we opened in Cork. Now with six stores in total, business was flourishing.

As the years passed, I found the day-to-day management of the business harder to handle. I was also burning the candle at both ends, and that never helps. In the late 70s, the first signs of a collapse in the economy were beginning to show. Two big Cork-based companies, Dunlop and Ford, shut their doors, with major job losses. Money was tighter and our shopping centre outlets were being squeezed on rent. It no longer made good business sense to have four shops operating within just a short walk from each other in the centre of the city. On the other hand, my concert promoting business continued to do well, and I had run a lot of major gigs in Dublin. I was operating as the local promoter for Asgard Agency's Paul Charles, who helped me to secure concerts with Elton John, Van Morrison and Paul Brady. Oliver sensed that I had lost interest in the shops and that I was spending too much time being a promoter.

He suggested we wind up the retail business and I agreed. It was a tough decision and a sad time for me. It broke my heart to walk away because I had some wonderful long-term staff in the shops. People like manager Catherine O'Brien, Noleen Dowling, Michael Murphy, Liz Murphy, Marianne O'Brien, Susan Tracy and Yvonne Murphy had all helped in advancing the business along its upward climb.

Ray Roche was a very dear friend whom we lost in recent years. One of the most popular guys in Cork, Ray, although employed at City Hall, had his finger in every pie in the city. He looked after the shops' security for me and managed any shows we took to Cork. I loved Ray, who was only in his early 50s when he died in April 2015. It was hard to hold back the tears when I met his lovely wife, Olive. Once again, all I could say was only the good die young.

As for the record shops, we closed or sold them off. Rainbow Records, our freehold building in Patrick Street, sold for over £400,000, which despite us having to pay off rent arrears on the other stores, left us with a sizeable profit. I now had enough money in the bank to look seriously at growing my concert promotion business.

11: QUEEN OF THE OLYMPIA

*T*n 1984, Brendan Smith, the legendary Dublin Theatre impresario and founder of the Dublin Theatre Festival, appointed me as a director of the Olympia Theatre. It was a great day for me. The eleven-year-old kid sitting with my sister Carmel in the gods at a Jack Cruise panto had a place on the board of a famous Dublin theatre. I was introduced to Brendan Smith by his assistant Pat Myhill, a very attractive blonde South African woman of exceptional charm who would later smash my life and heart into a thousand broken pieces. It all ended in tears, as Don Gibson sang in 1960. Once again, I was left drowning in a sea of tears, a sea of heartbreak.

Brendan Smith's actress wife, Beryl, Gerry Sinnott, Kevin Burke and Ronan Smith had taken over a theatre that, because of Brendan's illness, had fallen on hard times. The Olympia was in severe financial crisis, and without Brendan's renowned ability to pull a rabbit out of the hat when facing adversity, we were simply moving the props around on a sinking stage. Working alongside Ronan Smith was a pleasure. He's a lovely man and was forever trying to keep the peace at board meetings when sparks would fly over the theatre's never-ending mountain of problems.

Gerry Sinnott and I were appointed co-managing directors. It was a difficult partnership as were both pulling in different directions. Gerry, a lovely man with whom I became friends later in life, and who died in 2019, wanted the theatre to be a traditional performing house, with plays, musicals and so on. I wanted it as a concert venue because I felt that financially it was the only way of saving the theatre. Between Gerry's successful staging of shows such as *Children of a Lesser God* and *Run for Your Wife* and my concert promotions with the likes of Billy Connolly,

Shirley Bassey, Freddie Starr (and many more) we managed for a few years to keep our heads above water, but not for long. Eventually, I resigned and Gerry took over the everyday running of the theatre. Later, Denis and Caroline Desmond of MCD Productions bought Gerry out. The MCD concert policy has been a lifeline and has kept the 'Old Dame' alive; and for that, audiences can be grateful. I can honestly say that had Caroline and Denis not arrived to save the day, the Olympia might well have gone the way of the famous Royal Theatre and become nothing more than another theatrical memory of Dublin in the rare ould times.

During my time as a director and manager at the Olympia, I had many run-ins with the theatre union. Trying to introduce new work practices was a total nightmare. Without the help, support and loyalty of one very special lady, the job would have been impossible. Maureen Grant, a union shop steward, had spent her entire life working at the theatre. Time and again, she came out in support of my plans to streamline operations. Maureen's eldest son, Jimmy Grant, was the Olympia's house manager and his support was also invaluable to me. There was nothing but good in Maureen; her heart was always in the right place. It mattered not to her if you were Bono, Kris Kristofferson or a humble cast extra – she greeted and treasured everyone equally. Her care and concern for all the Olympia staff was legendary. My very good friend Rebecca Storm and I knew better than most the value of her love and friendship, and three great friends we were. Maureen started out as a sixteen-year-old usherette and bar girl in the late forties and rose to have the bar in which she worked, named in her honour, Maureen's Bar. All the great stars and entertainment names drank at Maureen's Bar: Shirley Bassey, Laurel and Hardy, David Bowie, Bono, Tyrone Power, and her own great favourite, Josef Locke. They all knew that once they entered her domain, there was only one star on show and that star was Maureen Grant. To say that I loved the lady would be an understatement. After 75 years at the theatre we lost her in 2021 and the Olympia bars will never again be as warm and welcoming.

Another great supporter from my Olympia days was Brian Whitehead, and I was delighted to see the former Olympia manager break big in 2019 with his band Picture This, which is now one of the hottest acts in the business. Brian's hard work ethic is another great example of what can be achieved without a university degree if you know your market inside out.

It was around this time that I ventured into something new alongside my directorship at the Olympia Theatre. From way back in the late

1800s, fly-posting had been the traditional way for travelling circuses and vaudeville acts to advertise their touring shows. Long before radio and TV advertising, an advance poster campaign was the best and sometimes the only way of letting the public know that a big circus or variety show was coming to town. In well over a hundred years little had changed. When I started posting for my concerts around 1979, I was like all the other promoters of the day – I was simply carrying on a practice that was part and parcel of staging any entertainment event. After securing the act and booking the hall, the next and most important move was to have posters printed and to get them onto the streets. Dublin in the 80s was very run down, and 40 per cent of the city was in a derelict state. There were lots of vacant shops and neglected sites abandoned by landlords, so finding space to fly-post was not a major problem.

The trouble began when three or four promoters went fly-posting all at the same time or on the same night. At around midnight, once the pubs had closed, I would load my car with posters for two or three upcoming gigs. Armed with a big bucket of paste and a pasting brush, off I'd go. I might start on the south side of the Liffey before heading northside, sometimes not finishing until two or three in the morning. Nine times out of ten, it was a clean sweep, but occasionally you would run into a bunch of rowdy nightclubbers heading home, who would mess with your paste bucket or nick a poster. A squad car might also stop to check that you were not posting IRA propaganda. Time and time again, after busting my gut posting a hundred or more posters, and then going to bed thinking I'd done a great job, MCD or Aikens would come out behind me and cover up all my stuff with their own gig posters. It was infuriating and soul-destroying. After a few weeks of hit and miss attempts, even leaving my run until 5 a.m., I was still losing out. I knew that if I over-posted MCD, they would send out a runner to pull my stuff down. The music and concert business needed to fly-post to create an awareness of shows and new record releases – we all needed the posters up to sell our gigs – but this was madness. Posters were being stuck up everywhere; on phone boxes, traffic light junctions and shop windows. The situation was getting out of hand and the once minor problems created by indiscriminate posting was

• •
In 1979, for their first ever Irish show, Queen arrived at the RDS Simmonscourt in four individual limos.
• •

becoming a major litter issue. Efforts by the city council to prosecute the culprits – which, of course, included me – were not working. Posters were the fastest way of getting the word on the street, but this mayhem was not in anyone's interest. And then I had, as the *Blackadder* character Baldrick would say, a cunning plan.

My idea was a long shot, but it would give all promoters a fair share of the derelict sites. First I had to get Dublin Corporation to go along with it. In 1986, I wrote to the then principal officer for the environment, Christopher Geoghegan, with a proposal to set up a poster company that would take responsibility for the proper distribution of all entertainment posters. The bigger promoters would pay £3 a poster and smaller independent gigs and bands just £1.50. The poster sites would be framed and painted in bright colours and would also be serviced every few days. I also agreed to provide a clean-up service that would remove all illegal and political posters from public phone boxes, shop for sale windows, lamp posts, etc. Because of the number of rundown sites owned by the Corporation, they were very keen to find a solution to illegal gig posting and I felt my proposal could solve the problem. Christopher Geoghegan liked my idea and agreed to put it before the council. Unlike some of his planners, he knew that high-quality, colourfully designed and properly displayed posters added to the city's visual life blood as well as projecting an alive, thriving and exciting image of the city as a place where music, theatre and the arts thrived. Over the years, I have fought many battles with the council to sustain Christopher Geoghegan's vision. Today, with little or no cost to the council or the developer, and with enormous ongoing development in Dublin, there is adequate room to accommodate, on temporary building hoardings, a striking poster platform showcasing Dublin's bustling nightlife. With a little imagination, event poster information could easily be incorporated into all builders' hoardings with stunning impact.

When Christopher Geoghegan mentioned my name to the councillors, there were complaints from some left-wing parties that I was a poacher turned gamekeeper, a pirate who had been breaking the law and now wanted the corporation to pay him to clean up the mess he helped to create. That was the general tone of their argument. However, 80 per cent of the councillors backed my idea. I appeared before the Keep Dublin Tidy council committee to make my case and lay out my plans. At first, the other promoters were reluctant to give me their poster business, fearing I would give my own gigs priority – which I never did. Anne Gara and

Noel McHale were instrumental in the early successful years of my poster operations. (Noel later became one of MCD's principal booking agents.) Promoters will always find someone to blame if a gig is not selling, and if the distribution of their poster campaign was not to their liking it was easy to blame me. If they saw my own gig posters or those of another competitor on a high street site where there was no sign of theirs, they would complain.

Dublin Corporation gave me a one-year contract to turn the situation around. It was never called in for renewal. Almost forty years on, Irish Poster Advertising is still in business serving the entertainment industry and continuing an entertainment fly-posting tradition that goes back over 120 years. While the ongoing development and visual improvements of Dublin city have continued on a daily basis, the event poster landscape continues to inform locals and tourists alike of great upcoming events and of the vast array of tourist attractions, galleries and museums that the city has to offer. Even in this new age of digital marketing, it's amazing how a city street poster campaign is still highly regarded as one of the best ways to announce the release of a new album or concert. Bands as big as U2 still use the street sites to announce the launch of tours or albums, and when the biggest acts in the world come to play Dublin their record companies will book campaigns welcoming them to the city.

In the early 1990s, I was invited to meet two visiting Belfast City councillors who were highly impressed with Dublin's street posting system. Fly-posting in Belfast was a chaotic mess, they said. They hoped to introduce something similar to what I was doing, sought my advice on how it might be set up, and then asked if I would be interested in running it. They had looked all over the UK and no council had anything in place that compared with Dublin. They were not the only people impressed with how the fly-posting in Ireland was organised. Several European promoters and acts had also complimented me on how well the system worked compared with other European cities. It is thanks to our great management team of Garrett Delaney and Caroline O'Neill that Irish Poster Advertising continues to offer the best fly-posting service in the entertainment business.

12: NEVER THE TWAIN SHALL MEET

*W*ith Sound Cellar doing great business, I decided to open up the first all-tape shop in the city. I had been blessed in Sound Cellar, having two of the most informed guys on the scene serve with me behind the counter. One was my lifelong friend John Miller, and the other was Peter Fallon, the internationally acclaimed poet (and creator of Gallery Press, which later published Phil Lynott's first book of poetry, *Songs for While I'm Away*). Peter is the brother of the legendary BP Fallon, and they both took turns looking after the shop. Their outstanding knowledge of the best music of the day was vital to in dealing with the madly enthusiastic customers.

Adrienne Foley, one of my favourite staff members in the early years, along with my first wife's sister Elizabeth Gernon, took on the initial management of the new cassette tape and 8-track cartridge shop. Based in Duke Street, I called it In Search of Tape after the Hawkwind album *In Search of Space*. At that time, the music business was all about the album, but cassettes and 8-track cartridge tapes were beginning to make serious inroads into album sales. It's incredible to think now that the CD had not been invented, and yet today, over 50 years on, CDs, just like cassettes and 8-tracks, are history. In Search of Tape was the first and only shop of its kind in Ireland. I also planned to use the shop as an exclusive concert ticket-selling outlet. Kevin O'Brien, who had designed the iconic Sound Cellar logo, once again came up with a brilliant design.

In the early 1970s, Kevin and Jim Fitzpatrick (the renowned designer of many Thin Lizzy album covers, and much more) were way ahead of the game as the only two local design artists who had successfully embraced the pop art form. Kevin's stuff had a touch of Roy Lichtenstein about it and I'm still using his original logo as our trademark. While In Search of Tape traded for thirteen years until the lease expired, I regretted not opening a bigger shop. It was too small and restricted and never reached the heights of Sound Cellar or Rainbow Records. However, what it did do was to establish my name among middle-of-the-road music fans as the place to buy concert tickets.

It was around 1975 that I opened my first promotion office on the top floor of 47 Nassau Street. In 1984, the same office also became the home of Irish Poster Advertising. Liz Gernon was instrumental in helping me set up Santa Anna promotions, the name I first used on all our early events. I had seen the movie *The Alamo*, as a kid in the old Regal Cinema and I had never forgotten the name of the Mexican general Santa Anna. There was something romantic and daring about his name, I felt. Without Liz's great support, hard work and input our concert business would never have developed into such a success. While I tended to be quiet and shy on the social and business level, Liz was the total opposite. Her lively personality endeared her to so many of the stars and managers who came to tour for us. While my awareness of developing trends and hit-making artists helped me to spot potential ticket-selling acts, Liz was the driving force in creating relationships.

Having moved to the UK in the late 70s as a personal touring assistant for Status Quo, Liz was very much in touch with what was happening in the UK record and touring market. She had become good friends with various managers, PR people, agents and promoters including Paul Charles, Judy Totton, Harvey Goldsmith, Alec Leslie, Steve Brown and John Reid. In the 70s and 80s touring was in its infancy and nothing like the sophisticated business it is today. With her ear to the ground in London, Liz would tip me off with details about various upcoming tours and which manager or agent to contact. I have never been a fan of agents, however – I always dealt directly with the managers. I viewed agents in the early years as being like second-hand car salesmen. The majority of them were blood-sucking piranhas, and it seemed to me the only qualification needed to be a showbiz agent was being rude, obnoxious and ignorant. This was something I never understood. I have always believed that it costs nothing but a few seconds of your time to listen to what someone has to say and treat them with respect. I never fail to take a telephone call or meet anyone who drops by the office, regardless of their standing. It's a good feeling to be polite and courteous and I make a habit of immediately calling back ticket holders who ring after a show with some complaint or other.

On the subject of agents, I still remember the agent for the ska band The Specials – Steve something or other from the Station Agency – roaring down the phone at me when I made a call to his office from a phone booth in London, 'Are you ringing me from a call box? I don't do business with people ringing from fucking phone booths.' He instantly hung up. I did eventually get to book The Specials in 1982 for an outdoor two-tone gig with the Selecter (and Dublin band Tokyo Olympics) at Dalymount Park for a fee of £10,000. I had picked the timing of the gig perfectly because eight or ten weeks before the agreed contracted date the group had released a song called 'Ghost Town', a monster hit that rocketed the group to number 1 and placed the ska revolution firmly in the main-stream. However, Station Agency Steve or whatever his name was now had the hottest act in Britain and no way was he letting them come to Dublin for some two-bit Irish promoter for the agreed fee because he knew I would make a big killing. He pulled the show on me with some flimsy excuse about recording commitments. I had to issue a court order in my long-drawn-out effort to have my £3,000 deposit returned.

One exception to the rule in those early days was Paul Charles from the Asgard Agency. All my early dealings were done with Paul, who came from Magherafelt, County Derry. Paul managed Fruupp, a psychedelic/prog rock band from Belfast. He later became an influential player in the development of the Irish concert business, and also managed, for a while, the careers of Van Morrison and Tanita Tikaram. In my early days at *Spotlight*, I had got to know Paul well. We were good friends and I looked up to him in the same way I did to Oliver Barry – as a guiding influence on my developing career. I liked him also as a pal and he became godfather to my son Graham. I helped him promote Fruupp in Ireland, as I knew he had invested heavily in the group. He and my sister-in-law Liz got on really well together, and in the early years of the Irish concert market, he gave me some of the greatest acts ever to play in Ireland, some true American, Canadian and Irish legends: Ry Cooder; JJ Cale; the Flying Burrito Brothers; McGuinn, Clark & Hillman (effectively The Byrds); Patti Smith; Emmylou Harris and the Hot Band; Loudon Wainwright III; The McGarrigle sisters; John Hiatt; Tom Waits; Paul Brady. Paul Charles, more than anyone else, helped to establish the name 'Pat Egan' as a concert promoter and for that I am eternally grateful. I was devastated, then, when our relationship soured. He and Liz had a falling out and he pulled all his shows from me. Extremely upset, I wrote to Paul begging him to reverse his decision not to work with me again, but to no avail. Paul had a ruthless side and I was on the wrong side of it. The loss of his friendship hurt just as much as the loss of business. I have always found it hard to separate the two and I have always been one to back down and face a loss rather than to lose a friend I valued. I have never been able to hold a grudge – yes, there are people I avoid by just saying 'Hello, goodbye' in the same breath – but I have always believed in living the door open. Unfortunately, I have never learned not to mix business with friendship.

Another lesson I learned too late was never to take anything for granted. I had promoted Status Quo for many years, including, with great success, our first-ever open-air show at Dalymount Park in 1979. Liz, my sister-in-law, hung out with Francis Rossi. They had a child together, Bernadette, and after Liz and Francis split up, Bernadette grew up in the same house in Toronto as my now distanced children, Graham and Deborah. My kids had no dad nearby but they did have two mums, my wife and Liz. I really loved Liz. She was a great sister-in-law, and I looked on Bernadette as a sister to my own two kids. I always tried to ensure that when I wrote or sent gifts or money to my own kids, which I did regularly, I included Bernadette. I would have done this regardless of whose daughter the child was, but we're talking here about the daughter of a millionaire rock star who, at that time, was not at all in his daughter's life. I knew Francis well from his many trips to Dublin to see Liz, and while we were not buddies, we had a decent relationship. (In fact, my ex-wife, Margot, had passed on to Francis a song she had heard on American radio – 'We're in the Army Now' – which Quo covered with huge success. Francis had produced two singles for me for Tokyo Olympics, a band I managed and in which I invested £25,000 trying to break the UK without success. A few years back Bernadette Rossi was fronting her own band and playing clubs in the Toronto area. She had, I was glad to hear, formed a special relationship with her famous dad.

Over the years, I had promoted some great concerts with Status Quo, at which I experienced some of the wildest crowd scenes of my entire career, including the night every one of the 400 floor seats of Dublin's National Boxing Stadium were smashed to smithereens by the manic air-guitar-wielding fans. And then there was the night at Belfast's King's Hall when the scheduled start of the show was delayed for an hour because the 12,000-capacity crowd were so tightly crammed against the stage front you could visibly see it move towards the back wall. Reinforced scaffold poles had to be lodged between the wall and the back of the temporarily constructed stage to prevent it collapsing. And the night at the Navan Exhibition Centre when yet another delayed start resulted in absolute mayhem. To this day I am still amazed that no one was injured. When the doors were finally opened the 5,000-strong crowd rushed to the front of house, resulting in the four entrance doors being blown off their hinges high into the air and then crashing down on to the floor, with broken glass flying all over the place. When Quo played Cork City Hall, I had to pull the security out from behind the front of the stage barrier as the steel bars holding it in place were starting to bend from the pressure of the crowd. Miraculously, no one was injured. These gigs in the 70s were really pioneering stuff. There were no health and safety rules, maybe one St John's Ambulance member in attendance, and no custom-built crowd barriers. I was, of course, flying by the seat of my pants and thank God no kid or bouncer got as much as a scratch. I think.

Imagine my surprise, then, when in the late 80s I bid for a Status Quo tour and was turned down without as much as a phone call from Francis to explain why I was being replaced by MCD as the Irish promoter. Twelve years of touring the act in Ireland was not worth as much as a phone call! I eventually called Francis, hoping he would sort it out, but he said it was not his call as they had new management. Instead, I got a call from London-based Agency Group chief Neil Warnock (now global head of touring music at United Talent Agency). Always far too self-important to be polite, he told me in no uncertain manner that it was no use using the 'old mates' trick with him. 'I'm calling the shots with Status Quo now,' he told me. 'You're out of the picture and Francis can't help you. Goodbye.'

13: 'HE'S MY BOYFRIEND, HE MANAGES THE BAND'

*T*n terms of the seated concerts we all know today, Jim Aiken was the pioneering music promoter of modern Ireland. Before him, in the late 50s and early 60s, there were other hit-and-miss Irish promoters who also toured international acts, but those appearances were mainly in dance halls and ballrooms. Music acts such as Jim Reeves, Johnny Cash, Slim Whitman, Charlie Pride, Hank Locklin and, a few years later, Roy Orbison, the Supremes, the Tremeloes, Status Quo and Marmalade all played ballroom tours and marquees in the football grounds of provincial towns. British-owned Irish cinema chains (and also Dublin's Theatre Royal) regularly featured seated concerts with major international acts. In February 1957, the Theatre Royal had the two wildest night in its history when the man credited with popularising rock'n'roll, Bill Haley, and his Comets, brought the house down (almost literally). In the 60s Cliff Richard, The Beatles, the Rolling Stones, Bob Dylan, and the Beach Boys all played Dublin's Adelphi Cinema. In the 1970s, when the trend for movie-going changed to triplex and multi-screen cinemas, movie house premises no longer ran live concerts. It was at this point that Jim Aiken began his pioneering run as Ireland's leading promoter.

In the mid- to late 50s, if you had access to a church hall, social club, school hall or hotel function room, you could clean up by running your own afternoon teenage hop, and then in the evenings there might be ballroom dancing with the likes of the Maurice Mulcahy or Mick Delahunty dance band. The secret for the smaller venues was to run a record hop or pay the group as little as possible, maybe £15 or £20. Few, if any, of the early Irish rock bands had managers, as there was no recognised touring circuit. All the gigs tended to be local and groups did not travel long distances. The only real touring musicians at that time were big bands and dance orchestras, and the very occasional international act. The first Irish beat groups to appear in the early 60s were the Viscounts, the Vic Mellows Quartet, The Caravelles (pre-Greenbeats), the Young Shadows and Four Keys. The Greenbeats had a television profile and were regarded musically as the best of the first wave of 60s groups. Ted Carroll was the pioneering group and club promoter of this period. Ted was always one step ahead of the developing trends in the music business. One of the nice guys, he was instrumental in Thin Lizzy's initial UK breakthrough.

If a band did have a manager, the chances were that on a good night he was picking up an extra tenner for himself from the venue owner or promoter as well as taking a cut of the band's poor fee. Parish halls, tennis, football and rugby clubs packed in as many bodies as possible at three shillings a head, and they were laughing, quite likely literally, all the way to the bank. It may have been peanuts by today's standards, but a guy running a weekly hop could clear over £150, which was big, big money back then. There was no such thing as a dance licence or insurance, no performing rights fees, no health and safety rules or building regulations to be complied with, and certainly no ticket commission or any kind of tax to be paid. Cash on the door has always been king at live entertainment events until Ticketmaster arrived on the scene in the 1990s. In the early 60s, the promoter or venue owner would employ two or three local gardaí as bouncers and two young women at the mineral bar. Advertising meant just a few pounds' worth in the neighbourhood news rag, and if he was lucky the local parish priest might be in on the act, getting a few shillings for his 'poor box' in return for announcing it from the pulpit after Sunday mass. Bands were lucky if a proper stage was provided, never mind a dressing room. Stage lighting was non-existent, three-phase power unheard of and you hired your speakers from the local radio and TV repair shop. The band would most likely have to put in a three-hour shift with just twenty minutes for a fag or, if they were lucky, tea and biscuits.

Things became a little more sophisticated in the late 50s and early 60s, when the Royal Showband kick-started the showband boom, taking the baton from the Clipper Carlton Showband, who are credited with being the original pioneers of the genre. Unlike the Clippers, the Royal were young and dynamic and had a teen idol frontman all of their own in

Brendan Bowyer. Bands at the top of the tree – such as the Royal Showband, The Capitol, The Freshmen and the Miami Showband – charged an admission price of eight or ten shillings, and would have been on a 50/50 split of the door. The band's manager would sit in the box office to keep an eye on everything to ensure he got his share (and it was still a great deal for the promoter and/or venue owner). The Royal Showband was the first act to charge over ten bob and introduce a 60/40 deal in favour of the band. On a St Stephen's night in the early 60s, at the Dreamland Ballroom in Athy, the legendary Royal Showband manager, TJ Byrne, broke all the admission rules by making his band the first ever to charge 15 shillings to attend a dance. It was unheard of at the time to break the ten-bob ceiling. Not that it made any difference to the turnout – the Dreamland was packed to the door, as was every other gig Brendan Bowyer and the Royal played. Bowyer was ahead of his time and probably one of the first ever tribute acts. He lacked Elvis's sex appeal by a mile but at the Arcadia in Cork on a Saturday night in 1962 he threw all the right shapes and the audience went wild.

Many of the minor names in the showband boom had to settle for a straight fee of £800–900, out of which they paid for transport to the gig and the hire of a sound PA system. They then split the balance between them. Musicians were working five and six nights a week for £50 – great wages in the early 60s when a storeman was on, at most, fifteen quid. The promoter/dance hall owner who got the numbers right could walk away with up to £1,500 or even £2,000 a night. That was very big money compared to what the bands were getting.

Red Hurley told me recently how he and his band went to London in 1970 to play a dance at the Hammersmith Palais ballroom and were paid a fee of £600. 'We could not believe it – six hundred pounds! – we thought all our birthdays had come at once. No one got that kind of money for a gig in 1970.' I remember meeting the late Paul Ashford in Grafton Street in or around the middle of 1967. Paul was a bass player in a really good beat group, the Chosen Few. He was over the moon with excitement, telling me he had been offered £80 a week to join the Dickie Rock Miami Showband and had just bought a new red BMW on the back of his new-found riches. I was in awe of him, thinking my £30 a week as a disc jockey – great money at the time – seemed like buttons. A year or so later, the recently deceased John Farrell, a brilliant lead singer and showman, and my best pal in the late 60s, was plucked from the promising rock band the Movement to front the Dreams showband. At just twenty-three years of age, he was delighted with his £90 a week.

The band management and promotion set-up in the showband days worked on different levels. There were co-op bands, where all the band members and the manager shared the door takings or fees equally. In other scenarios, the showband leader or the star frontman and manager 'owned' the band, and would pay a guaranteed wage to the musicians, regardless of how good or bad business was. In cases where the band was owned and operated by various businessmen and managers (people like Jim Hand and Mick Quinn), some musicians were on a straight weekly wage. These bands tended to have ongoing line-up changes, as guys dropped in and out looking to improve their earnings and profile. In a lot of co-op bands, the lead singer's rising popularity, inflated ego and star profile would lead them to believe they were worth more than everyone else. This resulted in original or founding members taking the hump and leaving or being bought out to be replaced by new players on a straight wage. This is what happened in the original Miami Showband when Dickie Rock felt he was carrying the other members and not getting the rewards.

For the younger showband musicians, the decent wage at the time and the glamour of being on stage in front of adoring girls was a big buzz to their egos. Few of them were thinking ahead – for them, it was all about living in the moment and overdosing on drink and women. But all the screams and adulation had to be balanced against the drudgery and the monotonous, never-ending cycle of eight hours a night on the roads between Dublin, Kerry, Cork and Donegal, perhaps only stopping along the way for dodgy fish and chips or hamburgers. There was no such thing back then as an overnight stay in a hotel or guesthouse – it was back into the minibus at 2 a.m. and then to Dublin by 6 a.m. You had a few hours' kip and then you started the same tedious routine all over again. This was not the generation of musicians and crews spoiled rotten by the luxury of sleeper coaches and supplies of cool beers and fresh prawn salads. There were no on-the-road caterers at every gig, no tour managers or roadies to help take the pressure off the performers. The band loaded and set up their own amps, drums, sound system, lights; and in the vast majority of venues, no decent dressing room facilities were supplied. It was seven guys plus a driver crammed into the back of a minibus. Night in, night out. Often the band members took turns at the wheel. It was a horrendous way to live and highly dangerous because of the appalling state of Irish roads in the 60s and 70s. Inevitably, there were road crashes, some serious, and many musicians never returned to the roads again.

I made many trips in Transit vans with beat groups in the 60s, either sitting on drum cases and amplifiers or on the floor with no room to stretch my legs. It really wasn't for the faint-hearted and I know I wouldn't have lasted such gruelling itineraries. If anything, the original beat groups were even more harshly treated by venue owners and promoters. I still have in my possession, from 1970, a written confirmation from the Star Club in Dublin's South King Street to pay Thin Lizzy a gig fee of just £25 and another in the same year from Premier Promotions in Tipperary for a fee of £33 for dancing 8 p.m. to 11 p.m. That's mind-boggling, especially when you consider that at the top of their game in the 90s, Phil Lynott and the boys were picking up £25,000 a night for their shows at the RDS in Dublin. By comparison, I went to Cork City Hall with Skid Row and the Movement in the late 60s for £5. The two bands picked up £30 quid between them. I got the same money when I went around the country with Phil making personal appearances at discos for *New Spotlight* magazine. Philo was picking up double my money at £10 a gig. Even in the early 80s, lots of groups played well-attended gigs in the provinces but the venue owner or promoter refused to pay them. Often confronted at the end of the night by a bunch of local heavies, they were thrown £40 or less and told to fuck off home to Dublin.

From the late 70s, the business became more sophisticated. The acts started to ask questions about where the money was going. Band managers got contracts from the promoter, checked the ticket stubs, counted the seats or tallied the punters walking through the front door with a sheep clicker. Some promoters even printed two sets of tickets with identical numbers so that they could get in an extra few hundred punters unnoticed by the act. Bouncers had to be closely watched to stop them running a scam by opening exit doors and pocketing hidden cash. The government eventually introduced value added tax on admissions, but by then it was too late to have any meaningful effect on the massive revenues that were

* *
'You sent a fucking taxi! We never travel to gigs in taxis.' – The Hollies' Tony Hicks to me when our limo driver went missing and we had no other option but to collect them from their hotel in taxis. The Hollies, a group I loved promoting, never toured for me again.
* *

creamed off the top. Those were the days before Ticketmaster arrived and changed all the rules. Right up until the arrival of Ticketmaster, there was no such a thing as a computerised ticket manifest. Hard tickets were printed and you relied on the printers' good reputation that they only printed the agreed number. At my Dalymount Park open-air gigs in 1979, 1980 and 1981, as many as five thousand counterfeit tickets were scammed for each show.

Like so many successful entertainment partnerships, the people making real bucks aren't on stage but in the background. This was especially true of Irish showbands. A handful or two of ballroom owners, promoters and managers made their fortunes on the back of starry-eyed young and inexperienced singers and musicians. By the mid-80s, the majority of showband musicians had returned to their day jobs. Drugs, drink, sex and rock'n'roll had taken their inevitable toll. Marriages hit the rocks, and dozens of the guys had emigrated to the USA and Canada in search of greener musical fields. There are endless stories of star showband players scraping around for a gig in their later years and even one of two of them dying penniless.

There is a widely held belief that the only star performers to have made their fortune out of the showband boom were Dickie Rock, Paddy Cole, Ben Dolan and Tommy Swarbrigg – by all accounts, they still have unopened Miami, Capitol, Drifters and Times pay packets under their beds! Some of the venue owners, promoters and band managers who became showband multi-millionaires were Con Hynes, Jim and Albert Reynolds, Tom Costello, Brian Molloy, Oliver Barry, Jim Aiken, Ben Dolan, Seamus Casey, Mick Quinn and Bill Fuller. The majority of them spread their millions across shrewd investments in property, radio stations, hotels and new venues.

As a teenager in 1964, I was a regular Saturday night dancer at the Crystal Ballroom in St Anne Street. I grooved to the sounds of the Dixies, the Pacific, the Capitol and the Cadets showbands. It was my very first introduction to the excitement of showband mania. Something that always stood out for me – and I can recall it vividly to this day – was the sight at the back of the hall, as you made your way upstairs to the minerals bar, of two very imposing characters standing a few feet apart and observing the buzz of the dance floor. One, in his early 30s, looked like a boxer, small and rough around the edges. The other was taller and stylish, just like a Hollywood matinee idol. They never danced, they weren't bouncers, so who were they? It was only when I asked a stunningly beautiful young girl named Anita to dance that she told me that one of them, the 'movie star', was Mick Quinn. 'He's my boyfriend, he manages the band,' she said, and I realised then that the two guys were taking care of business. Little did I know that these young dudes were to become two of the craftiest, most mysterious and most legendary operators of the showband years – the elusive Kerry man Bill Fuller and the debonair Mick Quinn.

Fuller had the reputation of being the smartest and toughest of them all. He was certainly the most connected and successful. At the height of his career in the 70s and 80s Fuller owned 23 ballrooms and clubs including the Electric Ballroom in Camden Town, the Crystal in Dublin and San Francisco's Fillmore West. Fuller was also a concert promoter and presented legends Billie Holiday and Patsy Cline in concert at Carnegie Hall. He was part-owner of the Holiday Motor Inns chain and had a big stake in an Eldorado gold mining company. In the 60s, when Las Vegas was controlled by the Mafia, Fuller was the only man who could get an Irish act (the Royal Showband) a headlining run at a Vegas casino. A strong supporter of the IRA, he died at the age of 91 leaving a vast fortune in property across the USA, the UK and Ireland.

Mick Quinn, or Quinner as he was known, came from the working-class Dublin suburb of Drimnagh. He chose a different route to invest his showband millions. When he died in 2016, the former manager of the Dubliners, the Pacific Showband, Red Hurley, and Maxi, Dick and Twink, was reputedly owed £7 billion – yes, £7 billion – by the Nigerian government for a failed oil pipeline deal. His estate is in an ongoing legal wrangle with the Nigerian authorities. It's a long, long way from the swinging 60s at the Crystal Ballroom St Anne St in Dublin to the mob-controlled casinos of Las Vegas or the black gold oilfields of Nigeria.

You have to hand it to Mick Quinn and Bill Fuller. Two absolute legends.

14: THE ULTIMATE DIVA

*S*hirley Bassey was a Cristal champagne lover and one of the original divas, a spell-binding performer with an incredible voice and stage presence, and certainly one of the greatest I have ever heard or seen. Sheer class. Only Barbara Streisand and, I must add, Rebecca Storm in her prime came anywhere near Shirley in terms of vocal ability, and no one, but no one, had her on-stage charisma. Standing in the wings for every show, I could actually feel the hairs on the back of my neck rise up as she poured her entire soul into songs such as 'I Who Have Nothing', 'The Impossible Dream' and the ultimate showstopper, 'Goldfinger'. On the three occasions I promoted her tours, I never missed a second of her performances. That's how great I thought she was.

In 1983, I had hung around, for three full days, the offices of MAM (Management Agency Music), Shirley's management company in London in the hope of meeting her manager, Barry Clayman. I was desperate to bring her to Ireland because I knew she would sell tickets. When I eventually got to meet her no-nonsense Jewish manager, his opening comments to me were, 'Shirley does not come cheap. You are looking at forty to forty-five thousand pounds to cover the orchestra, rehearsals, flights from Switzerland, where Shirley lives, local transport and deluxe hotel suites for three days – plus all her extras.' I didn't blink. I said 'No problem', but I knew I was getting in deep and that if the gig bombed I would lose my record shops to the bank. I needn't have worried. It turned out to be one of my biggest early successes as a promoter. For her show in the RDS Main Hall, we sold 4,300 tickets at £25–£30 each. The top ticket admission price of £30 was unheard of in the early 80s, but so was a gross box office of over £120,000.

Nothing and no one I had previously dealt with could have prepared me for the penniless kid from Cardiff's Tiger Bay who had risen from poverty to become a global superstar. She insisted on being called 'Miss Bassey', unless she told you otherwise. She had two full-time female assistants who did everything for her, and when I say everything I mean they satisfied her every whim. She was treated like genuine royalty, and everyone around her walked on eggshells for fear she would throw a tantrum. In relation to her hotel requirements, the suite had to be spotless, and she disliked anyone having stayed in the room the night before her arrival.

A letter from her management to the hotel and the RDS read: 'Miss Bassey is allergic to paint. Therefore, neither the hotel nor the venue should be painted in the two-week period leading up to the engagement.'

Miss Bassey stayed in Jury's Ballsbridge. At that time this very fine hotel was where I put all my visiting acts, who were always happy with it and with the exclusive VIP treatment that management provided. Not Shirley. I was summoned to her suite. 'The suite is beautiful and I love the embroidered towels,' she said. Embroidered towels are a touch I have always provided for our visiting acts. But there was more. 'But I can't go through that lobby again – it's like a bloody railway station. Make sure it's cleared before I leave for the show.'

'Yes, Miss Bassey,' I responded.

Jury's Ballsbridge Hotel was always busy in the 80s – even at midnight, the Coffee Dock was jumping. Harry McKeown, my security manager and lifelong pal, came up with a route out of the hotel through a banqueting room, into the kitchen, across the garden and out through the side gate, where Shirley's limo was waiting to take her five hundred yards across the street into the RDS. The venue wasn't to her liking, either. 'It's a shed and it's freezing,' she noted. Thankfully, she had no complaints about the show or the audience. Indeed, she was blown away by the audience – she received five standing ovations. She was on a high. I was called to the dressing room where she threw her arms around me, kissing me half a dozen times. 'Patrick, darling, what a wonderful, wonderful night! Thank you so much for bringing me to Ireland. We must do it again soon! And by the way, please call me Shirley!'

We did it again in later years at both the Olympia and the National Concert Hall. At the Olympia, she threw a tantrum and walked off the stage mid-set. *Fuck it!* I said, in a panic. She had to finish the show or I'd be up shit creek, what with having to pay refunds. By this time, though,

I knew her quite well. She would call me 'Pat, darling' and I would call her Shirley. In her dressing room she was hyper. 'My voice is in bits, I can't go on, Pat, darling. I am so, so sorry.' I asked her, quite sheepishly, if she could explain to her fans that her voice was suffering and could she just do an encore? Her response? 'I'm going to gargle this wine vinegar for a while and see how I feel. It normally works for me.' A few minutes later, her tour manager Steve Rayment called me aside and whispered 'She'll be fine. Make the announcement.' The orchestra had stayed on stage, thank God, and I told the audience that Miss Bassey would return in ten minutes. She did and sang two songs. We got a few complaints the next day about the shortness of her set – 65 minutes – but in general her devoted fans were just delighted to see her perform. She may have been trouble with a capital T, but I just loved everything about her.

In my early days as a promoter I encountered another temperamental prima donna, but in no way was she as likeable as Shirley Bassey. Dionne Warwick is the instantly recognisable voice of all those magical Bacharach and David hits – 'Do You Know the Way to San Jose', 'You'll Never Get to Heaven', 'Walk On By' – and the brilliant Barry Gibb song 'Heartbreaker'. Alongside Dusty Springfield, Dionne was among my favourite acts of all time. You know that old saying about never meeting your heroes for fear of being disappointed? I'm sorry to say it, but Dionne Warwick tops my list of stars who were rude, bad-mannered and ungrateful.

From the moment she arrived at Dublin airport she was complaining non-stop about everything. Without as much as saying hello, she wasn't impressed with the welcoming bouquet of flowers, dumping them instantly on her assistant. The short walk to the car upset her greatly – because of security concerns, it had to be parked a hundred yards from the front of the airport. The hotel suite was too small and cramped. And as for the venue, the Olympia, 'What am I doing playing in this dump?' she said to her tour manager. 'Just look at the state of the dressing room.' Admittedly, the Olympia was in the 80s in desperate need of a coat of paint and a general makeover, but the rooms were clean, and we had brought in bouquets of flowers, mirrors, sofas and heaters. But she still hated the place. My big problem, however, was that she sang only a few of her big hit songs and walked off stage after 55 minutes. When I requested an encore, she refused. The tickets had been expensive (£50) and she did not sell out the venue. The audience were incensed, and the following day the phone was hopping with complaints from punters looking for refunds. It was an evening to forget.

Even her opening act, the undiscovered Colm Wilkinson, was unhappy with his £75. 'Is that it?' he asked me, with equal levels of astonishment and disappointment. There I was thinking I was being generous paying a support act the not ungenerous fee of £75. Even though it was back in the early 80s, Colm knew his worth!

15: 'GIMME THE FUCKIN' MONEY!'

My first brush with crime and drug lords was at the National Boxing Stadium in 1979, at a concert I was promoting for Eric Clapton. The 2,000-seater hall was sold out. Just before the show got under way, I asked the bouncers to clear the aisles of people who were standing there and blocking the view of the stage for those already seated. The crowd moved into their seats as showtime was approaching, except for four guys who stood right at the centre of Block H, obstructing the view of the people sitting in Block D, which were the best seats in the venue. There was no way the people behind them would be able to see the show, so I ran down to where they were and said, 'Come on, lads, you have to move now.' Before I could utter another word, I was lifted off my feet by the lapels of my jacket. 'Do you know who the fuck I am, you little prick?' said the guy, inches from my face. 'I'm Shamie Dunne, and don't you ever speak to me like that again.' He dropped me to the floor. Now I knew why none of the bouncers had asked the four guys to stand aside. Like everyone else, I'd heard about the Dunne brothers, but to me they existed in another world, a world I had never come into contact with. At the end of the gig, as the hall was clearing, I saw Shamie talking to one of the bouncers, who was pointing across the hall at me. I stood frozen to the spot as Shamie approached with two of his mates. 'I didn't know you were the gaffer,' he said. 'Sorry for roughing you up, head. No harm intended.' I meekly replied, 'No problem', but he just turned on his heel and walked away. I hoped that I would never see or hear from Shamie again, but it wasn't the last time.

Shamie began to regularly call my office, asking to speak to me and requesting to be put on the guest list for various concerts. 'Pat,' he'd start, sounding like an old pal. 'How am I fixed for six seats for Joan Armatrading?' My reply was always, 'No problem, Shamie, you're on the guest list.' He would always ask politely if there was any chance of having a photo taken with whoever the headline act was. He seemed like a nice enough kind of guy, but I never hung around long enough to find out.

Fast forward to Dalymount Park, Sunday 6 July 1980, the day Bob Marley and the Wailers played their first and only Irish concert. It was around 1 p.m., and Bob and the band had just completed their soundcheck and returned to their dressing rooms. Ronnie Lane and his Slim Chance band (who had at the last minute replaced the Average White Band) were still on stage doing a line check. I noticed there was a commotion at the backstage area. One of Bob's own security guys, a large dreadlocked Rastafarian, was refusing entry to three guys who wanted to see Bob to give him a gift. *Oh, shit*, I said to myself, walking quickly away before I was seen, *it's Shamie Dunne*. A short time later I walked into the VIP bar, only to hear the dreaded words, 'Hey, Pat, it's me, Shamie.' He jumped up from his seat and walked over. 'Pat, I want to see Bob. I have something special for him.' How Shamie and his mates had even got into the VIP area in the first place was another story. At the top of their reign as drug lords of Dublin, it's safe to say that no dancehall, nightclub, disco or concert security man in the city would stand up to, confront or, God forbid, refuse the Dunne brothers and their gang entry into Dublin's thriving nightlife venues. From experience, I know that 95 per cent of major touring acts do not see guests before a performance. The social side of a gig is always after the show, as the acts simply do not want to meet people, including close family, before the gig. I can remember a number of occasions when even the band's wives were not permitted backstage before a show.

'Shamie, it's out of my control,' I said. 'I simply cannot let you in. It's not my call.' Shamie's response sent a chill down my spine. He said, very quietly, 'I'm not happy, Pat. Where's Bob's manager? I really want to talk to him.' Mick Cater, who was Marley's European tour promoter, arrived on the scene. At first, he said a very firm no – 'No one sees Bob until after the show.' At that point, Shamie got up from his seat, put his arms around Mick's shoulder and whispered something in his ear. Mick nodded, looked at me, and said, 'Leave it with me. I'll talk to Bob.' Ten minutes later, Shamie, on his own, was ushered into Bob Marley's dressing room to present the mysterious package. Terry O'Neill, who was the press officer for the gig, later told me what had happened. 'Pat, there must

112

have been a least a full pound or more of sugar [weed] in that bag. They couldn't have smoked it all. I wonder if it's still in the dressing room!' Terry was known to smoke a joint or two during his days managing Thin Lizzy, another bunch of guys who knew the value of a pound of weed. During my early promoting career, I had not come across a lot of heavy drug use. In the 60s, I knew dozens of guys who smoked pot; I'd been to parties with Phil Lynott, Henry McCullough, Bobby Kelly and numerous other musicians where a joint instead of a drink was the way to go. In the 70s and 80s, lines of coke were commonplace in dressing rooms before the act went on stage. I had seen, among others, some of Eric Clapton's US band doing serious drugs on their Irish tour. Almost every band and musician who toured in that period were smoking weed. I smoked the stuff a number of times myself but it didn't do anything for me. I much preferred a scotch and Coke and female company to a joint.

Twenty-three thousand fans had paid into the Bob Marley Afternoon in the Park gig at Dalymount. On top of that at least five thousand more had counterfeit tickets. It was also the first gig where parents were invited to bring along their kids free of charge. In total, the audience was well over thirty thousand. Running a concert of that size in 1980 was a walk in the park compared to what today's outdoor promoters are up against.

In early 1980 I had gone to London, having heard on the grapevine that Bob was planning a European tour for promoter Alec Leslie. I secured the gig in March that year for a fee to Bob Marley of $60,000, very big money in 1980. My original idea was to use the RDS Simmonscourt arena where I had presented Queen the previous year, but the RDS turned down me down on the grounds that Rastafarianism was a religious cult. I had also wanted to charge £10 a ticket but Bob Marley himself said no, the tickets must not go over £7. He did not want the fans ripped off.

Back then, no licence was applied for and health and safety clearances were neither sought nor given. In fact, it was only ten days before the gig that I dropped into Mountjoy Garda station to let them know it was on and that we were expecting at least twenty thousand fans to attend. 'No problem,' said the sergeant on duty, 'let me write it in the book,' which he did. As I said thanks, he asked, 'How many are you expecting?'

'Twenty thousand, I hope.'

'Oh, that many?' said the sergeant 'And will there be a few tickets for the lads?'

'Of course,' I answered.

The Dalymount gig that sunny Sunday in July 1980 has become the stuff of legend and I am very proud that it was such a great success. Bob was the first internationally acclaimed artist to headline an Irish festival. It's desperately sad to think that no one present on that historic day would ever have thought for one moment that within a year Bob Marley would be dead from melanoma cancer the age of just 36.

His final words to his son Ziggy were, 'Money can't buy you life.'

As Dublin's drug and crime trade continued to grow in the 1980s, so did the violence. Nightclubs and music venues were prime easy-money targets for Dublin's new crime lords. Shamie Dunne – maybe because of his egotistical need to mix with rock'n'roll royalty and to treat all his mates to the best free seats at my shows – saw me as a pal, but luckily for me, that was as close as the relationship got. I was not, however, as lucky in one or two of my other underworld experiences. I have been held up by a gunman twice, the most serious by far being an armed raid when a sawn-off shotgun was held only two inches from my face. The remarkable thing about these incidents is that they happen very quickly, so you really don't have time to think or react. Nor would you want to.

The most frightening and surreal moment happened in the late 1980s. It was 3.30 on a Sunday morning outside the AIB bank on a deserted Capel Street and I had just finished a bumper night at the Waterfront, the night-club I owned on Sir John Rogerson's Quay. It had been one of those great Saturday Disco Inferno nights, with the group Shush packing the place to the rafters and over four hundred punters raving the night away. Shush were one of the very best bands of that period, and they never failed to bring in the crowds. In the late 80s and early 90s there were very few late-night drinking venues in Dublin, and the Waterfront was one of the few places with a late-night dance licence. The venue (also known as Columbia Mills) originally opened as a restaurant but had failed to take off and was later converted to a nightclub. Because the premises held a restaurant licence, it was allowed to operate at later hours than a normal pub, simply by applying to the court every Friday for a bar extension. Once the pubs closed at 11 p.m., the Waterfront would start to fill up with punters chasing that last pint or gin and tonic. I changed the name of the club to the Waterfront Rock Café in the hope of giving it a broader appeal. It worked big time, and I secured a lot of private and business receptions. The filming of *The Commitments* at the venue was a major coup, as was a one-off appearance by David Bowie and his Tin Machine.

Bowie had played the Baggot Inn a day or so before the Waterfront. I received little or no notice that he wanted to play another club gig, but just one mention of it on 98FM was enough to have over four hundred people queuing outside two hours before doors opened. My good pal David Heffernan, one of RTÉ's best music producers, also used the venue to film the *On the Waterfront* rock music series. I had never really wanted to buy the place, to be honest. The previous owner, Gerry O'Reilly, had bought my Temple Bar venue, the Backstage pub (which became better known when its name was changed to Bad Bob's), and he offered me the Waterfront as part payment for outstanding monies due. Gerry was one of those maverick operators who had a funny-strange way of doing business, and even though I didn't really want to get into the nightclub business, his offer was 'take it or leave it', and so I reluctantly had to accept it. O'Reilly was a flawed genius and a brilliant visionary of nightlife enter-tainment, and Bad Bob's was one of the great venue/bar successes of the 90s. Run by the larger-than-life former DJ Derry Glenn, it revolutionised Dublin's nightlife with live music seven nights a week, turning the place into half Nashville saloon, half New Orleans speakeasy. The alcohol was legit, but the experience was totally off the wall.

Anyway, at the Waterfront on the night in question, I had been advised by my long-time friend Barry Gaster (who was at this point the manager of blues musician/singer Don Baker) that the renowned film director Alan Parker was in town and was interested in checking out the Waterfront as a possible location for his next movie, an adaptation of Roddy Doyle's book *The Commitments*. To say the place was jam-packed when Parker arrived with the Corrs' manager John Hughes was an understatement. Shush had done it again with a set that blew the place to pieces. I could not have picked a better night to show the place off. Parker loved the electric atmosphere and the buzz of the whole dockland area. Not only did he end up shooting major scenes there, but he also used the place as a base for auditions, rehearsals and the movie wrap and launch party. Funnily enough, I even got my face on *Entertainment Tonight*, the big US coast-to-coast Saturday night TV show, when they asked me to stand at the door with my manager and old pal, Shay Hession, and our bouncers, and pretend to refuse their presenter admission to the party. 'Sorry, VIPs and guests only,' was my line, which in fairness I didn't have to rehearse because I'd been saying it for quite some time! With 40 million TV viewers across the USA checking out the Waterfront, I had finally achieved my fifteen minutes of fame – or was it just twenty seconds? Regardless, I was over the moon that night following Parker's visit. John Hughes subsequently gave me the heads-up that Alan loved the place and would be back in touch about renting the Waterfront for a period of six weeks or more.

That night, by the time I got everyone off the premises and the place cleaned up, it was after 3 a.m. The routine we followed to deposit the night's takings was simple: we always used two cars to take the bank bags to the night safe at AIB's Capel Street branch. That night, the 'House Full' sign had gone up early and the bars were flying, so we had £8,000 in cash. Myself and our senior bouncer, Richie, split the cash into two bags. Richie and one other bouncer would travel half a minute ahead of me in one car, while I followed behind with one of the barmen in my car. It was a run we had done a hundred times without any incident, but tonight was going to be very different. The car with Richie and Sean was only a few seconds in front as we entered Henry Street from O'Connell Street. As Henry Street runs into Mary Street, the bank becomes visible. On the top left-hand side of Mary Street, 50 yards or so from the bank, is a small laneway. Richie's car had passed it, and just as mine did I heard a screech of tyres. Head-lights blinded me from behind, and the BMW driven by the gang slammed into the passenger side of my car, spinning it 180 degrees to face back in the direction of O'Connell Street. I didn't have time to be shocked. Before I knew it, a man wearing a balaclava and holding a sawn-off shotgun was at my driver's window. 'Get out! Get out!' the voice boomed into my face. As I opened the door, he stuck the sawn-off shotgun a couple of inches in front of my face and shouted 'Gimme the fuckin' money!' Out of sheer fear, I dropped the bag onto the road at his feet. Unfortunately, unlike my real action hero, Steven Seagal, I didn't kick him in the head. Frankly, I was scared shitless, riveted to the spot and quaking in my boots. All I could hear was the other armed raider shouting at Richie, 'Where's the other fuckin' bag? Give me the fuckin' bag!' Richie was one of the best

• •

The great American hitmaker Gene Pitney only wore his underpants in the dressing room right up to three minutes before going on stage. He only met guests before the show, which is the opposite to most other acts, and he always wore just his underpants. He never went back to the venue dressing room after a show, but walked straight out of the stage door into his limo and back to his hotel.

• •

bouncers I had worked with, a gentle giant, soft-spoken and polite, but as tough as nails. Like a lot of bouncers I'd met over the years, he had a short fuse that was not to be tampered with. I could see that Richie was actually considering taking on these guys, and not handing over the second bag. I shouted at him a number of times, 'Richie, for fuck sake, give them the bag!' Richie handed it over. It had all lasted less than a minute. I just stood there, at almost 4 a.m., in the centre of Capel Street, dazed and bewildered. I had survived, but I have never erased the image of the gunman holding the sawn-off shotgun next to my face. I had always known that the entertainment business was a magnet for criminals, so I counted myself extremely lucky to have walked away from the hold-up in one piece.

Intimidation and protection rackets were all part of the club and pub scene in Dublin in the 80s, and I had also come face to face with serious threats to my health and business when I opened the Backstage Pub in Temple Bar. This was three years or so before the redevelopment of what is now the Temple Bar Quarter. When I was a director of the Olympia Theatre, I spent a lot of time hanging around the theatre and surrounding area. One evening, passing what was then the Granary Bar on the corner of Sycamore Street and Essex Street, I stopped to speak to a nightwatchman at the door of the pub. He told me that the bar had closed down and that the bank intended to put it up for sale again the following month. I made immediate plans to put my own place, the Anglers Rest, up for sale and to buy the Granary, because at just £225,000 it was an absolute bargain. An A-listed freehold building in Temple Bar for less than a quarter of a million quid? It may have been the early 80s but it was still a bargain. It was a magnificent four-storey building that had been run by two well-known rugby brothers. The owner of the freehold was the brother of restaurateur John O'Byrne, who owned Dobbins, a trendy and popular Dublin eatery. I knew the Granary as the place where Paul McGuinness had signed U2 to a management deal. It was also the location for the 1967 movie of *Ulysses*, starring Milo O'Shea, Fionnuala Flanagan, Rosaleen Linehan and Jim Bartley, so it was indeed a historical building.

At that time, I had my own bar, the Anglers Rest, down by the Strawberry Beds on the banks of the River Liffey. I was never a publican and had no idea about running pubs. Only for the hard work of Noel Gernon, my brother-in-law, and his wife Marion, the Anglers Rest would have sunk without trace in no time. I had been making big money from concerts and my accountant told me to invest it in a bar. That sounded fine and dandy, but no one ever told me about the amount of work and the hours involved. My time at the Anglers Rest was enjoyable but was not without the constant shadow of fear. The previous owner's son had been shot dead on the premises, and that tragedy hung over the place like a curse. Ninety-five per cent of the clientele were salt-of-the-earth Dubliners and a sheer joy to know and serve. It was the other five per cent that you could never get away from – shadowy characters, drug dealers and two-bit gangsters who used the bar as a meeting place. There was always a sense that something sinister, tragic and dangerous was just around the corner. Pubs were a prime target for cash robberies and burglaries, and we had our share of them at the Anglers Rest, so again, I was lucky to avoid any serious criminal contact. The day I sold that pub was a happy one. I had come out of the deal with enough money to invest in a new property in town and I felt things were really happening for me. At just 38 years of age I had three serious businesses operating at one time – our concert division, our poster business and now our new city centre bar enterprise. Life was looking promising, and despite the pain of my children having emigrated to Canada without me, I still had big hopes for the future.

The prospect of moving into a marvellous Temple Bar building, right in the centre of Dublin City, was exciting and motivating. In the 80s Temple Bar was not the razzmatazz tourist centre it is today. I sensed the new bar was going to have to create and attract its own audience and I had to find a music formula that was going to make that happen. I had decided to call my new venture the Backstage Bar, and it was opened for me by the Academy award-winning producer Noel Pearson. However, the day the sale closed on the purchase of the property was a total disaster and the beginning of a nightmare. My first night as the owner was marked by a devastating burglary. All eight antique fireplaces and a dozen valuable mirrors were ripped from the walls. Antique bathroom fittings and lead pipes were also removed. It was soul-destroying. On the closing of the sale, I was also hit with an outstanding £20,000 rates bill that was due on the property. The solicitor for the seller refused to close the sale until the balance owing was cleared. I had not allowed for this in my figures. I was later to discover the amount in question was never paid over to Dublin Corporation and I had to pay it a second time! By the time I discovered this I was already in a major financial hole. I had gutted the entire building and was up to my neck in problems with the architect and builder. I had put aside £60,000 for renovations and decorating but I was already over £50,000 with the job only half completed. The builder was having trouble with one of the sub-contractors. He told me he was going to fire him and that I would have to stand over his decision, which I did. I ended up with a restoration bill of over £120,000 – double my original budget. Eventually, with problem after problem finally solved, I opened the doors, albeit two months behind schedule. Little did I know that my troubles were only beginning.

A few weeks after opening, I was alone in the bar one afternoon when I was approached by two respectable enough looking guys. After a bit of chit-chat, they asked if I had any security on the premises. 'I'm fine,' I said, thinking they were looking for door work. 'I have it sorted, thanks.' One of the guys looked around the room and said, 'Lovely premises. You should really look at taking out extra security cover. We can provide it at very reasonable rates, so have a think about it and we'll be in touch.' I knew at that instant they were not bona fide operators but part of a protection scam. Shaking and afraid, I knew the last thing I needed was this shit. I could barely pay my overheads and now I had real trouble about to arrive at my door. Over the following three weeks I received half a dozen or so phone calls, each more threatening than the last. The demand was for £1,000 a month. I repeatedly told them there was no way I could pay it and that business was bad. After selling the record stores in Cork, I had celebrated by buying myself a gold two-door Mercedes 350E from Johnny McCarthy Motors in Fermoy. Johnny was a great pal of my business partner Oliver Barry and at that time was a main Opel dealer in County Cork. He was a jovial, happy-go-lucky fella with a great person-ality, and he had bought the Mercedes himself for special occasions, race meetings and days out, but had rarely used it. 'I can't be seen driving around Fermoy in a Merc,' he told me. 'I'm the Opel man. What will the punters think? You take it, Pat. It suits your personality and image better,' he said, like a true American car salesman. It cost me close to £30,000, and I loved the car. Stylish and beyond my wildest dreams, it was the coolest set of wheels in town. A large tin of black gloss paint can do a lot of damage to a car like that, and that is exactly what happened. It was poured all over the gold Mercedes when it was parked outside my bar in Essex Street. This was followed by a phone call – 'Pay up or else because this is only the beginning.'

I still refused to pay because I just didn't have that kind of money and, to make matters worse, the Backstage Bar wasn't doing great business. Pat Douglas from Finglas, my bar manager at the time, was a lovely guy, an ex-army sergeant who couldn't do enough for customers. I felt secure knowing Pat was behind the counter and that he and Tom Dowling, the other barman, could handle any problems that arose. One Sunday evening Tom called me in near panic. 'Pat, you'd better get over here fast,' he said. 'Something really terrible has happened.' There had been only a few customers and three staff in the bar when two guys entered carrying sledgehammers. They made their way to the newly fitted-out ladies' and gents' toilets, where they proceeded to smash every piece of glass, every wash-hand basin, toilet bowl, urinal. Mirrors and windows were crushed to smithereens. Even the interior doors were smashed off their hinges – nothing was left in one piece. The call the next morning warned me to pay up or the place would be burned down. 'Last warning,' said the voice. 'Just pay up.' Again, I pleaded that I didn't have the money, but it was to no avail. I was reluctant to go to the Gardaí because I knew that unless they caught these guys in the act, nothing could be done. One of the benefits of being a concert promoter is that you move in an elite circle of specialist people: musicians, technical sound geniuses and lighting wizards, dedicated stage crews and, lest we ever forget, some of the very best security men. Because you give them a lot of work you have their loyalty and respect, and for me, the feeling has always been mutual. From the 70s to the 90s, running big concerts, both outdoor and indoor, I had worked alongside my life-long pal Harry McKeown, who was one of the senior security guys for the IABA (Irish Athletic Boxing Association) and Jim Aiken. I had also worked with Jimmy Connolly on the Dalymount Park shows and at the Point Theatre. Both Harry and Jimmy were highly respected professional operators. I contacted them and told them I was having major problems with a protection racket gang at my new bar and asked if they could offer me any advice. They did, and it was excellent advice, which I took on board. Without going into details, the problem disappeared overnight. The bar, which I'd bought for £250,000, was sold two years later for £600,000.

When you're young, naive and inexperienced and you're riding on cloud nine, way ahead of your life's expectations, you tend to think you can walk on water. You make decisions and choices, in both your personal and business life, without thinking them through, and without any idea of the consequences resulting from your actions. So, at just 38, with half a million in the bank, I needed someone to shout 'Stop'. Someone to tell me to step back and look at the bigger picture, and to say that it was not all about me. The reality is that right up until my mid-forties there had been people in my life telling me to do just that. To my regret, however, I was deaf to everything but my own self-centred importance.

16: 'SPEAK SOFTLY, LOVE'

Of all the acts I have promoted over the years, I have only had a handful of long-term friendships. Friendships were something I never pursued. More often than not, it was the managers I was interested in maintaining a friendship with. However, a few acts kept in touch with invites to gigs, after-show dinner celebrations, parties or just a hello in the dressing room following the performance. Billy Connolly, Gene Pitney, Freddie Starr, Graham Russell and Russell Hitchcock (of Air Supply), Sir George Martin, Jasper Carrott and Al Martino were a few of the people I got to know well. All of them wrote or sent a Christmas card or kept in touch at some point to ask a favour or just say how much they were looking forward to returning to Ireland. One of my favourites, however, was Al Martino, the Italian-American hit crooner who, along with singing, starred as the singer Johnny Fontane in the Francis Ford Coppola movies *The Godfather* and *The Godfather Part III*.

I did three shows with Al before he died in 2009. He was a charming man and, along with the Dubliners' Jim McCann, the best storyteller I have met in my fifty years in the business. I'm a massive fan of *The Godfather* (I've watched it twenty times or more), which for my money is the greatest motion picture in movie history. The hotels for Al's show dates were not booked by me but by the UK tour agent, the lovely and charming Debra Franks. Debra knows a thing or two about touring star names and she will tell you it's near enough impossible to please artists on tour. Al would tell me, 'They have me in these crappy three-star joints. Penny-pinching promoters – they're all the same.' Al had a tour day off in Dublin and I took him to lunch at the Shelbourne. 'Now just look at this place. It's a real hotel, and what a lunch,' he said, thanking me repeatedly. It was the first of three meals I shared with him, all of them immensely enjoyable.

The best story Al ever told me had me hanging on his every word – it was how he got the role in *The Godfather*. He told me that Francis Ford Coppola never wanted him in the role of heart-throb singer Johnny Fontane and fought to remove him from the cast. He was to be replaced by another US singer, Vic Damone. The film's Canadian producer, Albert S. Ruddy, insisted on keeping Al in the role, but Coppola refused and was adamant he didn't want Al. Another person who told him not to take the role was Frank Sinatra. Stopping by at his table in a Hollywood restaurant, Sinatra said, 'Al, you've played your last casino gig in Vegas, my friend.' Al also told me he had agreed to invest in a diamond mine fronted by Ruddy as part of the deal to secure *The Godfather* role. Al had his problems in the 50s with Mafia types, forcing him to flee America and spend three years in the UK and Europe, where he toured the theatre and summer season circuit. He topped the bill at the London Palladium and played a week at Dublin's Theatre Royal in November 1954.

'The Mafia took over my management contract in the States,' Al informed me. 'They wanted seventy-five thousand dollars from me upfront, as security for their investment, plus a fifty/fifty split on my earnings. I paid them the first ten thousand bucks but I was left with no option but to run away to Europe before they fleeced me. In 1958, a close friend of my dad's family, Russell Bufalino, my own godfather, became a crime boss and big hitter in the Pennsylvania Mafia.' Bufalino (who was portrayed by Joe Pesci in Martin Scorsese's 2019 movie *The Irishman*) was the long-time counsel for Jimmy Hoffa, president of the International Brotherhood of Teamsters. 'Russell had the slate wiped clean and arranged for me to return safely to the States and pick up where my career left off,' Al said. 'I was lucky to have one of my biggest hits at the time, in 1965, with 'Spanish Eyes'. It was a massive hit in the US and Europe, and that kept the work rolling in.'

In 1969, Al was sharing the bill with the Maguire Sisters at a casino in Atlantic City. 'I was friends with Phyllis Maguire, the youngest of the sisters. She had read *The Godfather*, the book by Mario Puzo, and she told me about this movie, which was to be shot and cast in New York, and that I should go for it. The mob, who were running the casino at the time, refused to let me have time off to go to New York for the auditions. Again, the family Mafia friend in Pennsylvania, who had saved my career by getting me back to the States in 1958, made a phone call. I was let out of my contract for two weeks on the understanding I would work a month for free in return. At this time, I had no idea that my friend Phyllis had started a relationship with Sam Giancana, the Mafia boss of the bosses, and little did I know it would work in my favour in achieving the role of Johnny Fontane in the movie.'

Al went on to tell me that Alfred S. Ruddy came under huge pressure from Coppola to drop him from the movie in favour of Vic Damone. 'I was shattered,' he said, 'because I was hoping the role would reinvent my career just like it had done for Sinatra in *From Here To Eternity*.'

According to the story Al told me over dinner at the Shelbourne in 2006, when he was refused the role he went to see his godfather, Bufalino, who in turn spoke to the heads of the New York Mafia families. By this time, Vic Damone had walked away from the role for fear the Mafia might make him an offer he couldn't refuse. In Al's words, 'Russell Bufalino called in a favour with the New York bosses of La Cosa Nostra, which resulted in phone calls being made to Francis Ford Coppola and Al Ruddy and the studio bosses at Paramount, telling them in no uncertain terms that Al Martino gets the role of Johnny Fontane or this movie will never be shot on the streets of New York.' Al finished the story by saying he had no doubt that his friend Phyllis McGuire also had a word in Sam Giancana's ear, and that this helped him secure the movie role. It is an amazing story, and I have no reason to believe it isn't 100 per cent true. What I do know is that when you place Al's fascinating tale alongside Mario Puzo's movie script and the role of Godfather Vito Corleone, played by Marlon Brando, in pursuing studio boss Jack Woltz to give his godson Johnny Fontane the movie role, the parallels between what actually happened and what the movie portrays are incredible and *almost* unbelievable.

My friend Al Martino died from a heart attack on 13 October 2009, six days after his 82nd birthday and not long after his final Irish show. I was privileged to receive a letter after his death from his wife, Judi, telling me how special the Irish shows were to Al and especially how much he loved the Irish audiences. Al will forever be remembered for the wonderful songs he turned into unforgettable hits: 'Spanish Eyes', 'Here in My Heart', 'The Story of Tina', 'Because You're Mine', 'Mary in the Morning', 'I Have But One Heart', and most of all for the magnificent love ballad, 'Speak Softly, Love', the theme song from *The Godfather*, written by Larry Kusik and Nino Rota:

Appearing in the controversial documentary *The Rocky Road to Dublin* in 1967.

Gig poster for Elton John – National
Stadium, Dublin, 1979.

Kevin O'Brien's logo for my second shop,
In Search of Tape, 1972.

eric clapton

ENTERTAINS

PERSONNEL OF EASTERN COMMAND

at his request

at Collins Barracks Dublin

on Friday, 16th March at 8 p.m.

Admission by Ticket Only

Ticket No. _____

PAT EGAN SOUND LTD

The ticket to Eric's
Collins Barracks gig.

The iconic Kevin O'Brien
logo for Sound Cellar, 1970.

Myself and Elton, Gresham Hotel, 1979.

A little under the weather, Eric Clapton joins the Irish Army – Collins Barracks, 1979.

With Elkie Brooks circa 1981 – one of our early touring successes.

The Waterfront Rock Cafe – Home of *The Commitments* and some of the wildest nights of my life.

With Meatloaf in 1982 in Dalymount Park. His room service bill for two nights was £1,300.

Eric on drums and in great form at an aftershow bash with Procol Harum's Gary Brooker and ace guitarist Albert Lee.

Last Supper portrait of Irish rock greats – Backstage Bar, 1988.

Status Quo's Francis Rossi with my sister-in-law Liz Gernon. They had a child together, Bernadette. Liz's contribution to the early success of my concert business was immense.

June 1993 – Freddie Starr and myself standing guard outside his band's dressing room at The Olympia after they had played out of tune.

Freddie Mercury on stage at Ireland's first arena gig – Simmonscourt, RDS, 1979.

Queen's 600 overhead lamps at the 1979 gig was the biggest lighting rig by far of its time.

Brendan O'Carroll, John McColgan, Gerry Brown and myself. Brendan's management company, 4 Q Tours, or as Brendan like to call it, 'four cute hoors'.

Presenting Mary Black with yet another gold record (inset the two of us with Mary's sister Frances).

Living the high life with the ultimate diva, Dame Shirley Bassey.

'What am I doing playing this dump?' – Dionne Warwick at the Olympia Theatre.

Marianne Faithfull with U2 sound legend Joe O'Herlihy at the Tivoli Theatre, 1986.

16: 'Speak Softly, Love'

Speak softly, love, and hold me warm against your heart.
I feel your words, the tender trembling moments start.
We're in a world, our very own,
Sharing a love that only few have ever known.
Wine-coloured days warmed by the sun,
Deep velvet nights when we are one.

17: 'BILLY CONNOLLY! YOU'RE THE SPITTIN' IMAGE OF YOURSELF'

When you spend forty years of your promoting career looking after Irish business for just one man, it's safe to say you gain a very close insight into the kind of character and personality you are dealing with. From 1978 to his last ever onstage appearance anywhere in the world at Dublin's 3Arena in 2018, I have been privileged beyond words to have had my name on the same poster as Billy Connolly.

The man has been an enormous part of my business life and there is seldom a day I don't look back at the memories of our tours together with deep and cherished affection. Billy is a very straight, down-to-earth human being. Yes, he's as internationally famous a comedian as they come, and rich, too, but he has never lost his working-class identity or values. He has, from my experience of working for him, not for one minute lost the run of himself. If anything, fame and fortune have only enhanced his ordinary, decent spirit. Knowing him has been one of the high points of my life.

I am not a close friend and I never regarded myself as one; I was simply the guy who put the tours together, did my job and minded my own business, and that was how Billy liked his promoters to be. I'm not saying that Billy and I didn't share a lot of close time together, we certainly did, but I always knew where the line was drawn and I always knew that crossing the line was never an option unless you were invited. And invited I was, many times. I was never one for sitting around in Billy's dressing room, because I knew he treated his dressing rooms as very private spaces. He did not like to be interrupted before a show, either, as he usually spent an hour or so alone in the dressing room meditating or reading a book to relax before going on stage. Like so many of the big names in entertainment, he never wanted to meet visitors or guests before a performance.

After a show was different. Then he would enjoy catching up with old pals. I would tell him which VIPs were in, and Billy would say things like, 'is Eddie Furey here? Oh, I love Eddie. Bring him in!' Whenever he heard Shay Healy or Phil Coulter or any of The Dubliners were around, he was always delighted. Billy loved Phil, who had been such a big part of his early career (he had produced his 1975 number one single 'D.I.V.O.R.C.E.' as well as the 1981 gold-selling album, *Pick of Billy Connolly*). Billy was distraught last year at the news of Shay Healy's death. He, like so many others, had great time for Shay and he would always tell me to call him and invite him to the Shelbourne for afternoon tea and scones. Billy was a perfectionist when it came to tea and scones. He loved his scones to be melt-in-your-mouth light and fluffy, and would get me to stop at good hotels to sample their scones as we drove across the country to a gig. I was never comfortable being Billy's driver as I don't regard my driving with a lot of respect, but when he asked me to drive I never said no. When it was a long tour, a hired driver took over, but not one who talked a lot. The instructions for hired drivers were simple. After a 'Good morning, Billy' and a few minutes of small talk you said little else unless spoken to. I had on two occasions in the early years of Billy's Irish tours replaced drivers who talked too much. (This was something I learned in my early days as a promoter, having once driven from Cork to Dublin with Van Morrison without one single word being uttered between us for the entire 160-mile drive.)

Jim McCann was Billy's favourite Dubliner. He had so much admiration for him as a performer and storyteller, but also as a man who had defeated his demons. Billy would tell me that he could 'sit all day just chatting to Jim. He's just such a lovely, lovely fellow.' Billy also had a very close relationship with Ronnie Drew and spent a few hours by his bedside the week before he died. Of course, they all went back such a long, long time together, as Billy was first and foremost a folk singer. He may have made his name as a comedian but deep down he was always and remains an old banjo-playing folk hippy at heart – all he ever wanted was to be the world's greatest banjo player. As a member of Glasgow folk group the Humblebums, Billy had met all the Irish musicians on the UK folk circuit of the mid- to late 60s, and he made it his business never to lose touch.

'How are Ronnie, Barney and John doing?' was the first thing he'd say to Brian Hand, The Dubliners' tour manager, who also worked with me on all Billy's tours. 'Have you seen Eddie Furey?' It was always Eddie he asked for, never Finbar, which always puzzled me. 'How is Christy Moore?' Billy's favourite Irish music act by a mile was Paul Brady. 'What a brilliant songwriter and performer,' he would say, and he always asked for Paul's CDs to be played on long car journeys. He also had a lot of time for Colm Wilkinson. 'What a performer – that voice is amazing.'

Over the years Billy was given many sizeable offers to switch promoters in Ireland but he never gave them a second thought. He would say to me, 'Why would I do that, Pat? You know me better than anyone else.' Artists' loyalty to promoters is very thin on the ground in 2021. Most of the big acts will chase the biggest offer, regardless of who the promoter is. In the 70s and 80s, things were different (and indeed, so were values such as loyalty and trust). If an artist built up a relationship with a promoter the chances are the agent was told that they would only work with that specific person. The pioneering Irish promoter Jim Aiken was a great man for cementing such relationships, with artists such as Tom Jones, Bruce Springsteen, Charlie Pride and many more spending their entire careers with Jim. Because they were well looked after, they subsequently moved on to work with Jim's son, Peter.

I have lost track of the number of tours I promoted for Billy. For over 40 years, he toured Ireland on average every two and a half to three years. The only show I did not handle was his very first visit for Jim Aiken in 1975 when he took his Big Banana Boots show to the Carlton Cinema in Dublin. It's true to say that he appeared in every major and semi-significant hall in the country, from early days venues like Connolly Hall, the Savoy, the Opera House in Cork, the INEC in Killarney, Belfast's Opera House and Waterfront, St Columb's and Millennium Forum in Derry, to UCH Limerick and Dublin's Olympia, Gaiety, Liberty Hall, The Point and, finally, in 2018, the very last gigs of his long career at 3Arena, for which he sold 27,000 tickets and a similar number in Belfast a few nights earlier, making

• •

At 82, Al Martino was the oldest act I ever promoted and the only person of that age I ever saw jump from the stage to sit and sing on the Steinway piano at the NCH. At 13, the wonderful Rachel Coyne was the youngest when she appeared at the NCH.

• •

it a total of well over 50,000 tickets. This tour – his final one – had never been billed as a farewell. Can you imagine the kind of numbers a farewell tour would have generated had the onset of his Parkinson's disease not arrived in 2019? It would have taken Billy five years to do a farewell world tour to meet the ticket demand from his millions of fans.

In all those years I toured Billy I only saw him fail to lift an audience twice. To say he died on his arse would be exaggerating, but in the late 1980s he found the audience at the Shinrone Community Centre in County Offaly very tough going. Maybe there were too many f-words on the night, but whatever it was he couldn't get them on board. Even some of his milder tales failed to get a laugh – like the itchy bottom piece, in which he wondered why they always occurred in public and at the least convenient times. Many middle-class Irish people who saw Billy on the *Late Late Show*, or with Michael Parkinson, expected the same routine at live gigs, but they were worlds apart. In concert, Billy offered a combination of songs, stories and some of the rudest material you would ever have the pleasure of hearing. He would tell an audience in his early days that he was 'going to curse and swear a lot tonight, but don't you worry about it because it's me that's going to hell'. Hecklers took their life in your hands, Billy had such rapid-fire responses. A few of my favourites include 'The last time I saw a mouth like yours, Lester Piggott was riding it'; 'You should get an agent, pal, why sit there in the dark handling yourself?'; and 'When they put the teeth in your mouth they spoilt a perfectly good bum.'

The other time I saw Billy fretting over a performance was on one of his last appearances at the Belfast Waterfront. Billy had what I can only describe as a pre-show trauma. He was not feeling well that night and was far from his usual happy self. He had been having trouble sleeping that tour and had been finding it hard to catch what the early show hecklers were shouting about. He was upset that he could not respond because his hearing had started to fail. I knew that in the past Billy had been prone to nervousness before a show, but that night was very different. He was unusually edgy and restless as he stood on the side of the stage. He simply did not want to go on. I could tell that having to face an audience was the last thing in the world he felt like doing, yet on the other side of the curtain were 2,200 fans waiting with great anticipation for the world's funniest man to keep them rolling in the aisles with laughter for the next two and a half hours. I realised then, maybe for the first time in my 40-year relationship with him, that living up to the reputation of being

Billy Connolly night after night on a 50-day tour was a genuine burden. As the announcement was made – 'Ladies and gentleman, please welcome Billy Connolly!' – he stepped out on the Waterfront stage to an almighty roar of welcome. If truth be told, he never got into the groove that night. His comedic instincts and skills, and decades of professionalism, carried it off for the capacity audience, but it wasn't vintage Billy. He could have cancelled the show at the last minute, of course, but knowing that he would have disappointed the fans it was never an option. In the true sense of the words 'the show must go on', regardless of his own personal wellbeing, he never failed to deliver.

What I always noticed about Billy's audiences was the generation gap being bridged over and over again. During my time with him, he reinvented himself so often that his appeal stretched from father to son, mother to daughter and on again to their grandchildren. No other comedian had that gift of making themselves relevant to three generations of the same family. The audiences were aged from 18 to 80 and many had returned tour after tour. Some of the Irish trips reached into six weeks, and one stint in the late 80s included a run of eighteen nights at the Olympia Theatre, Dame Street, and then, a short walk from there, to off-Grafton Street's Gaiety Theatre, where he added another six nights. In the early days, Billy didn't fancy playing big rooms. He liked to feel the audience was close to him as he believed it made for a more personal show and better feedback from the audience. 'I like being in someone's sitting room because you get to know them better,' he would say. When he first became successful and started staying in luxurious five-star hotels, he would look back at his Glaswegian tenement days and say 'I don't think I'll ever get used to big rooms. When I was a boy I could turn off the light and be in bed before it was dark.'

I was always amazed at how Billy could read an audience. He would sometimes peep out from behind the curtain five minutes before showtime to size them up and remark that the house seemed happy or subdued, or that the buzz on a particular night was electric, which always lifted his spirits. The mood of the audience seemed to determine how he would approach the opening of his set. It was the die-hard fans in the first ten or twenty rows, buzzing and chatty, who gave him his initial lift-off. As Bruce Dessau wrote in his 1996 book *The Funny Side of Billy Connolly*, 'Billy doesn't just feed off the audience responses, he also feeds off his own momentum. For a man so keen on language, the pauses are as funny and

130

as important as the words. It's during those pauses that Billy can often be seen laughing at his own punchlines, and that he is also going off on a mental tangent and continuously coming up with a brand-new segment of his act which in future years would become a classic.'

His last tour, The High Horse, was the only arena tour of his career. Prior to that, six thousand was pretty much the maximum number of his tour audiences. It wasn't that he couldn't sell out arenas, it was a personal and management choice. This may have cost him millions in revenue but it was how he liked it. With the exception of maybe one night, I attended every show Billy performed in Ireland – about 150 shows from the late 70s to 2018. The joy was that Billy's act was never rigidly scripted. The core of each performance would remain the same, but the opening twenty minutes could vary widely from night to night. Yes, he had his regular songs and set routine, but if you came to the show the following night, chances are you would hear some of the same material in a different order. Opening segments were classic ad lib, and usually included some impromptu remarks relating to the latest world news or to incidents or situations he had encountered on his many casual strolls around Dublin or whatever town he was playing in. One such was the Grafton Street flower lady who jumped in surprise when she saw Billy coming towards her. 'Jaysus! It's you – Billy Connolly! You're the spittin' image of yourself!' Or the Cork chancer on a bike passing Billy on the street who shouted, 'Hey, Connolly, sure you're only a bollocks yourself!' or the Belfast limo driver who told Billy never to bring an eejit to Belfast as the place was full of them. More often than not, in the middle of his set Billy would tell a standard joke told to him by another comic, but the joke was seldom included again for a number of performances.

My favourite one – even though I had heard it a hundred times – is Belfast-born comedian Frank Carson's tale of the building of the *Titanic* as explained to an American visitor. Billy tells it beautifully.

'So you're telling me', says the American, 'that no Catholics were involved with the building of the great ship?'

'That's right', says Billy, 'not a single one.'

'But what were all the Catholics doing when the Protestants were building the *Titanic*?' 'Ah,' says Billy. 'They were all up in Derry building the iceberg.'

Billy also never forgot to mention the Irish sports stars who were in the news. He was a big fan of cycling and would rave to the audience

131

about the Tour de France exploits of Sean Kelly and Stephen Roche and how much he admired them. If there had been a big soccer match on the day of a performance and Ireland had beaten England, or Celtic had hammered Rangers, he would get a good few minutes out of winding up the fans of the losing team.

The one thing about Billy Connolly that never ceased to amaze me was how he travelled about when he came to Ireland. Yes, he had a car and driver for the tour but it was the casual way he drifted through airports, big stores, city streets and coffee shops. His face was one of the most recognisable on the planet, yet, unlike so many stars who were far less famous, there was no hullabaloo or requests for VIP treatment. Over all the years I collected him from Dublin, Cork or Belfast airports he was the only act who arrived with no assistant and only occasionally a manager. He always carried his own case and walked through the arrivals terminal alongside the other visitors. On one occasion, when he arrived at Cork airport, without the slightest bother on him, we went directly to the coffee shop for tea and a scone. I can tell you with 100 per cent certainty that no other international star I ever worked with would come through arrivals alone or be caught dead having tea in an airport coffee shop. Of all the Dublin hotels we stayed at, he loved the Shelbourne best. He would have afternoon tea daily and I would be given a list of people, old pals mostly, who he would like to see. From the Shelbourne, he could easily access most of his favourite joints on his midday walks around Stephen's Green and Grafton Street.

Billy never asked for a suite in a hotel, but he was almost always offered an upgrade. More often than not his manager would end up taking the suite. 'I'm fine in a double room,' he would tell me. He loved the café in Nassau Street's Kilkenny Shop, where he would sit and talk to any stranger who so much as smiled at him. Maybe it was because he spent so many hours alone in hotel rooms that he just wanted, like most of us, to chat about nothing in particular. He also liked the Irish Tweed shop on Nassau Street. He would think long and hard about buying a new Donegal tweed jacket for £300 but at the same time would think nothing of giving £20,000 to a local charity. It may sound unlikely, but money never seemed to be one of his priorities. Never once in 40 years did he ever discuss business with me. I might say that the shows sold out in two hours, but he never asked how much the tickets were or asked about my deal with Steve Brown, his long-time manager.

Like Eric Clapton, Billy enjoyed visiting Cathach Books in Duke Street. The cigar store beside Trinity College was another favourite. He really loved his Cuban cigars and hated being told to stop smoking them after his Parkinson's diagnosis. He would saunter across College Green down past Bank of Ireland to the fishing tackle shop in Temple Bar. He always went out alone, with no fuss, no security. He would say he was just a bothered and bewildered old windswept and interesting hippy. 'What would I be doing with security?' he would ask. He thought his pals Ronnie Drew and Eddie Furey would think he had lost the run of himself if he had a body-guard. 'There were no bodyguards at the folk attic in Paisley in 1965.' This type of independence among major showbiz names was unique. No other international act who could sell 30,000 tickets in Dublin alone would be seen dead hanging around the streets without an entourage of hangers-on and minders.

The reaction to Billy across Ireland was phenomenal, and nowhere more than in Northern Ireland. Over the years, we played the 2,000-seat Waterfront Hall for eight nights each run. The very likeable Tim Husbands was the venue director, and he would tell me, 'Pat, I am not exaggerating but you have no idea of the demand for tickets; no one else comes near it. It's enough to fill the place for a month or more.' Billy, despite always having a go at Northern politicians, especially 'Big' Ian Paisley, was loved by one and all. Despite his no-holds-barred remarks and criticisms of the North's political masters during the deepest days of the Troubles his humour seamlessly crossed the divide. During the very dangerous years when other acts refused to come to Northern Ireland or were walking on the proverbial eggshells, Billy came to the Tonic Cinema in Bangor, County Down in the late 70s, and to roars of laughter from the 2,000-strong audience, he ripped into the local political establishments, both orange and green. 'Have youse no shame?' he screamed at them before lambasting Paisley and mocking his 'Ulster Says No' routine. After one Waterfront show in the 90s, Billy said to me, 'We have a special guest coming tonight, Pat, but I can't tell you who it is as I'm told it's top secret. He'll be coming in through the side entrance, so be sure to have someone on the door.' *Who could it be?* I thought. *Robin Williams? Elton John? Or maybe Paisley himself?* It was none other than Gerry Adams, who had often been the butt of Billy's critical wit but who came in peace to share some quality after-show wine and laughs.

Billy's manager, Steve Brown, was a music man who in his early days worked for Dick James Music, the original publisher of The Beatles' music. Steve had produced Elton John's first hit, 'Your Song', and worked closely with him at DJM records. He stayed with Elton for many years, working alongside John Reid when John Reid Enterprises managed Queen, Elton, Billy, and Kiki Dee. He later split from Reid and took Billy and Kiki with him to his new management company, Tickety-Boo (named after Billy's brand of tea, launched in 1999 to help raise money for orphans in India). Steve was a charming, calm, stylish, private man. He died just after Billy's last performance in Dublin. It was a sad time for our office, as Steve had been very good to me over the years, and a total pleasure to deal with. There was a touch of class to everything he did; I learned a lot about the business and how to treat people with respect from him. I'm glad to say I'm still in contact with his wife, Sam, and his daughter Hannah, a talented songwriter.

Over the years, Steve would keep us entertained with tales about his time with Elton and the singer's extravagant lifestyle. We had all heard the well-documented stories about Elton but to hear them from Steve was different. 'The first thing you need to know about Elton', he would say, 'is that he is the most caring and generous person alive and, yes, he's eccentric to the point of madness but no gift he gave was ever big enough.' As for the price? Price, said Steve, was immaterial. Steve had remained friends with Elton for years and said if he cared about you as a person he was your friend for life. His generosity was astounding. Once, on the spur of the moment, he sent a brand-new Steinway grand piano valued well over $100,000 to an unknown songwriter who had no piano to work with. Going shopping with Elton was another experience that Steve could never get his head around. If Elton went into a men's clothing store and fancied a Versace jacket in blue, he would buy the entire rack of about twenty similar jackets at around $500 each so that no one else would have one. It was the same with shoes. Elton insisted that fresh flowers be displayed every few days in his various homes around the world even though there was no one living in them. Up to £5,000 a week was being spent with florists and, yes, it was true: Elton often threw tantrums about all kinds of things. When on a concert tour no one in the tour party ever unpacked their bags on hotel arrival. They would all sit around their rooms or in the lobby waiting for word from the tour manager that Elton was happy with the quality of the never less than five-star accommodation. If he didn't like the suite provided or the colour of the wallpaper or the bed or – and especially – the room service menu, he would up sticks and move to another hotel. Steve recalled the management of one exclusive hotel summoning its five senior chefs to Elton's suite so they could give him a detailed account of their various degrees of experience and their awards in specialist cuisine. If he was not satisfied, he and the entire tour party would leave for another establishment. Yes, confirmed Steve, it was true that Elton hired the Orient Express for his birthday party, inviting a couple of hundred guests on a trip to some splendid European city such as Vienna or Venice. However, before arriving at their destination, Elton threw a tantrum about some minor detail, abruptly cancelled the trip and party and sent all his guests home.

It was thanks to Steve that I discovered the tiny island of Gozo, the Mediterranean Maltese island that has been my summer home for over twenty years. The city of Valetta, Malta's capital, is beautiful and pictur-esque, steeped in magical history, from its absolutely stunning grand harbour to the opulent cathedral home of the Knights of St John, and the resting place of a number of Caravaggio masterpieces. Outside of the Vatican's Sistine Chapel and the great domes of Rome, the Maltese Cathedral of St John must be one of the Catholic Church's greatest cathe-drals. I try to visit every year just to sit there in silence, marvelling at the presence of such bewildering beauty, enhanced by the spellbinding Cara-vaggio paintings. While Valetta is a stunningly beautiful place to visit, the remainder of Malta is disappointing, with dull and drab three-star holiday hotels very reminiscent of Spain in the mid-60s.

Thirty minutes from Valetta, the ferry takes you to the idyllic, paradise island of Gozo. I can only describe it as Connemara with sunshine, and although it's only seven miles by ten, there's a Catholic cathedral, basilica or sizeable church in every village. I counted almost fifty. In one village, Xewkija, the cathedral has a seat for every one of the 3,000 local inhabitants. Its dome is larger than that of St Paul's in London. My great friends Josef and Genevieve Buttigieg say to me often that if God exists he lives on Gozo, and I believe that to be true. Josef and Gen and their girls have looked after our home, Blue Bayou, for many years. I call them my Maltese family.

Over twenty years ago, I had told Steve I was looking for a holiday home and that my then partner Caroline was going to Malta to look for a property. 'Forget Malta', he said, 'come to Gozo. You will never regret it.'

How right he was. At that time, Steve had been living on the island for a couple of years. He had moved Billy's office to Malta for tax reasons and then fell in love with Gozo. A few years after I arrived, Billy also bought a house there – an old convent school in the village of Sannat that Pamela, Billy's wife, converted, using wonderful paintings and unique furniture, into one of the most beautiful homes on the island. I never went anywhere near Billy when I was staying on Gozo. I might sometimes have spent up to three months there without ever seeing him, which considering the size of the island is a remarkable achievement. Pamela did invite my ex-partner Caroline and me to their new home for dinner. They had a terrific local chef (who just happened to be the local estate agent – it seemed everyone on the island had two jobs, morning for 'real' work, afternoon for 'personal' work) who cooked us the tastiest Maltese dishes. Another wonderful invitation I received from Billy and Pamela was in 1999 for Caroline and I to come to Candacraig, Billy's castle home in the Scottish Highlands, just twenty miles from the Queen's estate at Balmoral. We were invited to join almost three hundred guests to celebrate Billy's 60th birthday.

The invitation read:

Doctor and Doctor Connolly
Request the pleasure of your company
To celebrate His Sexageniality
and his
Not giving a Saggy Arsed Fuck Thereof

In *Bravemouth*, the follow-up to her multimillion-selling biography, *Billy*, Pamela writes:

Guests had been summoned in entirely over-the-top posh invitations of gold-embossed script on heavy ivory Smythson's of Bond Street card. It was only after I arrived in Britain in 1976 that I learned such invitations are known in upper-class English life as stiffies.

In Australia, where I was raised, a stiffie is something quite different. I'll never forget a British acquaintance asking me if I'd received a stiffie from her friend, Oscar. I told her I was not in the habit of talking about my sex life and in any case, it was none of her business whether the poor man's penis worked or not. Michael Palin was one of the first to reply that I had mistakenly omitted to invite his spouse. 'Are wives invited? Helen is no trouble and I could keep her largely out of sight.' Stephen Fry replied, 'I ought to warn you I dance like an electrocuted pig.'

Nothing had prepared me for the beauty of the Highlands. It's an awesome place, and the scale and majesty of the rugged landscape is bewildering. The scenery alone was worth the trip. I had never seen anything like it and I vowed to return one day and spend a week or two discovering more of its secret scenic locations, of which there are hundreds. Their Highlands hideaway, Pamela said, was originally a forti-fied wooden castle but over the centuries had been rebuilt and converted into a magnificent pale stone mansion. The house and its façade and as many as forty rooms were destroyed in a fire in 1950. It was redesigned and reconstructed and today is a magnificent retreat with its own lakes. Billy and Pamela bought Candacraig from the founder of the Body Shop, Dame Anita Roddick, who died in 2007.

Caroline and I decided to make the trip from Glasgow to Aberdeen by train, and it was wonderful to pass many small railway stations with names I had only ever heard previously on the BBC's Saturday afternoon Scottish second division football results. At Aberdeen (the Granite City), we were met by one of Billy's drivers and taken on an hour-plus journey to a large, luxurious country house close to Candacraig that Billy had hired for me, Caroline, Phil Coulter, Geraldine, his wife, and their three daughters. We arrived early evening on Friday and although the party did not start officially until the following day, we were invited that evening to a lavish advance celebration dinner at the main house on Billy's estate. Once again, I was about to step out of my humble Eccles Street beginnings and into the pages of *Hello!* magazine. The dinner table in Candacraig was set for sixteen people, including myself, Caroline, Phil and Geraldine. The guests included the Duke and Duchess of York, Robin Williams and his wife, the actor Steve Buscemi and his partner, *Monty Python*'s Terry Jones and his wife, actor Aidan Quinn and his wife, and, of course, Billy and Pamela. Billy's party was listed as a two-day affair, so this dinner was a complete and magical surprise. We sat listening for hours to the funniest tales and stories that only Robin Williams could deliver. In fact, Robin took over completely that night and even Billy was left speechless by his great friend's side-splitting take on anything and everything.

The following day, the party began in earnest. For the first and only time in my life, I wore a kilt. To be truthful, it came from the dressware shop in Nassau Street, and it was a green tartan of which clan I had absolutely no idea. And, yes, I did also wear a pair of tartan boxer shorts. The party programme was as follows:

Saturday 17th August

6.30 p.m. Highland Welcome. Wee bevvies on the lawn. Pipe band
8 p.m. Dinner and special address to the Haggis
10 p.m. Dance a wild jig
Midnight. Stovies and champagne. Bare Bum Cavorting
Dress code. Formal black-tie kilt or windswept and interesting

Sunday 18th August

12 noon. Caledonian Brunch. Address to the Quiche
Afternoon. Fishing, caber-tossing, gorge walking, cycling, hiking, abseiling, banjo playing or shootin' the breeze. (Warning: all golfers will be fucked and burned)
4.30 p.m. Afternoon tea. Address to the scone. Falconry, archery, punting, pontificating or a vicious game of croquet (Glasgow rules full contact)
7 p.m. Barbecue campfire and music. Address to the Sausage
11 p.m. Tall tales and outright fabrications
Address to the Nightcap
Dress code. Jeans, Breeks or rumpled Intensit

Maybe it wasn't the biggest party marquee in showbiz history, but it was certainly the biggest I had ever seen. At its entrance was a 25-foot-high polystyrene statue of Billy looking like the Workers' Republic leader James Connolly. It was so impressive that it was hard to tell that it wasn't granite. It had been used in a series of television commercials Billy did for the UK National Lottery operator, Camelot. It was going to be dumped, but Billy said he'd hang on to it, and it had been rotting away in a garage until Pamela thought it would make an ideal prop for the entrance to the massive tent, and it most certainly did. As we arrived on Saturday evening, a welcoming pipe band played a new composition written especially for the event – 'The Connollys of Candacraig'. The buzz was upon us from the word go, and I kept bumping into faces I had only seen previously on the small or big screen. It was like a new TV game show or celebrity treasure trail. 'Michael Parkinson just said hello to me,' said Caroline, 'and Dame Judi Dench smiled at me when I responded.'

The inside of the marquee was a kaleidoscope of glowing tartan with a monster display of flickering candles and hundreds of pretty flower arrangements. A huge Harley Davidson motorcycle ice sculpture dripping into a silver tray was centre stage. After sitting with your partner for the first course, a simple lotto numbered system was then introduced whereby you got to meet and share time with God knows who for your second course. I was sitting beside Eddie Izzard for my main course, and for my dessert, I met motor-racing legend Jackie Stewart. At her table, Caroline had her main course with Pattie Boyd (aka Layla), and for dessert, she met ex-Celtic manager Martin O'Neill. Billy made a touching, sincere and personal welcoming speech about how proud he was to welcome so many of the people he loved to his home. Speaking with such pride about his love for Pam and his children was real and emotional. Robin Williams gave the Ode to Haggis and Fiery Bums toast. Pamela and Billy got the dancing started, and on and on it went until the small hours. As we networked the big tent, Geraldine Coulter, Phil's wife, had a go at Bob Geldof for having voted her single a miss on *Juke Box Jury* in 1975. The poor man was flabbergasted, lost for words for perhaps the first time in his life. As we waited to have a birthday photo taken with Billy, I enjoyed a laugh with his Australian and New Zealand promoters. It was special to meet two guys who, like myself, took enormous pride in being associated with the world's greatest comedian. The evening ended with a spectacular firework display, but the weekend wasn't over just yet.

As we roamed around the beautiful estate after Sunday brunch, we bumped into celebrity faces by the dozen. We watched clansmen do battle, marvelled at experts flying beautiful falcons, eagles and buzzards, and enjoyed fly fishing specialists giving lessons. Pamela had indeed laid on the most wide-ranging attractions. The evening barbecue in the woods brought everyone together for a feast of grilled delights such as prawns, lamb chops, hamburgers. As the campfire blazed, Paul Brady gave a brilliant performance; Ronnie Drew, Anna Friel and a great Irish trad band had everyone dancing and singing along. The craic was 90, and as the rain started to pelt down and fireworks blazed across the sky we unfolded our large Billy Connolly original souvenir brollies and with all the guests followed the torchlight procession, the pipe band and medieval clansmen back to the main house. So ended a fairy tale, a once-in-a-lifetime three nights and two days of celebration. Alongside my trip to Windsor Castle, Billy Connolly's 60th remains one of the great social events of my life.

After the event, Billy wrote:

Although I don't like birthday parties, although I don't mind other people's, I found I absolutely loved my 60th, which took me by surprise. The house looked fantastic and the tent was brilliant. I liked absolutely everyone who came. It was an extraordinary feeling being with friends from childhood, from my youth, music and drama … from all departments of my life. They were all linked by the fact that they were my friends and had remained my friends. Many of them had enriched my life, and some had even changed it. They made the atmosphere very extraordinary. To have so many delightful people I love being in one place with me was heaven. I only wish we could have invited more. What did I like best? Och, to stand in the woods and listen to delightful music, to warm myself by the campfire and tell funny stories to my pals. Oh and to see Paul Brady blowing people away. A lot of people had never heard of him and were completely flattened. Ronnie Drew telling stories about a Dublin that they'd never heard. It was wonderful stuff and not really show business … far more real joy to watch them, people laughing and dancing by the campfire, and to watch Geldof being so proud of the Irish band because they were outstanding.

Billy's great friend and producer, and a man I have been proud to represent for many years, Phil Coulter, summed up the thoughts of many of Billy's lifelong pals.

I was bursting with pride for you as I stood outside your fairy tale castle on Saturday evening, listening to the pipe band welcome a succession of the great and good, and I couldn't help asking myself is this the same Billy Connolly who, thirty years ago, was told that people would never understand him outside Glasgow. I think the begrudgers have been well and truly fucked.

On the very last shows of his glittering career in Dublin and Belfast in 2018, Billy walked out on stage as the enormous sound system boomed out Jerry Lee Lewis's classic 50s hit 'Whole Lotta Shakin' Goin' On'. On those nights Billy knew in his heart – but told no one else – that these Irish performances were the end of his touring days. He told the audience that he had Parkinson's, gesturing to them by shaking his right arm about and pretending he couldn't hold it down. For me, it was the most iconic moment of my promoting career. I was the last promoter ever to bring him to an airport in 2018, the shows I promoted the very end of his life on the road.

It was just the two of us at Dublin airport, standing in line at the Ryanair check-in. He was not well in himself that morning, a little disoriented and distant. He looked sad and a little lost. I knew in my heart that this was the end and that I might never see him again. With tears in my eyes, I told him that morning I was worried about his health and wellbeing and what he had meant to me and my life. I told him that I was so grateful for the pride I felt just knowing him and the honour he had bestowed on me by allowing me to be his man in Ireland for over forty years.

Sir Billy Connolly gave me a big hug and told me to be off about my business.

Billy Connolly played the longest stage performance of my promoting career – three hours, twenty minutes on stage at the Savoy, Cork in the early 1980s. Dionne Warwick played the shortest set – fifty minutes at the Olympia Theatre, Dublin in 1984.

18: 'WHAT ABOUT MRS ROONEY?'
'FUCK HER, SHE CAN WALK.'

'*F*uck off,' said Mickey Rooney to the National Concert Hall house manager, Aidan Quinn, as he reached out to shake hands and welcome the legendary Hollywood actor to the venue. 'Just fuck off and leave me alone.'

Aidan, a perfect gentleman, could not believe his ears and was left in shock with his mouth wide open. In all his years at the NCH, no artist had ever spoken to him in such a manner. There was more to come, however. An elderly gentleman who had been waiting at the stage door to present a shillelagh and box of Irish roses to the movie legend was told in no uncertain terms where he could stick them.

I had no idea what was going on behind the scenes when I welcomed Mickey to Ireland in 2007, but it was very easy to see that all was not well. 'Are you in charge?' he asked me as I helped him into his limo at Dublin airport. 'Yes, sir,' I said. 'I'm the promoter.' Mickey looked at me. 'Come closer,' he said. I stepped nearer to him. He whispered into my ear, 'Keep your eye on that step son of mine, he's a creep.'

Rooney was a genuine screen legend right out of Hollywood's golden pages. *Vanity Fair* called him the original Hollywood train wreck because of his chaotic life and business affairs. In a career spanning nine decades and 300 movies, his estate should have been worth hundreds of millions, yet he died penniless in 2014 leaving just $18,000. He died owing thousands in medical bills and taxes. Contributions were solicited from the public to cover his bills. He had suffered beatings, humiliation and poverty at the hands of his eighth wife, Jan, and one of her sons; both were accused of elder abuse. Rooney's stepson, who was supposed to be minding his fortune, spent it on his own extravagant lifestyle. I had no idea when I booked Mickey if he would sell tickets. In Hollywood movie-making terms, his name was truly legendary and his fee of $10,000, plus all extras, wasn't a major risk for me. And at the very least, I thought, I would get to shake hands with the man who married my all-time favourite movie star, the world's most beautiful woman, Ava Gardner.

My immediate impression was that at 86 years of age Rooney was not a fit person to be out on tour. Meeting some of the great stars from classic eras of music and film was fairy-tale stuff for me, but with him it was different. I instantly felt sorry for him being dragged around theatres in the UK and Ireland when he should have been tucked away in an exclusive Hollywood retirement home reminiscing with some of his old pals. He just wasn't enjoying the experience and it was written all over his sad, old face.

Mickey stayed at the Conrad Hotel, which is less than one minute's walk from the front door of the National Concert Hall. I was driving the car myself and arrived ten minutes early for his 7.15 p.m. pick-up. He was waiting in the lobby.

'You're late!' he shouted at me.

'No', I said, 'it's just five minutes past seven.'

'You're late,' he repeated. 'Let's go.'

'What about Mrs Rooney?' I enquired. He didn't even look at me this time.

'Fuck her, she can walk.'

The eighth Mrs Mickey Rooney, Jan, was an ex-Las Vegas show girl and torch singer with a quality voice and good personality. She was by far the longest partner Mickey ever had. At the NCH, they performed duets together, but the highlight of the evening was a cabaret song and dance routine that he did with a live on-screen Judy Garland. He spoke about his love for Judy with great sincerity and it was only then that you fully realised what an iconic legend this little old guy really was.

Showbusiness can be the most magical, wonderful and rewarding profession but it can also be the dirtiest, most degrading and cruel. Mickey Rooney was a genuine Hollywood legend, his movie career unique and unmatched in screen history. His fortune after a lifelong gambling habit and eight marriages, however, was well and truly gone. What a comedown from appearing on screen with legends like Sinatra and Garland and being the biggest movie star of Hollywood's golden age to ending your career in England playing panto at provincial theatre venues.

Mickey Rooney died on 6 April 2014 at the age of 94. His eight surviving children said in a statement that they were barred from seeing him in his final years.

19: THE BEST CONCERT IN THE WORLD

So said Elisa Lanza, the only surviving child of the great Italian-American tenor Mario Lanza. Elisa was speaking in 2008 at Dublin's National Concert Hall after the first performance of *The Loveliest Night of the Year*, a celebration concert I was privileged to produce and present for the International Mario Lanza Society.

In 2008, I was approached by Dublin-born Geraldine McCann about doing a celebration event a year before the fiftieth anniversary of the great tenor's death at the age of 38. Geraldine, a gentle, kind, wonderfully elegant lady, was the president of Mario's Irish Appreciation Society and not only had been a devoted Lanza fan all her life but was also a close friend of Elisa. Geraldine did not want the fiftieth anniversary of Mario's death to pass without a fanfare concert of some kind and believed I was the person to stage it. I was very aware of Mario Lanza due to his enormous popularity through the generations of Irish fans from the 1950s onwards, so I didn't need much convincing. It would, I believed, be a sure-fire winner.

The show starred the outstanding Galway tenors Seán Costello and Frank Naughton, along with baritone Ronan Egan and much-loved soprano Sandra Oman. It was a major hit for our company. We had also drafted in the superb violinist Vladimir Jablokov and a dozen members of the Slovak Festival Orchestra. I paid Sony Music a royalty to use spoken word recordings (by the famous actor Christopher Lee) of Lanza's life, so as to set the correct tone, against a huge screen that showed clips of Lanza's exceptional career and movies. It was one of the first concerts in Ireland where the cast had no speaking roles whatsoever. Christopher Lee's brilliant narration and Lanza's timeless hits worked their own magic.

145

It was a pleasure to meet Elisa on a number of occasions. In fact she flew from Los Angeles to Dublin five times to celebrate with us the cherished legacy of her father. I had not known that Mario's wife, Betty, Elisa's mother, was part-Irish, a fact that she was enormously proud of. The standing ovation that Elisa received on that very first night when Geraldine McCann introduced her to the NCH audience said everything about how much Irish people loved her father. In the late 1950s and early 1960s, Lanza had only one competitor for Ireland's favourite recording artist and film star, and that was Elvis Presley. There was surely not a home in the entire country that didn't have a copy of 'I Walk With God' or 'Be My Love', and when Lanza played the King's Hall in Belfast in 1958, over half the 6,000-strong audience had travelled north to catch his one and only Irish concert. The show was so oversold that chairs had to be placed along the back of the stage to accommodate the huge numbers.

The actress Dolores Hart (real name Dolores Hicks), a first cousin of Betty Lanza, co-starred with Elvis in two of his early and better movies, *King Creole* and *Loving You*. Having made ten films, including *Come Fly With Me* with Hugh O'Brien, a Golden Globe winner, and a box office hit with Connie Francis in *Where the Boys Are*, Dolores walked away from Hollywood at just 24 years of age. She gave away all her earthly possessions and became a Roman Catholic nun, joining an enclosed order at the Benedictine abbey of Regina Laudis in Connecticut, of which she became prioress in 2001. In October 2008 the Holy Trinity Apostolate held a celebration breakfast in Hollywood in her honour, her first time in public and back in Hollywood in 43 years, at which she told her story about turning her back on fortune and fame. 'He led me out into an open space, he saved me because he loved me,' she said. Reverend Mother Dolores, now 83, remains a member of the Academy of Motion Picture Arts and Sciences, the only nun ever to be an Oscar voting member.

In the late 50s, at my grandmother Cox's house in Leo Street, Mario Lanza was king – as he was in thousands of Irish homes – and no one was allowed to talk or go near the radio when he sang. His 1951 movie *The Great Caruso*, had been one of the biggest screen successes in Hollywood's history at the time and featured members of New York's Metropolitan Opera. Being the first time that opera had ever been presented on the big Hollywood screen, it was a landmark picture in more ways than one.

The Loveliest Night of the Year series of concerts will remain one of my greatest achievements as a promoter. The show is already scheduled to return to the National Concert Hall in the near future. The Lanza celebration special has now played to well over 25,000 fans. The icing on the cake for me was our show being strongly featured in a Mario Lanza tribute special on Sky Arts in 2017, a show that is still featured regularly on that arts channel. The other great compliment is that Elisa Lanza, her husband, Bobby, Lanza's biographer Derek Mannering and their families, have, thanks to Geraldine McCann, my co-producer, returned again and again to Ireland to celebrate The Loveliest Night of the Year.

20: THE FIFTH BEATLE

*O*ne morning in late April 2016, a black envelope with an attractive silver border dropped through our mailbox. Since I was a kid in the 50s I have always loved receiving big or fancy envelopes from the postman. The surprise and excitement of opening something unknown have always been a joy. But this one was something extra special.

Lady Judy Martin requests your attendance at a service to celebrate the life and work of
SIR GEORGE MARTIN CBE (3rd January 1926 – 8th March 2016)
At 11am on Wednesday 11th May 2016
ST MARTIN-IN-THE-FIELDS

Helena and I were deeply touched to be asked to attend the service in the company of Lady Judy Martin, Giles Martin, Adam Sharp, Paul McCartney, Yoko Ono, Julian and Sean Lennon, Elton John, Paco Peña and dozens of other famous names. I felt truly humbled that Lady Judy had thought to invite me to this memorable service. She had a reason, though.

On 23 October 1999, as we walked in the door of the Trocadero restaurant, the velvet tones of Matt Monro singing his great number 1 hit 'Portrait of My Love' filled the room. 'Ah', said Sir George Martin to me, 'you had them play that for me.' I could have lied, of course, but I said no, I hadn't. In fact, I had no idea of the connection between Matt and Sir George, nor did I think the Troc's charming owner, Robert Doggett, had any awareness that the man accompanying me to his restaurant had produced the song that had made Monro an international star. I'm not sure even to this day that Robert knows Sir George – the most successful record producer in popular music history and absolutely the fifth Beatle – dined in his establishment, and was probably one of the most celebrated diners to ever grace Dublin's popular showbiz eatery.

In over fifty years of promoting shows and concerts and meeting many great stars, I have never met any celebrity so untouched by fame as Sir George Martin. Celebrated and acclaimed across the world for his enormous creative contribution to almost the entire Beatles catalogue, he was a complete gentleman; welcoming, courteous, graceful, charming, modest and down to earth, with a softly spoken, mellow personality devoid of grandeur or ego. He stayed in the big suite in the old Berkeley Court Hotel. 'Pat', he said, 'the suite is beautiful, but really there is no need for it at all. Lady Judy and I are happy in a good double room.'

In 1998, I went to London to meet Sir George's manager, Adam Sharp, and Giles Martin, George's son. I had an idea to pitch to them – a gala Beatles celebration concert in Dublin. I wanted Sir George to come to Ireland and conduct a 75-piece orchestra with guest singers in an evening of Beatles classics at the National Concert Hall. Having watched over so many years his close and crucial association with John Lennon and Paul McCartney, I wanted desperately to present this great producer in concert. There was no doubt in my mind that his vision for The Beatles had created a musical revolution never to be equalled.

Sir George was 74 when he came to Dublin, and after so many years in the studio his hearing was fading fast. Giles took over much of the preparatory work at the rehearsals, but Sir George would regularly intervene to conduct and offer guidance to the various singers. He was especially taken by two Dublin lads, Fran King and Scott Maher, of the Classic Beatles, a band way ahead of their time and arguably the best Beatles tribute act ever in these islands. So impressed was he that he spoke about using them in other Beatles orchestral projects. He also loved the voices of guest singers Leslie Dowdall and Seán Keane and paid great compliments to the Irish musical director, the late Pat Fitzpatrick.

After finally pulling it all together we did three sold-out shows at £60 a ticket. Sir George's fee was a modest £20,000, but the extras (which included the orchestra, one week of hotels and three days of rehearsals) left a very small profit. But it was honestly never about making a profit and much more about the experience and the thrill of being able to say I had worked with and promoted this unique man and musical legend. Over the years, Sir George and his office kept in touch, and he also wrote to the boys from the Classic Beatles. He said that he and Lady Judy had wonderful memories of their trip to Ireland, and so I was chuffed to be asked in 2006 to organise the music for Giles's wedding reception when he married the beautiful Dublin film producer Melanie Gore-Grimes.

The list of acts Sir George produced and was associated with is utterly phenomenal. His status in popular music history is without parallel, but his work ethic and innate character are also insights into a wonderfully kind and considerate man who, despite his fame and reputation, would take the time to write to me – a minor Irish promoter – not once but three times, personally expressing in great detail his gratitude for the good work we did in presenting his Irish shows. I feel it is important to present this list of his associations to give an insight into just how highly this man was regarded by the great and good in popular music. It is the most staggering list.

Sir George Martin's full list of associations and collaborations is as follows:

Larry Adler, Aerosmith, America, Benny Anderson, Eamonn Andrews, Richard Attenborough, Burt Bacharach, Dame Shirley Bassey, Mike Batt, Jeff Beck, The Beatles, the Bee Gees, Elmer Bernstein, *Beyond the Fringe*, Cilla Black, Jon Bon Jovi, Eve Boswell, Gary Brooker, Glen Campbell, José Carreras, Jim Carey, Cheap Trick, Eric Clapton, Phil Collins, Ray Cooper, Peter Cook, Bernard Cribbins, Jim Dale, John Dankworth, David and Johnathan, Celine Dion, Geraint Evans, Ella Fitzgerald, Geoff Emerick, Flanders and Swann, the Fourtune-Tellers, the Fourmost, Peter Frampton, the Frog Chorus, David Frost, Judy Garland, the George Martin Orchestra, Gerry and the Pacemakers, George Gershwin, Stan Getz, John Gielgud, Ron Goodwin, Rolf Harris, George Harrison, Sidney Harrison, Goldie Hawn, Mary Hopkin, Anthony Hopkins, Hurricane Hugo, Michael Jackson, Dick James, Antônio Carlos Jobim, Elton John, Quincy Jones, Tom Jones, the King's Singers, Mark Knopfler, Billy J Kramer and the Dakotas, Gene Krupa, Cleo Laine, John Lennon, Dick Lester, the Little River Band, the London Baroque Ensemble, Sophia Loren, Humphrey Lyttleton, Paul McCartney, Kenneth McKellar, John McLaughlin, Henry Mancini, the Mastersingers, Brian May, Spike Milligan, Matt Monro, Dudley Moore, Carl Perkins, Jon Pertwee, The Police, the Prince's Trust, Jonathan Pryce, Cliff Richard, Ralph Richardson, Kenny Rogers, Harry Saltzman, Seatrain, Harry Secombe, Neil Sedaka, Peter Sellers, Jimmy Shand, Paul Simon, Frank Sinatra, Johnny Spence, Ringo Starr, Tommy Steele, Rod Stewart, Sting, Roger Taylor, the

20: The fifth Beatle

Temperance Seven, *That Was the Week That Was*, Dylan Thomas, Sidney Torch, Pete Townshend, Björn Ulvaeus, Midge Ure and Ultravox, Peter Ustinov, the Vipers Skiffle Group, Alfred Waterhouse, Jimmy Webb, John Williams, Robin Williams, Brian Wilson, the Paul Winter Consort, Steve Winwood, Chris Wright, Stevie Wonder, Catherine Zeta-Jones.

21: 'NO FULL MONTY? IT'S A RIP-OFF!'

The Bad Girls were a five-piece, high-class stripper outfit from Australia's Gold Coast who toured a female version of the Chippendales' show. It was a high-quality Las Vegas-style production comprising a variety of dance sketches played out to the big chart hits of the day. I had previously seen the LA Centrefolds (a US stripper troupe) pack out Dublin's Olympia Theatre for promoter Kieran Kavanagh, and I knew the Bad Girls would be a winner. Nobody, however, told me about the public outcry that would ensue when the dates were first announced for late March 1998. The *Irish Star* ran a story about the Australian strippers coming to Ireland 'to drive the men crazy', which soon created a media frenzy resulting in an OTT pushback from local politicians and clergy. All the press and local radio wanted to know was whether the girls would be doing the full monty, the answer to which was that I had absolutely no idea. Shows were advertised for Dublin and provincial towns, which included Drogheda, County Louth.

The then Lord Mayor of Drogheda went on LMFM radio to declare that this type of cheap low-life show was not what the young people of Drogheda wanted and that it should be banned. He asked the local Garda superintendent to intervene and ban the performance. I had previously promoted the Chippendales at the Tallaght Basketball Arena without much fanfare, but the fuss over the Bad Girls took me by surprise. Had nothing changed in holy Catholic Ireland, I asked myself, since the day thirty years previously when Hollywood sex kitten Jayne Mansfield's risqué cabaret show had been run out of Tralee because the local bishop said she was not a proper person to entertain the local males. Poor Jane, God rest her soul, had sex appeal written all over her, but she was far from a Bad Girl stripper.

Billed as a payback gig for the men whose women friends fancied the Chippendale goons, the almost 100 per cent male audience at each venue went berserk as the ladies changed from lavish stunning gowns to skimpy party dresses and then to bikinis – and the rest. It wasn't rock'n'roll, and my mother would have turned in her grave had she known I was promoting such filth (as she would have called it), but to be fair to the Gold Coast beauties the show was visually stunning and professionally presented.

The 70-minute show played to a packed midnight audience at the Olympia Theatre on Saturday 28 March. A number of smaller out-of-town gigs were also rammed to the rafters. It was at the Rosnaree Hotel, just outside Drogheda on the main Dublin Road, that the issues started. Close to six hundred guys were packed into the function room, which had a low stage just two foot off the floor. I could foresee trouble on the horizon long before the show started, and I asked the venue's head bouncer to position some of his ten men around the front of the stage.

The problem arose when the Bad Girls appeared for the first number and the bouncers left their strategic places and starting raving with the rest of the punters. At least a dozen guys tried to touch or grab the girls and had to be forcibly pulled away by their trouser legs and shirts and dumped on to the side stage dance floor. For the first fifteen minutes, it was total mayhem. The worst, however, was yet to come. A mass shout-out started calling for the full monty, and before I knew it the entire house was screaming 'Monty! Monty! Monty!' The Bad Girls did not oblige. The tour manager tugged my jacket hard, and told me that unless the stage security was improved, he would pull the last act of the set. Had that happened there would have been a riot. Somehow or other we got through the show. It had been a frightening and almost out-of-control situation.

• •

Peter Green, the famous Fleetwood Mac guitarist, asked me to drive him back to Dublin after a gig in Cork. He then went on to tell me the music I was playing on the car cassette player (Clifford T. Ward) was crap and to turn it off. About five miles from Portlaoise he shouted at me to stop the car – he wanted to walk the rest of the way to Dublin. I let him out and when I looked in my rear-view mirror he was walking in the opposite direction.

• •

The majority of the crowd were not happy that the Bad Girls had not done a full monty. 'Are you the promoters?' myself and my friend Barry Gaster were asked at least a dozen times. 'No!' I lied, feigning a how-dare-you look. 'I'm just picking up my son.' One guy close to me said, 'No fuckin' full Monty? It's a rip-off!'

The following night at Dublin's Olympia, the Bad Girls put on an incredible gig; 1,300 punters, almost all guys aged between eighteen and forty, brought the house down and gave the girls a roaring Dublin welcome. The place was throbbing but because of the high number of security personnel on duty, and the big orchestra pit gap between the stage and the performers, we had no problems like the previous night. But, as had happened in Drogheda, the call went up close to the end of the show – 'Monty! Monty! Monty!'

Again the girls resisted. As a promoter, you don't get involved in telling the artists what and what not to do during their act. The contract for almost every show states that the promoter has no input into the production, and even if you did try to tell an act something, chances are you would be told that it was none of your business and to fuck off.

The problem at the Olympia that night was that it seemed to me to be one in a million. When the shouts went up again and again, 'Monty! Monty! Monty!', guys in the gods or gallery, the theatre's third tier of seating, started to throw small coins down on to the stage. I was frozen with fear that someone in the lower tiers would be hit on the head. With coins still raining down, the tour manager could see the problem and agreed with me. He was afraid that the girls might get a coin in the face. At that point, one of the girls made a quick 'be patient' gesture to the crowd and the coins immediately stopped falling. During the very last number, and as quick as you could say 'Jumpin' Jack Flash', the house roared as the Bad Girls did the quickest full Monty in history.

You might say it was a very close shave, but once again I had escaped with my life.

22: BRIEF ENCOUNTERS

The Golden Bear

In 2002, I set up In-Person International. The years before the 2008 crash was a boom period for corporate and after-dinner entertainment. I had achieved great audiences with the Paul McGrath branded dinner events and I wanted to continue that success story. Along with using our own stable of acts, who included Rebecca Storm, Phil Coulter, The Dubliners and the Celtic Tenors, I also wanted to secure some big-name Irish personalities to add to our list. I managed to secure Irish radio's greatest-ever star, Gay Byrne, as a regular client. The elegant and sophisticated queen of Irish fashion Barbara McMahon was our most continuously in-demand personality across TV, radio and personal appearances. Football legend and writer Tony Cascarino was our busiest sports client.

One of the very best people I ever had working with me, Elaine Tiernan, headed up the In-Person department of my business and set up dozens of celebrity appearances, booking leading Irish and UK stars into events across the world. Elaine secured a personal performance by the Celtic Tenors and the Vard Sisters for US President Bill Clinton at Dublin Castle. Among the international celebrities who came to town for In-Person events were Joanna Lumley (who presented the Eircell Awards) and Liverpool footballing legend Alan Hansen (for the Smithwicks Head-to-Head promotion). We also hosted Beatles producer Sir George Martin for Visa Card, Roy Keane for Champion Sports, and Enya (in one of her exceptionally rare stage appearances) for the Golden Plate Banquet International Achievement Awards. Other personalities included Anthea Turner, Jayne Torvill, Bill Bailey, Alison King, Jodie Kidd, Tamzin Outhwaite, Nick Leeson, David Bellamy, George Best and so many more.

The greatest and most acclaimed jockey in racing history, Lester Piggott, came to Dublin in 2005 for a special Legends lunch in celebration of the career of the immensely highly regarded commentator Sir Peter O'Sullivan. Along with looking after Peter, we also organised Lester's trip. I needed a compere for the event, and who better to do the job than Lester's daughter, Tracy? 'How do you feel about interviewing your dad?' I asked her.

'It will certainly be different,' she said, 'if I manage to get him to say more than a few words.' We needn't have worried – it was a highly successful lunch attended by the great and the good of Irish racing. JP McManus and his family were delighted with the event and thanked me for organising the tribute to Sir Peter. Peter himself was over the moon and wrote to me thanking me for the brilliant arrangements on what, he said, was truly a day to remember.

In July 2006, the world's greatest golfing legend, the Golden Bear, Jack Nicklaus, eighteen times a Major winner, came to town for a Legends dinner sponsored by A&L Goodbody Stockbrokers. I was pleased to have on board as a co-promoter CSL events, run by Liz McHugh, a very dear pal from my days at *Spotlight* magazine. Liz, like myself, had moved on to greater things after our wonderful years at the magazine. Another old pal from my days at the Five Club, Tony Johnston, was instrumental in helping me secure Jack through his connection with Killeen Castle, which – justifiably – boasted of its Jack Nicklaus-designed course. I had taken a lot of big gambles in my time with music acts, but this one was different. For Jack to appear as the special guest at the dinner in the Burlington Hotel he requested a fee of $250,000, plus an additional $20,000 to fuel a private jet from the USA to Dublin and back again. He also insisted on Australian golfing legend Peter Thomson being his interviewer, which cost another $10,000. By the time the hotels and transport and other related costs were totted up, we were well over the $300,000 figure for a one-hour interview! He would, we were informed, supply only twelve signed photos and that was it – no other autographs. At €5,000 a table, it was breaking new ground for corporate events, and while we did not sell the full target of 100-plus tables, we also didn't lose money. Thank God!

While not in the same financial league as Jack Nicklaus, I also had the pleasure of booking what Gay Byrne said was his 'most rewarding ever personal appearance'. He was paid a large five-figure sum – 'money for old rope, Pat', Gay told me. The gig? Gay and his wife, Kathleen, flew first-class to Singapore for a four-day trip to open a new Irish bar. 'I made a short speech and after that we were wined and dined like royalty. We stayed in the most fabulous hotel suite. It was marvellous! I'll take a few more jobs like that if you can get them,' said Gay, laughing at least some of the way to the bank.

After 2008's financial crash, the bottom fell out of the after-dinner speakers' market and has never recovered to anything like the same level since.

I put my money where my mouth was when, in association with former Cork Opera House manager Gerry Barnes and Andrew Flynn from Galway's Decadent Theatre Company, we presented at the Gaiety Theatre Martin McDonagh's *A Skull in Connemara* and *The Pillowman*. Andrew Flynn did a brilliant job directing both productions and McDonagh's growing international reputation as a writer and film-maker made them seem like a good bet. What upset me most about those productions was the unwillingness of McDonagh to support the marketing in any way whatsoever. *Skull* did good business but *The Pillowman* left me with a €70,000 hole in my pocket.

As a concert promoter or producer, big financial losses are very much a fact of life. You simply cannot win every time. The secret is to know when to cut your losses and walk away, but that's easier said than done. I have promoted some shows where I lost €150,000 or more and I have also taken other sizeable hits on gambles that just went wrong. My biggest loss and biggest win were with two top international acts.

In May 2014, at Dublin's 3Arena, I lost €180,000 on the former Spanish professional footballer turned heartthrob singer Julio Iglesias. I knew the polished crooner was past his sell-by date but at a straight fee of $250,000 plus local extras, it looked a good bet. The 9,000-seat arena had a gross potential of close to €800,000 if I sold every ticket. With a top price ticket of €85, I would break even at less than 60 per cent business. However, the show bombed with fewer than 4,000 tickets sold. Despite the loss, I enjoyed the show if only to experience the OTT behaviour and shenanigans of Julio and his entourage. He flew in on his 20-seater private jet with his three stunning Brazilian backing singers and full band, plus five or six assistants. The first thing his personal tour manager said to me on seeing the all-new SUVs waiting to drive him into Dublin city centre, was, 'Julio only travels in black transport, these cars are blue. Please have them changed.' I had to supply an ice-cooling van to take the fridge with his personal wine collection to his suite at the Shelbourne Hotel. I was asked to book a fish restaurant near the sea for his after-show dinner. I said to the tour manager that it would be dark by the time the gig was over and he wouldn't be able to see the sea. 'No, but he will smell it,' she answered abruptly. Having secured a table at a high-quality restaurant in Howth, the tour manager asked to speak to the chef to inform him how Julio like his scallops and monkfish cooked. After all that, and with everything in place, she later told me Julio would have dinner in the hotel instead. Julio had a serious hip problem and was unable to stand without being propped up next to the piano and amplifier, where he stood and sang for the entire performance. It was comical to watch and yet, somehow, he pulled it off. Julio and his full entourage didn't even stay a full night at the Shelbourne. They disappeared without any farewell or thank you, and stepped onto his private jet at 4 a.m. He had been on the ground in Dublin for less than 24 hours. His hourly rate was a few cents over €10,000. Easy money if you can get it.

The biggest one-off winner in my career, outside our annual Christmas panto, came about through a fault on the part of a German touring company, who undersold to me a very hot property. In 1999, 'Time to Say Goodbye' was, and it still is, one of the world's favourite songs. The hit duet, featuring one-time Hot Gossip dancer and 'Starship Trooper' Sarah Brightman, and the brilliant Italian tenor Andrea Bocelli, captured the hearts of millions and launched Sarah, the former wife of Andrew Lloyd Webber, to superstar status in the USA and across the world. The popularity of the song was phenomenal; it sold over 12 million singles. I knew that Sarah Brightman would sell tickets and I got on the case at once to try to secure an Irish tour date. I got tipped off early on that a German company, CoCo Tours, was putting together Sarah's first ever world tour, Eden, named after the success of her multi-million-selling album of the same name. After a trip to Frankfurt to meet the promoters, I had an oral agreement to the rights for an Irish show. The show fee was set at £40,000. After receiving the contract, I was surprised to see that the deal didn't include any back-end cut or percentage for Sarah of the show's profits. Most big acts will always include an extra cut for themselves once sales have reached a certain level. *Very unusual*, I thought to myself, but I kept my mouth shut and said nothing.

The 5,500 seats flew out the door at £40 a ticket, which was at the very top of the scale in 1999. Almost immediately, I added an extra show and it sold out in a few days. I then went back to the Germans and asked for a third show, and again it sold out. I had sold over 16,000 tickets, grossing £660,000 with an artist fee of just £120,000. On the final night of our three dates, the tour accountant from the German promoter went over the figures and was happy, before mentioning the back-end split. I said there wasn't one. 'Look at the contracts. It clearly states three shows at £40,000 per show. There is no back end mentioned anywhere.' He scratched his head and said, 'You're right, somebody has cocked up and it's not your fault.' He smiled at me and said, 'Good for you, you're a winner this time.' After sorting all our local costs – venues, hotels, promotion and so on – I walked away with a whopping £350,000. It was the last big concert deal I did before the introduction of the euro, and the chances of seeing the likes of it again are nigh on impossible. It was the biggest one-off profit of my entire promoting career.

Walking on the wild side

The very first thing Lou Reed did after his flight from the USA touched down at Dublin airport was to call me aside and ask, 'Are you the main man?' When I said I was, he put his arm around my shoulder, took me to one side and said 'I need you to pick up a special lady, she's on the eight-thirty p.m. flight from Amsterdam. Do it yourself; I want you to treat her good, bring her right to the gig.'

'No problem, Lou' I said. It had become something of a regular occurrence over the years – trips to the airport to meet glamorous ladies of the night – but this was my first one from Amsterdam. It was April 1979, and when Lou went on stage at the National Stadium at 8 p.m., I was standing at Dublin airport arrivals waiting to pick up a hooker from Holland. Lou's only other remark to me afterwards was, 'You did good, my man. Thank you.'

Lou's taste in whiskey was another problem. It had to be Chivas Regal, which wasn't something the off-licence on the South Circular Road knew much about. We must have tried twenty joints for the stuff, with no luck. Exotic whiskey in Dublin in the 80s was a rarity. We eventually bought it across the bar counter at the Shelbourne. Expensive, yes, but at least Lou got his walk on the wild side that night in Dublin.

Arrested by UK police

I booked the legendary poet Gil Scott-Heron, the godfather of rap, for a date at the old Wexford Inn in the late 90s. The show was booked out. The fee was £4,000 pounds, with 50 per cent paid upfront and 50 per cent on the night. At around 5 p.m. on the day of the gig, there was no sign of Scott-Heron or the band. The airport pickup driver called to say they never got off the plane. I was just about to put up 'Cancelled' notices when two cabs pulled up in Wexford Street, outside the Inn. It was the band. They had gone to the bar in the airport and forgot I had a driver outside. But there was no sign of Gil Scott-Heron; he had been arrested by UK police before boarding the flight. The band wanted to play the gig without him, but I said, 'No way; I'll be lynched if he doesn't appear.' The tour manager, a big six-foot-something fifteen-stone black guy, pulled me aside and said 'We turned up, we want to play the gig and you owe us the balance of the fee.' By this time the almost 500 fans were waiting to get inside and becoming very impatient. I pulled the gig and stood my ground and said 'I'm not paying the balance.'

My security had to hide me away in a back office for nearly three hours until the band finally left the premises. I never did get my £2,000 deposit back.

$2500 to see Miss Streisand

In 1999 RTÉ's *Late Late Show* asked me if I had any contacts in Las Vegas. They were trying to buy two tickets for the Barbara Streisand Millennium concert at the MGM Arena that was taking place on Friday 31 December 1999.

The tickets were for Gay Byrne to give away on a *Late Late* special to celebrate the millennium year of 2000. 'Yes,' I said. 'I do know someone who just might be able to help.' The show was the hottest ticket in America and if anyone could deliver, it was my old friend Vicky Hamilton, who had discovered Guns N' Roses and Mötley Crüe. Vicky knew everyone in the US business. She called me back and said, 'Pat, the face value on the best seats is two thousand five hundred dollars each, but it's going to cost you a lot more than that.'

Vicky delivered all right, but by the time I'd paid a string of commissions and extra handling charges the tickets finally arrived in Dublin, at a cost of over $5,000 each, double the face value. I charged an additional $1,000 a ticket. Total cost to the *Late Late Show* – a shade over $12,000 for two seats in the front circle at the MGM arena.

The tickets for the Streisand Millennium concert remain to this day the most expensive concert tickets in showbiz history. Maybe I'm wrong, but I imagine it's highly unlikely that any other show host than Gay Byrne would have been allowed to pay this kind of money for two concert tickets.

'Betcha By Golly Wow' – It's The Stylistics

I have been The Stylistics' Irish promoter for almost twenty years and it has been a total joy on so many levels. Every January, like clockwork, my great old-school agent pal in the UK, Roy Hastings, one of the original 10 per cent showbiz hustlers of the early 60s, calls me to tie down the contract for The Stylistics' annual year-end trip to Ireland. The only problem is that Roy is no longer a 10 per cent man – he's moved with the times, and if you are not up at cock crow and on your guard, the fee will jump by a thousand quid a show every year. But thanks to Roy and his mate, the legendary English promoter Danny Betesh, The Stylistics never fail to arrive in Ireland to play a short Irish tour.

When you consider that they were one of the first international groups ever to play an outdoor gig – at the RDS in Dublin in November 1975 – it says a lot about their durability and longevity. Their string of 70s hits became the soundtrack to the lives of so many young Irish people in their twenties and thirties who now come back every year to welcome this truly legendary Philadelphia group to Ireland.

The run of successful Stylistics hits seemed endless. They became much more than just another pop group, they were the romantic dream weavers of the 70s and early 80s. Their Top Ten hits over almost eight years truly defined an entire generation.

It all started in in 1971 with their first big hit, 'You're a Big Girl Now', and seven years later the hits were still coming – 'Stop, Look, Listen', 'You Are Everything', 'Betcha By Golly Wow', 'Break Up to Make Up', 'I'm Stone in Love with You', 'You'll Never Get To Heaven', 'You Make Me Feel Brand New', 'Let's Put it all Together', 'Star on a TV Show', 'Sing Baby Sing', 'I Can't Give You Anything (But My Love)', 'Funky Weekend', 'You Are Beautiful', 'Rockin' Roll Baby', 'Na Na Is the Saddest Word'. In 1975 the *Best of the Stylistics* became the biggest selling album ever in Ireland.

It sold well in excess of 100,000 copies when John Woods at Polydor made it the first television-advertised album by a mainstream artist. In 1976 The Stylistics did it all over again when the same album went back to number 1 in the UK charts and again sold massive numbers in Ireland.

Fifty years on the group still features two original members, Airrion Love and Herb Murrell. Their longevity and immense popularity (they always sell out every single seat) is down to their impeccable attention to detail. I always standing stage side during their performances and I have never failed to be impressed with the quality and professionalism of their show. Musically, little has changed since their many performances on *Top of the Pops* in the 70s, except continued reinvention of a brilliant stage act. Simply put, The Stylistics are a lesson in how to stay at the top of your game as a touring act.

In recent years, long-time vocalist Eban Brown moved on to a solo career and was replaced by former Temptations lead singer Barrington 'Bo' Henderson, who fitted seamlessly into the line-up. When you've been fifty years on the road and you're still selling out tours across the world, picking up $20,000 and more a night, you must be doing something right.

Joining the press gang

I had no intention at any time to recall my history and cherished memories in writing. It just happened one day during the pandemic. With no shows to promote, no posters to paste across the city, my two companies closed and an office operating with just two loyal staff, I discovered a hand-written note from my old friend John Boland about a review of the Beach Boys gig I did at the old Point Theatre in the 1980s from the *Evening Press*, which was at that time the biggest selling evening newspaper in Dublin. It made me realise I actually had a history and a story to tell, and so with too much time on my hands I told myself *Why not give it a go?* During my early successful years as a music promoter, I became close friends with John, a great journalist, poet and television critic. At that time, John was the star writer with the *Evening Press*, although he later moved to the *Irish Times* and the *Irish Independent*. One of the highlights of my week was meeting up with John and some of the paper's editorial crew every Friday evening at Brady's on Aston Quay – there was always a great buzz in Brady's on a Friday evening. Eamonn Brady, the bar owner, was the man who ejected Sex Pistols' singer Johnny Rotten onto the pavement outside when he had drunk more than his share of the black stuff and had become troublesome. At that point, I had written a few concert reviews for the paper, so being able to mix in the company of editor Seán Ward and writers such as Noeleen Dowling, Mary Kerrigan, the *Sunday World* editor Joe Kennedy and gifted award-winning photographer Eric Luke was magical for me. John was inspirational and a wonderful storyteller who could quote the literary giants of the top of his head. He gave me a lot of advice at a time when my life was in pieces, the kind of stuff I needed to know about supporting my kids as my marriage fell apart. Despite having written thousands of words in my column and across the pages of *Spot-light*, I never for one minute considered myself for one moment as a real writer or journalist. So being accepted into this close circle of very talented people was a wonderful bonus for my always low self-esteem.

23: THE IRISH CONNECTION

No show like a Joe show

Over the last twenty years, there have been dozens and dozens of cases in the US courts relating to tribute acts infringing artists' copyright. There are simply not enough courts in the world to shut down the 50,000, give or take, Beatles, Elvis Presley, Bee Gees, George Michael and Pink Floyd imitators playing in bars, concert venues and, lately, arenas across the globe every night of the week. I'm not saying it doesn't happen, but it's now extremely rare for a tribute band to end up in court for reproducing the music and images of their heroes without permission. The majority of the big original acts are now happy to pick up their performing rights cheques for the use of their music and to take the rest as an ego-boosting compliment. When I was seeking rights to do a television special for our successful Carpenters touring show, Karen so Close, Richard Carpenter had no problem with us doing the show – in fact, he wished us well but refused to participate in the programme. While Australia gets credit as the home of the original really successful tribute act, Bjorn Again, the early Elvis imitators like Brendan Bowyer were really the first, followed closely by the Fab Four. I sometimes feel the best tribute acts don't get the credit or standing they deserve for bringing to life what in a lot of cases is classic music long past its sell by date. An actor or actress will get five stars from critics for playing a dead or legendary star in a movie, but the best tribute acts – which are every bit as good, if not better – are relegated to being just another tribute act.

I believe it's wrong because I have seen close-up how serious the very best tribute acts are when it comes to dedication to their performances. The problem with these acts is that the best ones are brilliant (there are probably only fifty of them worldwide), while the other 49,950 are shoddy, musically rubbish and, if anything, are killing the tribute phenomenon. Along with creating our own tributes (I prefer to call them celebrations) for the over-50s at the National Concert Hall for the likes of Burt Bacharach and Joe Dolan, I also have had the luck to exclusively promote four of what I consider to be the best tribute acts on the planet. These acts put as much time, effort, dedication and attention to detail into their performances as the original acts. The big concert promoters have toured hologram shows that are not a patch on the very best tributes. I know – I have seen the Roy Orbison hologram show, yet the Dean Bourne tribute to the man is closer to Roy than any recreated image could ever be. The best tribute acts I have promoted are Stephen Triffitt and the Definitive Rat Pack, Belinda Davids, Dean Bourne and Toni Lee. Triffitt is amazing as Frank Sinatra; not only can he sing at the same level as the great man, but he has perfected Sinatra's mannerisms to a point where you really can imagine you're watching the leader of the Rat Pack live from Las Vegas. South African Belinda Davids is simply spellbinding as Whitney Houston; Australian Dean Bourne bears a remarkable closeness in voice and image to Roy Orbison; and as Karen Carpenter, England's Toni Lee has the only voice I have heard that can reproduce, to perfection, Karen's smoky tones.

In Ireland, I am delighted to say, and not because he is my pal, that Ronan Collins' interpretation of the Joe Dolan songbook is brilliant. No other singer in Ireland can perform the great hits of Joe Dolan like Ronan. While he does not try to imitate Joe, he is the only singer who can reproduce Joe's range and falsetto vocals to near flawlessness. Backed by Eugene McCarthy's eight-piece band, the Sugar Cubes, Ronan delivers the most stunning tribute to the great Mullingar man – it's so good it gets ovation after ovation every time it plays the NCH and across Ireland.

Which reminds me of a phone call and solicitor's letter I received at my office telling me that I was in breach of copyright by using a photo of Joe Dolan in the background of adverts for Ronan's shows. Seamus Casey, a gentleman and Joe's former manager, was on the line to say he and Ben

● ●

After a Joan Armatrading gig in Dublin in the mid-80s, her tour manager, Pete Wilson, was arrested at Dublin airport and relieved of £7,000 by Irish customs. They thought it was drug money. It took close to six months to have it returned.

● ●

Dolan, Joe's elder brother, were unhappy with Ronan. They felt that he should not be touring this show, and that I had no right to use Joe's picture (which, to be fair, was true). I had an artist produce an original painting of Joe that visually 'faded' into the background of the show artwork. Thankfully, I heard nothing more, but I was really baffled by their complaints. I couldn't understand such short-sightedness on their part. Not only does Ronan do great justice to Joe Dolan's music, but he is endlessly reminding people of what a truly great talent Joe was. He also regularly plays Joe's original hits on his daily RTÉ Radio 1 show. No one was or is doing more than Ronan to keep the music of Joe Dolan alive, so why would Ben Dolan want to kill off the one man who is keeping his brother's legacy alive? I really have no idea.

Aonghus McAnally, one of the truly nice guys of the Irish music business, is another former RTE producer with a real hidden talent. A great stand-up comic and presenter, he has inherited many of his famous father, Ray's, stage skills.

His most outstanding musical achievement is his tribute to Christy Hennessy, which won widespread acclaim, selling out to over 2000 people on its last tour at the Board Gais Energy Theatre in 2019. This was a major achievement as the tour also included five or six other nationwide sell outs. The secret was the combination of Christy's great songs and the unique way Aonghus - a close friend of the late singer - presented the show. I was delighted to be the promoter who helped Aonghus take this great show on the road. The family of Christy Hennessy expressed some reservations about Aonghus doing a tribute. But I can assure you, that this was a brilliant celebration of the career of Christy Hennessy which was presented with great respect to the legendary songwriter. Not unlike what Ronan Collins has done to keep Joe Dolan's legacy alive, Aonghus has championed Christy's music both on air and on stage, which has contributed hugely to Christy's continued popularity. If you were a fan of the great Tralee songwriter, this is a show that comes with a five-star review.

Robert DeNiro walked in

Two great singers with the most incredible voices who I have taken great pride in promoting and representing over the years are Red Hurley and Colm Wilkinson. Both are now in the twilight of their careers, and their prime days on the concert stage are now rarer, but when they do appear on stage the opportunity to see them should never be missed. What is remarkable about both men is that their voices have remained forever young; and they still have the same power and magnificent performing ability.

Colm Wilkinson's international career success is unparalleled in the history of Irish entertainment. No other Irish singer or stage star has achieved such heights of acclaim across the world. I suppose you know you have really made it when a leading university presents you with an honorary doctorate and names a scholarship in your honour. That's what happened to Colm when Ryerson University in Toronto honoured him for his outstanding contribution to Canadian entertainment.

Colm has appeared on more than 70 albums throughout his career; he has shared a stage with such legends as Frank Sinatra, Aretha Franklin, Stevie Wonder, Quincy Jones, Elton John and John Williams. Colm was the first singer/actor to play the leading role in *The Phantom of the Opera* at Sydmonton, the country home of Lord Andrew Lloyd Webber. He had to turn down the lead role in *Phantom* because he was committed to playing Valjean in *Les Misérables*. Lloyd Webber also honoured Colm with another theatre scholarship in his name. Few people know that Colm's signature song, 'Bring Him Home', was written especially for his incredible falsetto voice – 'a voice from God, like no other,' said Cameron Mackintosh, producer of *Les Misérables*. Academy award winner Eddie Redmayne remembers him walking onto the *Les Misérables* movie set. 'I will never forget it. All the other actors, having grown up being beguiled by his staggering talent, were silenced. Completely silenced. Everyone just stood there with dropped jaws as if Robert De Niro had walked in. That's it, really – Colm is the De Niro of the musical theatre world.'

I was blown away way back in 2014 when Colm called me and said, 'I see you're doing a good job on a lot of other people's gigs. Will you work with me on some shows?' It was the biggest compliment of my more recent career. We have done two Irish tours and several one-off shows that have also been high points in my showbiz life. Colm also entrusted me with the responsibility of putting together *The Essential Colm Wilkinson*, the anniversary three-CD box set that was released in 2018 by my old pal Cathal Tully at Beaumex. Unlike so many showbiz stars, Colm has little or no interest in the celebrity side of things. In fact, the further all those people are away from him the better he likes it. It's almost like singing has been just a nine-to-five day job and once the show is over, he retreats to his home, family and anonymity. It's great to be able to say that Colm has become more than just another music act to promote – he and Deirdre, his lovely wife, have become close friends of Helena and me. A friendship to cherish.

Red Hurley's string of big ballad quality recordings in the mid-70s put him right at the top of the Irish showbiz list of A-rated performers. His many Top 10 hit songs include 'When', 'Kiss Me Goodbye', 'Sometimes', 'Isadora', 'Love is All', 'Hey' and 'Broken Promises'. His heart-breaking ballads made him unique at the height of the showband years. Even in those early days, Red had all the hallmarks of becoming a vocalist of the highest standard. Since Red graduated to being a big stage concert act, I have promoted many of his sell-out nights at the National Concert Hall and the Gaiety Theatre. A really lovely modest and down-to-earth guy, he is an absolute gentleman and a joy to work with. Over the years I have never seen him fail to get standing ovations time and time again. His career longevity is down to the high quality of his performances and his meticulous attention to detail. He is a wonderful singer with the ability to craft any great song in his own style. In recent years Red has reinvented himself several times, headlining the highly successful Reeling in the Showband Years touring show, but most successfully as a gospel performer. His soul-chilling take on such classics as 'I Walk With God', 'You Raise Me Up' and 'Bring Him Home' ensures that he will remain at the very top of concert attractions for as long as he continues to perform. I am looking forward to working with him on a special series of spiritual concerts celebrating the life of the Italian saint Padre Pio which are planned for late 2022.

I am proud also to be good friends with him and his beautiful wife, Norma.

Yet another cherished friendship.

A man for all seasons

I have had the honour of being Phil Coulter's booking agent and concert promoter for twenty-five years or more. Phil is easy to work with as long as you do your job and get results. Professional to his fingertips, he puts immense effort into everything he touches. I love working with Phil, and to say he is the oldest swinger in town is not far off the mark. But even at the age of 80, which he reached in 2021, Phil shows no signs of calling it a day. He is as eager and hungry as ever. If you want to unlock the secret of success in the entertainment business, look no further than the great Cool Filter himself.

It was the elusive Maurice Cassidy, the silent impresario who helped launch *Riverdance* and Abba's *Mama Mia* internationally, who once said to me, 'There is no one in entertainment worldwide that works as hard as Phil, he is addicted to giving great performance and receiving applause.' Looking back at his career, he has delivered every aspect of the all-round performing genius. Songwriter for two of the greatest names in pop history – Elvis Presley and Cliff Richard – and album producer for Van Morrison, James Galway, Sinead O'Connor and his great pal Billy Connolly; musical director for the legendary Richard Harris; a major touring star with Sir James Galway; a Eurovision winner; and teen idol creator (Bay City Rollers). He sails every year on his own Phil Coulter-themed Caribbean Tranquillity Cruise. Not forgetting a string of sell-out solo concert tours starting from his huge-selling *Tranquillity* album days in the 1980s right up until 2019. His songs 'My Boy', 'Scorn not His Simplicity', 'Remember Me', 'The Town I Love So Well' and 'Ireland's Call' will live for ever.

Phil always knew that success is fleeting and the only way to sustain it for sixty years has been to keep working his ass off. Phil is a master of self-promotion and creative reinvention, so no interview or promotion opportunity will be dismissed without due consideration. He is a truly great inspiration to young performers – I'm always telling aspiring stars that if they want to see what real long-term show business success looks like, all they need to do is to look at the career of Phil Coulter.

One very special evening I spent with Phil and his wife, Geraldine, at their country mansion in County Wicklow, 24 November 1999, will live for ever in my memory. It was an evening of great food, wine, shenanigans, craic and stories to die for. In truth, I was a gate crasher and photographer that night, as I was driving Billy Connolly on a tour night off. Phil had pulled together some of Billy's greatest Irish pals for what he titled on his menu 'The Night of the Dinosaurs – A rare chance to view these noble but threatened creatures at play before they face extinction.' So we had Phil, Billy Connolly, Ronnie Drew, Jim McCann, Ralph McTell, Shay Healy, Paul Brady and Christy Moore reliving their life and times on the road in the most hilarious tales. Nobody could ever match the wit and wisdom of either Ronnie Drew or Jim McCann. How sad it is that we have lost such great guys as Ronnie, Jim and Shay. It was a real privilege that night to be in the company of such giants of Irish music and one that I will never forget.

On the subject of great arrangers and pianists, one man I must pay tribute to, who has worked on all my shows, is Eugene McCarthy, our musical director and arranger. Eugene is the kind of guy everyone needs as both a friend and workmate Without Eugene's brilliance I would never have been able to produce some of our most successful shows – The Carpenters Love Songs, Burt Bacharach at 92, Roy Orbison Reborn, Ronan Collins Sings Joe Dolan, the Bobby Darin and Connie Francis specials, the hits of James Last, and the Definitive Rat Pack. Eugene has worked closely with Aled Jones, Red Hurley, Colm Wilkinson, Stephen Triffitt and Ronan Collins and is highly regarded by Phil Coulter as one of the country's best arrangers. He is, in every sense of the word, a true gentleman and very dear friend, one of the kindest guys I know. Thanks also to the great backing singers Maeve McCarthy, aka Karen Black, and the lovely Aileen Pringle. The Sugar Cubes big band of Ronan Dooney, Carl Geraghty, Adam and Terence Taylor, Karl Breen and John Swan contributed so much to the success of our many shows. The guys and I have shared some magical nights together over many years at almost every theatre in the country.

No Frontiers

I was very proud to be Mary Black's promoter during her highly successful early years. Mary is an elegant, stylish lady who never let the need for a commercial or showbiz persona interfere in her quest to be the perfect female voice of Irish folk and contemporary music. It was a wonderful experience to play a small part in the developing years of a truly brilliant artist.

From her earliest traditional folk years to her exquisite covers of Jimmy MacCarthy's best songs, Mary was unique among Irish female hit makers of the 80s. Her 1989 album *No Frontiers* remains the definitive recording by which all other Irish female singers are measured. Spending well over 52 weeks in the charts, it was the pinnacle for both her and Jimmy MacCarthy's song-writing careers. Mary and Jimmy were not unlike the Dionne Warwick–Burt Bacharach partnership of so many magical hits – each brought the very best out of the other. Mary also championed the great songs of Noel Brazil and Mick Hanley, and she gave opening spots on all her concerts to dozens of younger songwriters such as Sinéad Lohan and Eleanor McEvoy. As I've often said, there is only one Mary Black.

One of the most cherished memories of my time with Mary was the night my co-promoter Denis Desmond and I hosted a wonderful 40th birthday celebration for her in the Back Lane restaurant behind Cork Opera House. It was a wonderful night. Although she had hits around the world (including Japan), dozens of successful tours, and was selling out major venues like the Royal Albert Hall, her attempts to cross over into the soft rock US market with her 1997 album *Shine* fell short. That was such a pity because quality and artistry oozed from her. I don't get calls very often from the world's most famous concert promoter, so I never forgot in 1986 our receptionist saying that Harvey Goldsmith was on the line. 'For me?' I asked in surprise, for once in my life feeling important. I pressed the phone extension button and picked up the line.

'Hi, Pat, tell me about this girl Mary Black. I'm hearing a lot about her, is she as good as they say?'

'Yes, Harvey, she's the best ever.'

'Will she do a tour for me in the UK, say eight to ten dates?'

'I think she would be delighted.'

'Check it out for me.'

Joe O'Reilly of the Dolphin music family, Mary's husband and manager, is a nice guy who has always played his cards close to his chest and he always gave me the feeling he didn't quite trust me when it came to promoting Mary's shows. Joe has protected Mary's career like armed guards protecting gold bullion in Fort Knox, and to give him his due, she did brilliantly under his management. However, we can only guess if Mary's career missed a defining moment by turning down Harvey Goldsmith's offer to launch her in the UK over 35 years ago.

It's hard to talk about Mary Black without including her master songwriter, Jimmy MacCarthy. I have known Jimmy from the first moment he came ranting and raving into Kate and Anna McGarrigle's dressing room at Connolly Hall, Cork, way back in the mid-70s. Jimmy was the support act on the night and was livid with the Canadian folkie sisters for not giving him a decent soundcheck before his gig. As he stormed away, he let off a bark. 'Big stars my arse!' Jimmy has serious history when it comes to soundchecks. He is a total perfectionist and goes through soundmen at an alarming rate. He will often take a full hour, sometimes two, to perfect his sound before a show, and when he gets everything right and rosy, he may well insist on starting over again to tweak what might be an imaginary tiny blip. One day the soundman can do no wrong, yet a week later he's gone. Perfectionism aside, Jimmy's solo concerts can be the most joyous and personal; it's like sitting next to him in his sitting room while he's tuning his guitar in the middle of telling a story about his early days as a jockey. His eccentricity aside, let me tell you about the other side of Jimmy MacCarthy: he is a lovely, kind, soft-mannered, caring person with a heart of gold who is generous to a fault. While we fell in and out of friendship about ten times over the years, I love the man dearly, and to me, he has been a loyal friend. In his book *Ride On in Song and Story*, he paid me a treasured compliment: 'With Pat Egan as my manager, I had for the first time truly professional representation, a commodity that is in very short supply in the Irish music business. Pat's work as my promoter was also impeccable.'

I helped him with many deals, including a major publishing contract with Universal Music. After an hour of negotiating my 20 per cent fee downwards he eventually paid me an amount I was happy with, but Jimmy still felt I was overpaid. The very next morning, my daughter Layla was informed that a brand new, pedigree pony named Starlight, which I understand cost well over £1,500, had been delivered by Jimmy MacCarthy to her riding school in Newtownmountkennedy. Layla no longer needed to hire a pony – she now had one of her own, given to her by a man who knew more than a thing or two about our four-legged friends.

Despite spending hundreds of thousands (and I really mean hundreds of thousands) recording on what might well be his last album with acclaimed producer Donal Lunny, it never saw the light of day. 'It just wasn't right, Pat,' he told me. 'It never got off the starting blocks.' I had advised him and offered my services on the financial end of things before he started recording the album, but Jimmy, being Jimmy, wanted to do it his own way. I felt very sad for him when it was all over; he was in a very low place, disappointed and regretful, and seriously out of pocket that the project had not produced a string of new hit songs. In terms of his song writing, Jimmy is right up there in an exclusive club of his own. Nobody - and that includes Van Morrison, Phil Coulter, Bono, Paul Brady, Brendan Graham, and the Edge – could weave a tapestry of lyrics and melodies even close to Jimmy's best work. I like to call him the W.B. Yeats of contemporary Irish song-writing. Just read the genius lyrics of 'Adam at the Window', which is a genuine but sadly uncelebrated masterpiece. Mary Black's version of the song is sublime and for me one of her best ever recordings.

Adam's at the window staring at the apple trees on fire
Waiting for the windfall that brings the smile of kings and their
desire.
Door blows in behind him, a floral pattern, summer dress so gay
Burning in the sunlight, too late to wait, for darkness won't delay
To steal her cherry lips away.
For while the careless tongues of sunlight slowly trickle down
The curve of hips, her fingertips, in kissing sips we drown
In kissing sips, we drown.
And Adam will have his way
Adam will have his way.

(© Jimmy MacCarthy. Reproduced by kind permission of
Jimmy MacCarthy/ Universal Music)

Or 'Bright Blue Rose':

I skimmed across black water, without once submerging
Onto the banks of an urban morning
That hungers the first light, much much more
Than mountains ever do.
And she like a ghost beside me goes down with the ease of a dolphin
And emerges unlearned, unscathed, unharmed.
For she is the perfect creature, natural in every feature.

(© Jimmy MacCarthy. Reproduced by kind permission of
Jimmy MacCarthy/ Universal Music)

The only comparison I can make to Jimmy's kaleidoscopic stream of lyrics is to step back into the 60s and play Jimmy Webb's classic, 'McArthur Park', Gary Brooker's 'Whiter Shade of Pale' or Bob Lind's 'Elusive Butterfly'. Jimmy, however, did not write his best work in a haze of alcohol or marijuana, but from the deepest part of his soul, a place that only a true genius knows how to discover. It's my belief that Jimmy's work is not and has never been fully appreciated by the Irish media. Yes, Mary Black has paid the ultimate vocal tributes to his songs, but Jimmy is more than that, by far. To me, he is, plain and simple, a song-writing poetic mastermind unmatched anywhere in popular Irish culture. Knowing and working for him has been a high point of my life. Cork City Council should pay tribute and erect a statue of Jimmy MacCarthy in Patrick Street – because he truly is the Contender.

Trust is a two-way street

Mary Coughlan is one of the finest jazz and blues singers in the entire world. She is also a really lovely person, kind, caring, and so considerate of others. You can't help but love the lady. She is also a difficult act to represent as a manager, promoter or agent. Twice I tried and twice I failed miserably and it hurt. Things fell apart because trust went missing.

At the height of her popularity in the 80s no other female rock or blues singer anywhere in the world could touch Mary's mesmerising vocals and her on-stage charisma. She was truly brilliant, leaving the competition in her wake. *Melody Maker* hailed her as the white Billie Holiday and the best blues singer of her generation. Denis Desmond, Mary's first manager, had put everything perfectly in place for a long and successful career at the very highest level as one of the world's great blues and torch singers. Mary has had some top managers, agents and record companies in her day, and some of the biggest in the business, including Denis Desmond, Mattie Fox (ex-manager of Christy Moore), Barry Gaster (the Corrs' co-manager) among them. Smart guys well on top of their game who could buy and sell you with one eye closed.

So why do some acts spend an entire career with one manager and others constantly jump ship? Artists need stability if they are to achieve their ultimate career goals. Trust is the most vital thing in a relationship between artist and manager and when that evaporates the manger is lost and on a hiding to nothing. It often happens in the music business that the greatest talents fall shy of their deserved financial rewards, not always through any fault of their own, but because they lack an understanding of the logistics of a career in performing, and the attention to business and financial detail that is so vital in making a career in music work. What you think you see on stage when a top artist like Mary Coughlan is appearing in a major concert hall is not, unfortunately, what you get.

The perception when people see full rooms is that the artist is rolling in cash all the way to the bank. That's not true – it really only happens in the world of the Eagles, Coldplay, U2 and the like. The reality for 85 per cent of touring acts is a very different ball game all together. Mid-level concert performances and tours have to be bankrolled by someone, whether it's the artist themselves, their manager or a promoter willing to risk their bucks in the hope of a full house, because anything less will cost them money. It often takes selling the last 200 seats in a 1,000-seater hall for the promoter to see a profit. Ticket commissions, sound, lighting, trucking companies plus engineers all have to be paid. The venue will take 30 per cent of the gross as a rental charge. Advertising – posters, press, radio, social media –costs a lot of money. Unless you're a Christy Moore or a Tommy Tiernan, you will need musicians at anything between €300 and €500 a gig or more, depending on their status in the industry. Insurance is now a major cost factor in running any gig. By right the musicians should (but more often than not don't) have their own insurance cover. They simply can't afford it. For some years now the big insurance companies have seen the flashing dollar signs in the rock'n'roll business and, like everyone else, they want their share, and it does not come cheap. Even if a promoter buys an act at, say, €20,000 a show, the artist still faces sizeable bills for their sound and light crew and musicians, and don't forget the manager of the act and their agent who between them are taking as much 30 per cent of the fee. The old 10 per cent commission days have long passed. Everyone wants to grab a bigger piece of the action, and unless the artist is micro-managed to perfection their chances of living in Monaco are slim. The bottom line here, of course, is that to cover all the high costs of staging a concert the price of your admission ticket to a show continues to soar.

I must tell you a story that Eric Clapton's tour manager told me about the fee charged by one of America's top sound engineers. Eric was very keen to have this guy doing sound on one of his big American tours way back in 1991. I can't remember his name, but seemingly he was right at the top of his game and every big touring act wanted him. His fee per show was, wait for it, a whopping $10,000 a show for sitting at the sound desk. Some of the top-notch musicians on the same tour came in cheaper per show. Can you imagine now, thirty years later, what the same sound and lighting engineers are being paid by the world's biggest acts? It's true what they say, you know, there is no business like show business.

Larger than life

'Oh, Jesus, what have I gone and done! Fuck it! The leg is cracked and I don't have a replacement!'

The soundcheck had been progressing nicely. It was 4.30 p.m. at the National Concert Hall. The star billing on the night was Ronan Tynan and his 30-piece orchestra. It was his first solo Irish concert since the Irish Tenors' amazing US success story. The hall was sold out, and the President of Ireland, Michael D. Higgins, was due to attend.

'What am I going to do?' he howled. 'I can't go on with only one leg!'

Larger than life in more ways than one, and easy to like, Ronan has an extremely funny, bubbly, likeable personality, but boy is he complicated. Nothing is simple or straightforward with Ronan Tynan. He had been enjoying the soundcheck and was clowning about the stage with the orchestra musicians. He was in such good spirits he decided he would leap up and sit on the Steinway piano, but he misjudged it and one of his artificial legs (he has two) went from underneath him and he landed on his arse on the stage floor.

Why does Ronan have two artificial legs? He was born with phocomelia, a rare birth defect characterised mostly by severely shortened, sometimes completely absent, limbs; and both of Ronan's lower legs were underdeveloped. In 1980, at the age of twenty, following a car accident in which he sustained a back injury that made it impossible to continue using the prosthetic legs he had, a decision was made to amputate each leg below the knee. The operation was so successful that within a short time Ronan was competing at the highest level in track and field. He went on to represent Ireland at the Paralympics in 1984 and 1988, winning four gold medals, and between 1981 and 1984, he won eighteen gold medals in various competitions and set fourteen world records. He subsequently became the first person with a disability to be admitted to Limerick's

• •

In 2018, when Billy Connolly played his last ever gigs at Dublin's 3Arena, it took three 40-foot articulated trucks to bring in his stage set. I really thought I have seen it all but, no, a comedian with three trucks of gear is now quite normal. God be with the early days when comedians such as Tommy Cooper arrived for a gig with a small suitcase and a few decks of cards.

• •

National College of Physical Education, and he later went to Trinity College Dublin and became a physician specialising in orthopaedic sports injuries. He was also an accomplished horseman. In other words, Ronan had more smarts, ambition, dedication and resilience than most. But not right now, because, as he exclaimed, one of his artificial legs was cracked and he didn't have a replacement.

While Ronan was having good laugh at his own expense, he suddenly realised there was no spare leg available anywhere in Dublin. We now had a major problem, and showtime was just three hours away.

'I don't have spare legs,' he said, 'they're all in America. Don't worry, Pat, let me think.' A few seconds passed. 'I have a pair of riding ones at home in Kilkenny. They're not the best but will work if we can get them to Dublin on time.'

Like I said, complicated is not the word for Ronan, but this near disaster of losing a leg three hours before a performance – well, truth really can be stranger than fiction. In my moment of panic, I could just see the morning papers headline: 'One-legged Tynan fails to appear for the President.' Frantically, a plan was put in place to get Ronan his riding legs from Kilkenny to Dublin in time for the performance. We had a little under three hours to get the big man mobile. Lo and behold, twenty minutes before showtime, with the help of a Garda motorcycle rider, the spare legs arrived at the National Concert Hall. I was very relieved when Ronan walked on stage at 8 p.m. and gave the performance of his life, followed by a handful of standing ovations.

Working for Ronan as a promoter can be frustrating. It's a kind of no-win situation. Despite agreeing to a deal in advance and issuing a contract, Ronan is rarely happy with the outcome, and when he sees the 'Sold Out' sign going up he is even less happy. 'I should have got a bigger fee; you're making too much money, Pat.' He says this without having any firm idea at all as to what you are making, or the costs involved, such as orchestras, flights from the USA for his musical director and star bass player, five-star hotels and limousines, not to mention a large five-figure guarantee. He compliments you on a job well done by saying it was a great tour, but in the next breath informs you he will have to get more money next time!

During the 90s, the Irish Tenors – Ronan, Finbar Wright and Anthony Kearns – were the biggest Irish act in the USA, after Enya and U2. They played massive tours in 20,000-seat arenas and sold millions of records.

They are undoubtedly a great act with a huge over-50s international following. I did a short Irish tour with them in 2018, selling out the 2,000-seater INEC in Killarney, as well as two nights at the National Concert Hall in Dublin. It was a high-priced ticket event with a full orchestra, yet I often wondered why the act did not work together more often as there was no mistaking their appeal. At the after-show signing sessions, hundreds of middle-aged women acted like teenagers, swooning all over the boys. I had no doubt they could play to 5,000 or even 10,000 fans a year in Ireland at €60-70 per ticket, but it was never going to happen.

I have been working for a number of years as Finbar Wright's promoter. Finbar, a lovely man who it is easy to like, has a very strong core audience who enjoy his wit and charm personality and adore his singing. He is a very grounded guy and a total perfectionist. He is demanding in that everything related to his performance, including his on-stage sound must be 100 per cent. His manager, the charming and attractive Angela, a tough cookie, ensures that no one gets to steal Finbar's thunder. Over the last twenty years, his regular tours have seen his dedicated audience return time and time again.

If Finbar has an ego, he keeps it well hidden, and while I have not toured with Anthony Kearns I have been made aware that he considers himself the star voice of the trio and won't let the other two lads forget it. I have toured with Ronan, who I know loves to be the centre of attention, and if he is not, then he is not at all happy.

So here we have an undoubtedly brilliant winning combination of three great voices and the ability to fill out large venues, sell millions of records and make loads of cash, yet the chemistry just doesn't gel. In simple marketing terms, three very smart guys just can't seem to see the bigger picture. It's an incredible situation that when so many other acts are breaking their backs to find a winning formula, a terrific act like the Irish Tenors allow minor trivialities and personality issues to derail the high-speed success train that everyone else is clamouring to board. As I said, truth can be stranger than fiction.

Say it's not true

You can be a great singer/performer/songwriter in Ireland but you don't always get the acclaim you deserve. It all depends on what department of the business you are selling your wares in. Showbiz musicals, variety and theatre artists tend to get overlooked simply because they don't grab the same level of attention from the press, radio, television and social media that contemporary acts do. It is for that reason I feel some are overlooked or underachieve, despite being world-class performers. It is into this category that I place the brilliant vocalist Rebecca Storm. While Colm Wilkinson achieved his deserved rewards going down the international route to New York's Broadway and London's West End, Rebecca has always stayed closer to home. Yes, she had West End starring roles in *Evita* and *Blood Brothers*, but deep down she's a home bird (although UK-born, at heart she regards herself as Irish). She is in my opinion a far better stage performer, actress and singer, with a far greater voice range, than Elaine Paige (another diva I was privileged to present in concert on two occasions).

I have had the delight of being Rebecca's promoter and Irish agent for a long number of years, and I can honestly vouch from my experience of working with her that Ireland has never produced a female artist with her range of talents. At her prime in the 80s and 90s, no other singer came near her impeccable vocal range. The quality of her vocal delivery and ability to craft any song to her own faultless style was mesmerising. I have stood side-stage for dozens of Rebecca's performances and having had the experience of working close up with Shirley Bassey (plus my lifelong admiration of Barbara Streisand) I can say without fear of contradiction that Rebecca at her supreme best was operating on the same level of excellence.

One of the reasons she may not have always had the Irish media on her side is that in her earlier days she came across as a bit of a temperamental diva, which did not endear her to television producers. RTÉ should have been using her far more regularly over the years but her perfectionism and attention to detail was often misunderstood. Yet she has singlehandedly contributed to making *Blood Brothers* the biggest and longest-running musical touring success story in Irish theatre history. No other international musical has toured Ireland so frequently, and just adding her name to the starring role resulted in years of continuing sell-outs for it at every theatre in Ireland. Her recent association with Take That's Gary Barlow and her starring role in his touring version of *Calendar Girls* was a roaring UK success but went under the radar across Irish media. I am very proud of my association and friendship with this great singer, who genuinely is the first lady of Irish musical theatre.

'I don't think anyone wants to hear me sing anymore'

When I met Sonny Knowles at the National Concert Hall in 2007, he was approaching his 74th birthday. He had just recovered from a second battle with cancer and as far as he was concerned his singing career was over. Two old pals of his, Sil Fox and Roland Soper, had dragged him along to see one of our original West End cast Rat Pack shows, and lucky for both of us that they did.

I had first seen Sonny way back when I was a teenager in the mid-60s, when he was singing with the Pacific Showband at the Crystal Ballroom (which would morph into the rock venue McGonagle's in the mid-late 70s). I remember thinking his laid-back style was polished but not cool enough for me. After six years on the road and a couple of big hit songs ('No One Will Ever Know', 'We Could'), he moved on from the showbands and in the 70s established himself as Mr Easy Listening, the cabaret king of Irish entertainment.

That night at the NCH, Sonny said to me, 'I'm reluctantly packing it in, Pat, as I don't think anyone wants to hear me sing any more. I've had a great career and I'm grateful for that. I can't complain.' Knowing the MOR (middle of the road) market well, I knew Sonny was wrong and I told him he must be joking. 'There are thousands of people out there who love you and will come out to see you, and to prove my point I will pay you €10,000, I'll get Ronan Collins to put together a big band at my expense, and we will play a night here at the NCH.' Sonny looked at me as if I were insane. 'You'll be wasting your money.' I told him that I'd be the judge of that. Within a day of the tickets going on sale I had, thanks to Joe Duffy and Ronan Collins having mentioned it on their RTÉ radio programmes, added a second show with ticket sales close to €80,000. We also crossed town and added yet another sold-out show at the Helix Theatre in DCU.

The NCH shows gave Sonny the biggest paydays of his entire career by a mile. Ronan Collins had joined up with MD Eugene McCarthy, and together they delivered a great live band that Sonny felt comfortable with. My lifelong friend, Paul O'Reilly of Dolphin Records, one of life's gentlemen, came to me with an idea of an album (*The Very Best of Sonny Knowles*) to tie in with the concert dates. Paul played me some of the tracks going back to the 70s and 80s and I was amazed not only by the brilliance of Sonny's voice, but also by the outstanding arrangements by Johnny Tate. It is no exaggeration to say these arrangements were right up there with the best from Hollywood and would have sat comfortably with the great Tommy Dorsey's or Harry James's bands. Sonny himself had that effortless, easy listening, laid-back Perry Como-style delivery. At the top of his game, coupled with the high quality of his work, he could easily have given the likes of Como and Bing Crosby a run for their money. The hits album was a huge success, selling over 20 000 copies and giving Sonny, at 75 years of age, the first platinum album award of his career.

Sonny was one of those quintessential Dubliners with a level of popularity to match that of Ronnie Drew or Paul McGrath. Modest to a point and devoid of ego, he knew he was popular but he also knew not to get above his station. By playing every major pub and cabaret venue over many years, he had become Dublin's number one working-class showbiz hero. Whether it was in a shopping centre or on a bus, he could not escape the trademark window-cleaning wave routine that he made famous in his stage show. Housewives, binmen, young kids, even at football matches, the players would salute Sonny with a window-cleaning gesture.

Sonny was quite timid when it came to the financial side of his live performances. As a singer he knew his own value, but as a businessman he did not. During the height of the cabaret boom in the 70s and 80s he was drawing big numbers but was poorly paid. He would settle for three or four hundred quid a night when he was worth at least three or four times that. He also signed record deals that were so lopsided he never saw a penny. 'I would go to the record company and ask how sales were going and was always told very slow, but when I asked for free copies to sell at shows or for friends, I was told none were available.' He found it extremely hard to say no to any kind of charity or community event, and he would also do birthday parties for friends and neighbours for a hundred quid, sometimes for nothing.

During my short time managing his affairs, I had first-hand experience of his softness and generosity being abused, such as when a top showbiz personality paid him just €250 for an opening spot on his show at a major Dublin theatre. Sonny was not the only old-timer being harshly treated by the same act. I later discovered that Sean Dunphy, the former Eurovision star, was also working for €250 a gig. It was my feeling that both men, close to the end of their careers, deserved more respect. I confronted the person in question and told them Sonny wouldn't be playing those shows again for that money, that it was an insult. At the time Sonny had two shows on sale at the NCH where he was top of the bill and earning

€15,000-plus a night. Sonny being Sonny, however, was worried about upsetting this showbiz personality, a person he regarded as an old friend, but who in my eyes was anything but. Sonny eventually received a decent four-figure sum for the theatre spot, but this was still well below his market value.

Another welcome windfall for Sonny came not long after he stopped gigging. I got a call at my office from a French film company who wanted to use Sonny's version of 'Roses of Picardy' in a forthcoming movie (2014's *Before the Winter Chill*, starring Kristin Scott Thomas). The producer told me that he had listened to all the other versions of the song and felt Sonny's version was streets ahead. It said a lot for Sonny's voice, brilliant arrangement and recording technique when you look at the list of other acts who have recorded the great standard (they include Buddy Greco, Mario Lanza, Frank Sinatra and Perry Como). For me, Sonny's best recording bar none is the beautiful James Last song 'Music from across the Way', best known, perhaps, as a hit for Andy Williams. Sonny was in his vocal prime and his velvet tones handled the lushness of the song beautifully. It's right up there with the best.

> *I shared the golden sun with her in days that are no more.*
> *I used to love to run with her along the sandy shore.*
> *She had a special prayer for me to help my world go right.*
> *Her hand was always there for me the coldest winter night.*
> *I hear music from across the way, across the bridges of my mind.*
> *I lift the misty shades of yesterday to catch the dreams I left behind.*

> (© James Last/Carl Sigman. Reproduced by kind permission of Polydor/Universal Music)

I was very proud to represent Sonny during the final years of his career. I only wish we had got together earlier. He was much more than just a lounge singer – he had an unmistakable class that was never fully nurtured and progressed, and he deserved to play bigger venues, like the London Palladium or the Las Vegas casinos. Sonny did his final show in the John Field Room at the NCH a few years before his death in 2018. He shared the bill with Sil Fox. It was sad to see his unique stage presence and memory fading, as he struggled to complete his set, but his lifelong pal Sil was with him all the way and ensured that Sonny's farewell show was a triumph. Let's hear it for Ireland's best-ever crooner!

'All the Lies That You Told Me'

I first met Frances Black way back in the mid-80s when she played a weekly gig at my Backstage pub in Temple Bar. In those days, when few women drank pints, she'd have a pint of Harp and would sit for hours after her show at the back of the bar, reading and enjoying the craic. It's awfully hard not to like Frances – she is very much a case of what you see is what you get. Her endearing charm is in her no-frills, bubbly personality. She cares about other people and even in those early days I could see that beyond her music interests she had deeper, more heart-felt concerns. Hits and fame would be great but there were clearly more important issues at the back of her mind. The problem with her career in music is that she started at the very top and it was difficult for her to repeat her massive debut success. Yes, she had been part of the Irish music scene before that, touring with Arcady and Kieran Goss, but the *Talk to Me* album success was in a different league altogether – it sold over 100,000 copies, which was astonishing for an Irish album. With the single 'All the Lies That You Told Me' at number 1 her popularity was reaching, albeit for a short time, beyond that of her more famous sister, Mary. Her down-to-earth, girl-next-door image worked in her favour on the concert stage and she sold out every concert hall and major venue in Ireland and the UK. I got involved as manager with Frances for a couple of years, and despite Sony Music spending big bucks on an image reinvention and a pop-oriented album, *Don't Get Me Wrong*, Frances never again hit the heights of the huge success of *Talk to Me*.

She never really felt comfortable with showbiz celebrity, and trying to turn her into a pop star with 'Love Me Please', a reworking of the Yvonne Elliman hit, worked well but it just wasn't Frances. She won't rate her multi-platinum album successes as her greatest achievement. Her Rise Foundation charity for the families of addiction sufferers and her successes for social justice and equality for the vulnerable will be her greatest legacy. Now an independent senator, she continues to tour once or twice a year to big crowds. Her love of music remains, but it's a secondary issue behind her committed mission with the Rise Foundation.

One of her great strengths is her long-time partner, Brian Allen, who I still regard as a great friend – a more caring and decent guy I have yet to meet. It is also wonderful to see Frances's son and daughter, Eoghan and Aoife Scott, making big waves on the traditional and folk scene. What a wonderful family.

Sadly, a one-hit wonder

The Vard Sisters, Cathy, Wendy and Lisa, sold over 80,000 copies of their first album, *Heavenly*, in a matter of weeks in 1997. It also produced a major hit single: their version of the 'Flower Duet' raced to the top of the singles chart. The Vards came out of nowhere and overnight they were a sensation unlike anything the Irish market had previously produced. The girls had class written all over them and there was no way anything was going to stop them breaking internationally

It was John Sheehan, the former boss at Sony Music, who discovered and launched the sisters into becoming one of the biggest selling local acts of the decade. Eighty thousand albums is no mean feat with a brand-new act, and it was the kind of lift-off that should have ensured a lifelong career at the top of Irish music for the three stunningly beautiful sisters. So what went wrong? Despite having discovered a unique niche market in the rapidly growing gospel, Christian, spiritual and new age fields, the sisters never got to release a second album with Sony. John Sheehan told me once, 'Pat, it was a disaster. The girls could not agree a formula to move forward, there were all kinds of disagreements and in the end, I did a solo album with Cathy which came nowhere near the success of *Heavenly*. It was a great disappointment for me and Sony.' Sparks were flying in the Vard household; Cathy walked away and three promising careers dissolved overnight.

In mid-1999, I got a call from Dave Pennyfeather, the popular and highly respected head of Universal Music, telling me that he had signed two of the sisters, Wendy and Lisa, to make a crossover classical-influenced pop album, to be produced by Denis Woods, and asking if I was interested in taking on the girls for agency. I had been a good pal of Wendy's for many years, and she lived near me in Ranelagh. Both sisters have quality soprano voices and marketing-wise they were a dream ticket. My only reservation was that if they had Cathy, the elder sister on board as well, they would really be a very unique act. Having said that, Wendy and Lisa produced a terrific crossover album, with some brilliant semi-classical tracks.

The albums' big song was to be a duet with Westlife on 'If I Had Words'. The tune was taken from the main theme of Saint-Saëns' Third Symphony. It sounded and looked like a real winner. With Westlife riding the crest of a wave and the two girls singing brilliantly, the track had all the makings of a chart-topping number 1. However, someone at Universal had jumped the gun and the release was delayed for weeks. When it did finally come out, the Westlife name did not appear on the label – this had been the reason for the long delay. It appears that when the boys agreed to duet with the Vards, no one had asked their record company, RCA, for clearance, and when they did, it was rejected out of hand. The album produced by Denis Woods featured some brilliant tracks, every bit as high class as the original *Heavenly* album. While Universal spent big money recording the album, the marketing fell flat and despite its quality it sank without trace.

I did manage a year or so later, to get the three sisters to reunite and they were still one of the most stunning acts visually and musically. They toured and made a TV special in Germany with the Celtic Tenors. They also played the Queen Elizabeth Hall in London on a special Celtic Tenors EMI showcase, and appeared at a gala dinner for former US president Bill Clinton. I was also privileged to present them at a sold-out concert at the National Concert Hall. It was a high-maintenance act to promote and manage. The girls were classy dressers and would wear only the best designer evening gowns, shoes and diamonds. In fact, the very best of everything, including Wendy's bottle of Cristal champagne in her dressing room. 'Where's my must-have Cristal, Pat, darling?' she asked as I put a bottle of Dunne's best sparkling wine on her dressing room table.

I loved working with the girls but they needed a bigger stage than Ireland and without a major record company behind them, it was never going to happen second time round.

The producer blew £350,000 down the drain

Alongside Deutsche Grammophon, Decca Records was greatest classical music label of the millennium years. Decca was home to the Three Tenors, Luciano Pavarotti, Dame Kiri Te Kanawa, Renée Fleming, Cecilia Bartoli, Angela Gheorghiu and Dame Joan Sutherland. To be offered a recording deal by such a great company was in itself a brilliant achievement for any artist. And so it was for Ireland's 1996 Eurovision winner, Eimear Quinn, who won the competition with Brendan Graham's great, haunting song, 'The Voice'. Eimear is a very beautiful, elegant and sophisticated young lady with a unique classically trained soprano voice. In every sense of the phrase, she was a marketing dream. Decca knew they were on to a winner and were prepared to throw everything, including the kitchen sink, into making her a star. The global president of Decca, Costa Pilavachi, came to Dublin in 2000 by private jet to oversee the signing of the deal, and promised Eimear that no expense would be spared in marketing her debut album for the label – it was to be Decca Classics' biggest ever launch of a new artist. There was, however, no recording budget – the label was so confident of its success that nobody seemed to be keeping tabs on the outrageous spend that in the end came close to £350,000. The album, *Through the Lens of a Tear*, would be released across all international markets. So why did Eimear not break through? What went wrong? The search for a producer was spread far and wide, and after much head scratching Decca went with the talented Clannad member Pól Brennan.

My hope for Eimear's career was that Decca would turn her into a Sarah Brightman of sorts by producing an outstanding classical-influenced crossover album. It made great sense – just two years previously, Brightman had released *Eden*, the biggest-selling crossover classical album ever, and had little or no competition in the marketplace. I believed Eimear had everything it took, and more, to do likewise. We just needed a couple of radio-friendly classical-themed commercial tracks suitable for mainstream radio. In my opinion, however, somewhere along the way the producer lost the plot entirely and what we ended up with was a new age wasteland of ragbag elevator music. There was not one single song that had radio play potential. I made an effort, later on, to introduce a great American crossover song but it was rejected by the producer. Despite our misgivings, the album was launched with great fanfare at Dublin's Guinness Storehouse, but within a week we were in deep trouble and Decca pulled all the promised marketing plans. From that moment on, *Through the Lens of a Tear* and its extravagant budget sank without trace. The entire project had, from the highest of expectations, fallen spec-tacularly flat on its arse. It was a truly major disappointment for Eimear and me. But I am happy to say that, while she is no longer working with our office, Eimear's career has flourished and she is now one of the great voices in contemporary Irish music. She has performed in recent years at all of Europe's greatest concert venues to kings, queens, presidents and her legion of fans. No one deserves her success more.

'I don't want to do this anymore'

From 1995 to 1999 I managed the career of Sinéad Lohan, the brilliant Cork-born singer–songwriter. Sinéad was a lovely young lady, and very special, not just as an artist but also as a person. She played the game by her rules and if that did not suit you, then so be it. Despite being on the verge of cracking the US market in 1999, having sold over 300,000 copies of her second album, *No Mermaid*, she was not prepared to compromise her artistic integrity for the sake of commercial success. In the middle of a big US tour, she woke one morning and over breakfast told Mark Spector, my American manager/partner, that she wanted to go home and would not be touring ever again.

She was not enjoying the touring experience anymore and felt that the commercial element of the business was not for her. I had no doubt whatsoever, and neither had Mark, that if she'd continued to pursue an American career she would today be a world superstar.

Mark Spector was a great guy, a serious but smiling gentleman. He was the best thing that could have happened to Sinéad. He had a long history of success, having managed Joan Baez and Graham Nash, and had opened so many doors at the top of the business for Sinéad. He was in a position of power and could have cut me from the US deal, but he knew I had worked hard for Sinéad, he was very fair and reasonable in every way and my admiration for him lives on, twenty years after our great adventure.

No Mermaid was critically acclaimed, Sinéad's tours were starting to click, she was beginning to sell out 3,000-seater rooms, and was picking up serious airplay. After a bidding war between the major labels, she signed to Interscope, which paid millions of dollars up front for a long-term deal. Her songs were showing up everywhere, from the Kevin Costner movie *Message in a Bottle* to the hit TV shows *Buffy the Vampire Slayer* and *Dawson's Creek*. Another of her own songs, 'Everything Around Me Is Changing', was the lead track on the Golden Globe-nominated hit *Anywhere But Here* starring Susan Sarandon. Her songs had been covered by Joan Baez, Shaye and Nickel Creek, and she had become a Hollywood insider, her music being considered for dozens of movie soundtracks.

When she walked away from it all it was a tough blow to take after some years of building a career. While I respected Sinéad's right to call it a day I felt very low, very sad and terribly disappointed. Not so much for myself but for Mark Spector, who had paved the way for the storming of America. But that was Sinéad – it was her way or the highway.

The day Sinéad called it quits was the end of my dream of managing a genuine international superstar. I have met Sinéad a few times over the years; she and her husband, John, have a beautiful family at home in Cork. I did try once or twice to entice her to return for gigs but, Sinéad being Sinéad I knew it would only ever happen on her terms, and sadly it was not to be.

EMI Classics turn down 'You Raise Me Up'

The second time I came close to having a hit act under my wing was in 1999, when I signed the Celtic Tenors to EMI Classics. Four of us – Niall Morris, Mathew Gilsenan, James Nelson and myself – walked into the boardroom of EMI Classics in London and walked out with an international deal. The boys did an on-the-spot audition for the label head, Sir Richard Lyttelton, who within minutes of the audition ending pulled a contract out of a drawer and signed them right there and then. The Tenors were a strong act with great cross-over potential. They were also well ahead of the game with their mix of classical pop, long before the emergence of Il Divo.

The Celtic Tenors achieved double platinum status with their debut album, but I still feel that EMI Ireland sold the lads short when it pulled the TV promotional campaign. I asked the then EMI boss Willie Kavanagh why EMI had done this, when the album was about to break really big. I really lost my cool – the decision made no commercial sense whatsoever. 'The album was halfway up the charts, so why pull the support?' I fumed. Willie, a tough operator, refused to listen to my ranting. I made my feelings known at a number of EMI meetings in the UK, but to no avail.

• •

'The pillows in my bedroom are not soft and puffy as requested. And the curtains do not close completely. I can only sleep in total darkness.' – Elaine Paige to me following an inspection of her suite at the Shelbourne Hotel.

• •

Happy days with the Queen of the Olympia – the wonderful Maureen Grant.

98FM's bus design for the City of 1000 Bands Dublin Rock Tour.

Bad Girls – the Australian Gold Coast strippers come to town.

Rebecca Storm with her hoard of Barbra Streisand personal memorabilia.

At the Legends of Sports dinner with Paul McGrath, George Best, and his wife, Alex.

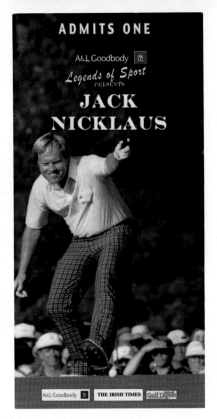

Jack Nicklaus – $250,000 for a dinner date, and don't forget the jet fuel money.

Al Martino. He used his own mafia connections to get the Godfather role.

Another sell-out tour for Billy.

Mickey Rooney poster for his National Concert Hall show in 2007. Very sad end for a true Hollywood legend.

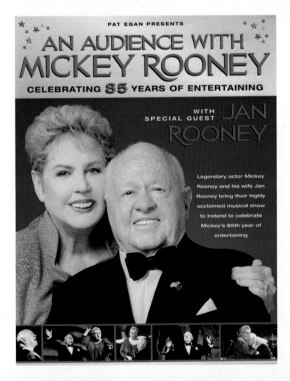

The cast of Spotlight Productions' *Annie* during its successful run in Dublin and Cork in 2009.

Meeting the real-life *Layla* – with Patti Boyd at Billy Connolly's 60th.

Phil Coulter and myself with Billy at his 60th birthday party at his home in the Scottish Highlands.

My tribute show in honour of Mario Lanza sold out 12 nights at the National Concert Hall. 'The best in the world' said his daughter Eliza.

Sinéad Lohan turned her back and walked away from success right on the verge of enormous stardom.

Danny Ellis's *800 Voices*. The best Irish album ever.

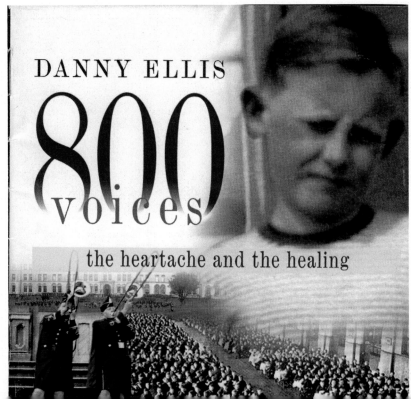

Sir George Martin at the National Concert Hall, 1999. Three sell-out shows with Brian Kennedy, Seán Keane, Leslie Dowdall, Eimear Quinn, Liam Ó Maonlai and Jimmy MacCarthy.

The brilliant Donna Taggart – 220 million hits online worldwide but Irish radio refuses to play her.

in person EXCLUSIVE

Acts Sing For The President

Pictured are exclusive **In Person International** acts The Celtic Tenors (Niall Morris, James Nelson and Matthew Gilsenan) and The Vard Sisters (Cathy, Wendy and Lisa,) with Bill Clinton. Both acts entertained the former President at a special dinner held in his honour at Dublin Castle in May this year.

The Vards and The Celtic Tenors with President Bill Clinton.

The world's most expensive concert ticket.

My page in Brendan O'Carroll's monthly comic strip.

I only got to know Willie in later years and he's a straight-up guy. It was all about fighting for the act with me – it was never personal – and yes, Willie, I was a bit of an asshole thinking I was managing The Beatles.

While the first album did well in Ireland it made a much bigger splash in Germany, entering the Klassik Chart at number 6 just behind opera legends Cecilia Bartoli and Maria Callas. After four weeks it reached the top spot. It was number 2 in the UK charts when it was announced that the boys had won Germany's Classical Echo Award (the German Grammys) as best newcomers. We all flew to Germany to appear on national television alongside opera diva Angela Gheorghiu in a special awards ceremony. It was looking like the lads were becoming very hot property when they were asked to shoot an American public television special in Hamburg. However, it was a false dawn. EMI Germany were having financial problems and it dropped a bombshell, firing the head of the label and dropping the Celtic Tenors overnight, despite very promising sales figure.

I had always wanted to manage a group with a hit on the American Billboard chart and the Celtic Tenors obliged when their first US release entered the classical chart at number 12. The group's second UK album, *So Strong*, failed to live up to the initial success, but EMI Classics stuck with us for album three. They also gave us the artistic freedom to produce and record the album as we saw fit. It was an opportunity we were waiting for and the lads delivered a brilliant third album.

Myself and David Munro, the group's musical director, delivered the new tapes at a meeting of all the department heads at EMI offices in Baker Street in London. I was so proud of the lads and I went to the meeting with really great expectations. In his Edinburgh studio, Blue Nile producer/engineer Calum Malcolm and David Munro had turned out twelve ground-breaking classical cross-over tracks that were commercial and, in some songs, revolutionary.

The album included one sure-fire hit, a great version of the Brendan Graham classic 'You Raise Me Up' with a guest performance from Samantha Mumba, who had just scored a number 5 hit in the American Billboard chart. Not only was the Tenors version of the Brendan Graham song outstanding, but Samantha was currently the darling of the tabloid and television media. It was a marriage made in heaven in terms of profile and publicity. In my mind it was a winner for all involved. I am not sure if stories of my outbursts at the previous EMI encounter with Willie Kavanagh and label boss Theo Lapp had preceded me to the London meeting, but

David and I were met with a stonily negative response. This was early 2004 and the Josh Groban version of 'You Raise Me Up' was only beginning to make inroads into Europe; it was not yet the spiritual anthem it was later to become. In my opinion the Tenors had delivered the best cross-over classic album of all time, featuring at least two sure-fire hits. But to my utter despair the EMI suits were stuffed so full of shite they could not hear the cash registers ringing. They let their personal opinion of me as a troublesome manager get in the way of business. 'This song is a number one', I shouted, 'and you won't fuckin' release it as the first single, you bunch of morons.' I was losing it again, but I felt it was my job to fight for my band.

I was so upset I told Sir Richard, the chairman of EMI Classics, where to stick his £40,000 advance for the recording and that I would personally repay it. I said I would take the album to Decca and prove them all wrong. I picked up the tapes off the boardroom table and stormed out.

'Do you think that was wise?' asked David Munro as we made our way out into Baker Street.

'I have no idea at all, David,' I answered. 'No fuckin' idea at all.'

Within six or so months Westlife were number one with 'You Raise Me Up' and within a few years the entire EMI company was on its knees, broken beyond repair. The Classical division was sold off to Warner for a song. When I think back now, I do so with great regret that the ears at EMI that day in 2003 were so deaf to a great group and an even greater song.

The Celtic Tenors never made tens of millions, but they built a very substantial and rewarding career across the world, and they are still going strong twenty years on. Great guys, Matthew James and Daryl; I was proud of our achievements together and I still am.

It's truly a masterpiece

The best, yet the most under-achieving Irish album of my entire lifetime is *800 Voices* by Danny Ellis. I make this statement without any hesitation whatsoever. In all my years selling records across the counter and my lifelong involvement in the local scene, no other Irish songwriter has produced a work of such brilliance.

Danny, one of the most talented musicians from the showband era, spent his early years in the Artane Industrial School in the 1950s. Danny writes, 'Late one night in December 2001, while singing ad lib at the piano, I got the surprise of my life. Tired and alone, I let my guard down. Decades of protective layers fell from my soul and for the first time I allowed the abandoned child within me to express himself in a song.' At first, his memories were overwhelming. 'My mother's betrayal, the loneliness, and the brutality of Artane. But I knew I'd abandoned him like everyone else and it was time to bring him home again. Later, song by song, the broader picture of my childhood emerged. The tomfoolery on the playground, the friendships and the mischief, the blessing of music and the astonishing courage of the lads. These songs changed me for ever and for better. Now the circle is complete, the adult reaching across the past to the lost child within saying 'Hang in there, kid, this is going to work out fine'.'

The songs are brilliantly constructed, telling the tale of a kid without hope saved by music through joining the Artane Boys' Band. How Danny manages to fit a pictorial vision, an entire tale, into just a three-minute song is as extraordinary as it is brilliant. Here is just a flavour, from fellow international professionals and reviewers, that says everything I want to say, but much better than I ever could:

> *If musicality was the only bar by which an album was judged, then Danny Ellis' debut would hold its own alongside other worldly voices such as Brian Kennedy. But 800 Voices is much more. It is a searing testament to the resilience of the human spirit and the depths to which the spirit can sink. Ellis is an Artane Industrial School survivor. His tales of childhood, innocence shredded asunder, of the divine inspiration of a fellow inmate's angelic singing, and the refusal to yield to a consuming bitterness, elevates this chronicle to a place where the listener can savour the musicianship while never losing sight of the murderous mayhem that forged it. A musical healing and lyrically breath-taking debut.* **Siobhan Long, *Irish Times***

> *This album is amazing. It exceeds any sort of expectations in that it's varied, always musically interesting, melodic but above all honest and amazingly revealing, unsentimental, and not bitter, I played it at home on Saturday night, the way you do when you have a pile of cd's to work through. When it got to the end I played it again start to finish and then again.* **Jim Lockhart, founding member of Horslips and RTE radio/television producer**

It's truly a masterpiece, and I mean that in the ancient sense of the word, when the masterpiece was the work an artisan or artist did, to demonstrate the mastery of his craft. Every song is a gem, every emotion clear, three-dimensional and so truly expressed by the music and lyrics, so beautifully woven together. Not a false note, musically or emotionally, all the way through. The lyrics alone are worth the price, completely personal and at the same time universal. Such a gifted storyteller. And his voice tugs at my heart in every song, some are almost unbearably poignant. **Erika Anderson, Proteus International**

This is one of the best CDs to cross my path in a long time. Beautiful, unique voice, loaded with emotion. The writing is excellent, very powerful song writing weaves traditional Irish melody, rhythm and instrumentation into contemporary song writing so beautifully. A very original unique work, the production is exquisite. **Aubrey Atwater, songwriter**

It's rare that my eyes well up several times while listening to an album. Each song is like a poem that tears through the mundane. Their imagery is extraordinary, the vocals are intricate, natural and free. A true testament that pearls are created from the fiction of sand. **Kim O'Leary, songwriter**

A few years back I tried to float *800 Voices* as a potential stage musical. I attempted to go down the successful 1970s route pioneered by Noel Pearson's productions of *Jesus Christ Superstar* and *Joseph and the Amazing Technicolour Dreamcoat* by using star singers like Jack L, Maria Doyle Kennedy and Luke Thomas, but without success. In recent times the great Colm Wilkinson, who loves *800 Voices*, has expressed an interest in doing the show. As I write, I am, along with producers Stuart and Ciara O'Connor currently looking at putting a stage version into development.

'That fella wouldn't hurt a fly'

For fifteen years, Stuart and Ciara O'Connor and I have been staging the Olympia panto, which has been one of the great successes of my career in entertainment. Way back in 2006, Brian Hand introduced me to Ciara and Stuart and it was, I have no hesitation in saying, a lucky day for me. Stuart, who looks like he just walked out of Don Johnson's shadow in *Miami Vice*, is a slim-built guy with boundless energy and huge enthusiasm for everything he does. Hard work runs off him like water off a duck's back. He sets no limits on his commitment to any project, and behind all that he is one of the nicest, most approachable guys in the business. Stuart's wife, Ciara, is a softly spoken, pretty as a picture brunette who, while shy and reserved, has a serious, less trusting side. This makes her perfectly suited to taking care of the business end of their growing showbiz empire, Spot-light Productions, which includes running two stage and dance schools, along with the Three Rock Irish summer cabaret, a class act that draws thousands of tourists from April to October every year. They also have an international touring Irish dance show. The Irish cabaret show that Stuart co-promotes with Three Rock owner Johnny Keenan also opened in Edin-burgh in recent years. They have also been responsible for producing the fantastic in-store entertainment in Brown Thomas at Christmas, and to top all that Stuart is the creative force behind RTÉ's *Late Late Toy Show*, Ireland's most high-profile television spectacular.

Our first promotion together was a very successful stage version of Alan Parker's great kids' movie *Bugsy Malone*. This great show was enough for me to realise that hanging on to Stuart and Ciara's coattails was going to bring me some very rewarding years as a panto promoter. My job on the panto is to just sit back and, as Stuart might say, 'stay out of the effin' way, Pat.' Seriously, though, our job at the office, with the help of the wonderful PR queen, Aine Carmody, is to ensure that every seat in the theatre – all 40,000 of them – across every performance is sold out. Caroline O'Neill is the superwoman who takes care of all the budgets and finances. She ticks all the boxes and, most important, makes sure that everyone gets paid. Pat Egan Sound Ltd could not run without her attention to detail and lead-ership. Our two people on the ground during every performance for a long number of years were my lifelong friends Brian Hand and Michelle King. On the production side, Stuart has a very loyal support crew who bring their talent and expertise to the show year after year. These include panto first lady Natasha O'Hanlon who, along with Ciara, looks after everything from kids to costumes; our brilliant MD David Hayes and music provider Chris O'Sullivan; the ageless Terry Heron and Doreen Meehan on sound. Damo O'Connor is the lighting whizz kid, actor Simon Delaney is the panto director, and the production boss is Killian Collins. In addition to a fantastic backstage crew and creative team, some of the country's greatest talents work tirelessly on stage to make sure every member of the audience, young and old, laughs non-stop from beginning to end: *Dancing with the Stars* heartthrob Ryan Andrews, the outstanding Maclean Burke, social media star James Patrice, crazy blogger Erin McGregor. Along with the terrific voice of Rob Vickers, the beautiful dance princess Michaela O'Neill, and up to a hundred singing and dancing kids, they make the Olympia panto a magical place to be every year. One young man, Alan Kavanagh, later to be known as Al Porter, originally appeared in the stage version of *Bugsy Malone* as an eleven-year-old tough-talking gangster, and has, I am happy to say, featured in almost every panto in the fifteen years since. His buddy and on-stage sidekick, *Fair City*'s Ryan Andrews, has also been part of the panto cast since day one. Al and Ryan also write a brilliantly funny script every year. I am grateful to each one of them – a really solid team of people who we could not do without.

Dustin the Turkey, one of the highlight features of our Panto's for a number of years never failed to raise a laugh and the odd eyebrow. In 2015, he was so concerned that he might end up on the table at someone's Christmas Dinner, that a request was made to President Michael D Higgins to grant him a pardon. Alas the President's office informed us that he can only grant such a pardon on the advice of the government, and as no such advice was received, no pardon was possible. We were assured by President Higgins that he would never include Dustin as part of his Christmas dinner. He wished him, and all of the Olympia Cast the best of luck with the Panto.

I want to tell you about the fall and rise of Al Porter and how becoming the biggest star in panto since Twink and Maureen Potter has turned out to be the making of the guy. Al fell from grace in 2017 when he was wrongly accused of inappropriate behaviour. This led to a full two years of living in limbo with his career in freefall and his bank account empty. Even though he was not charged with any offence, this long two years in the wilderness had all but broken him. The nineteen-year-old Al was living the dream, having cracked the live stand-up comic scene on a huge scale. Overnight he became hot property, in fact too hot for a guy of his age to realise that fame brings with it a darker side, one inhabited by people whose only mission in life is to bring winners down a peg or two and knock them off their perch. From having his TV quiz show to selling out eight nights at Vicar Street, Al had fallen right into the gutter. But it was in his darkest hours that Al's panto family gave him strength. Now that he has been fully vindicated, that strength has enabled him to plan his return back to where he belongs - at the top of the top of Irish showbiz. Surrounded by some of the best young people in the business, led by actor Ryan Andrews, the close-knit panto cast and crew never stopped supporting and believing in Al. With so many good people cheering for him, Al found out who his real friends were and, thanks mainly to Stuart and Ciara, that support will help him find his way back not only to treading the boards but also to the success he deserves in the years ahead. I have said it before and I will tell anyone who listens that Al Porter is the most talented, off-the-cuff compère and stand-up comic this country has produced, and that includes Tommy Tiernan. Of the many talented young men I have met over the years, Al is unique, a genuine, caring, appreciative and modest young man. As my mother would say, 'That fella wouldn't hurt a fly.' Far from being some kind of 'Look at me, I'm top of the heap' kind of guy, Al's feet are now firmly planted on solid ground and his future as a star is guaranteed if and when he decides to return to the stage.

I presented three other big theatrical shows with mixed success. Our version of *Annie*, produced by Stuart and Ciara and starring my pal Rebecca Storm and a wonderful supporting cast, did great business in Dublin and Cork in 2009. Again, Stuart and Ciara excelled with a super production that highlighted all their skills and experience when working with a young cast.

City of 1000 rock bands

A project close to my heart, which sunk without trace much to my great disappointment was the 'City of a Thousand Rock Bands' tour of Dublin. Denis O'Brien, thanks to Lucy Gaffney, had given me upfront cash to purchase and launch Dublin's first ever rock tour. 98FM had come up with a brilliant design and Ireland's most famous chauffeur, Mick Devine, had paid a deposit for me in the UK on a former rock tour bus, which had been used by Status Quo and Black Sabbath. We had been allocated our own bus stop in O'Connell Street just across from the Gresham Hotel.

The idea of the tour trail was to start at O'Connell Street and travel to the grave of Phil Lynott in Sutton. The return journey would first pass the house in Artane where Enya did much of her recordings with producer Nicky Ryan, then on to Mount Temple comprehensive school - the birthplace

of U2. The tour would then take you across the Liffey, passing the Prin-
ciple Management offices of U2's Paul McGuinnes. Next stop would be
The Waterfront Rock Café, home of the Bafta- and Academy-Award-nom-
inated *The Commitments* movie. Here you could also have your photo
taken with one of U2's East German tour relics, a real live Trabant used
on the Achtung Baby tour. A walk around the corner to Windmill Lane and
you could scrawl your message to the band on the famous Windmill Lane
Studio wall. For many this was to be the tour highlight, followed by a quick
drop into Bono's favourite pub, The Docker's, for a glass of Guinness.

The tour bus would then travel to downtown Temple Bar, which
included a free burger at the Bad Ass Café, where Sinead O'Connor once
worked as a waitress. There were also stops at the Dubliners' favourite
pub, O'Donohue's, as well as a stop at the famous Baggot Inn, where so
many of Dublin's bands quick-started their careers. The tour would finish
off at Captain America's, where Chris De Burgh once played piano. Each
tour ticket would include a 10 x 8 photo of your favourite Irish rock star
plus a free pass to the Waterfront rock cafe where a tribute band did a U2
unplugged gig every night.

Having pulled it all together and spent over £15,000, I got cold feet
and decided to put it into cold storage – a decision that I later regretted
big time.

Michael Devine, one of the Irish concerts business most popular guys,
who has provided transport for every major touring act to come into the
country, later launched his own version of the rock tour. His coach concept
was different to my idea and was more of a virtual, video-driven experience. It, I am sad to say, had a short life. I felt my idea was more realistic
but regretfully we will never know.

Tony (Como) Jones

We lost the brilliant singer Tony Jones in the first week of October 2021.
Only 65, Tony was one of the finest crooners and big band singers to grace
the National Concert Hall stage. He played the leading role of Perry Como
in two sell-out nights at the Hall. His low, soft, lush velvet tones were
perfect in bringing the great hits of Como back to life. Tony also stared
as Matt Monro in another of our Celebrations concerts. A total gentleman
and lovely guy, he will be very sadly missed by his lovely wife, Orla, and
all his pals in the music business.

24: TIME FOR AN IRISH MUSIC BOARD

During the early summer of 2021, I read an interview in *Hot Press* with Bren Berry of Aiken Promotions. Formerly a member of the highly rated Irish band Revelino, Bren is very much on top of his game and is held in very high esteem by everyone in the Irish music business. Few people have a clearer picture of what's going on in Irish entertainment. The line that caught my eye was Bren reflecting on a dream he had about Irish radio stations and how they suddenly realised the damage they were doing to Irish artists by refusing to play their music. The dream also included Irish radio stations coming together to collectively agree on playing Irish music on one day of the week and 50 per cent Irish music on the other six. Bren went on to write that such a scenario was simply too weird. Sure, why on earth would Irish music stations play music by our own people and champion our own music and culture? That'd be far too weird. Wouldn't it?

In 1982, The Dubliners' manager, Jim Hand, a guy who called a spade a spade, was practically carried out of RTÉ 2FM by the station's security and dumped on the pavement. He could be heard shouting at the top of his voice: '2FM is Radio Fuckin' Burbank!' Jim was protesting at 2FM's refusal to playlist Paddy Reilly's new single, the definitive version of the Pete St John classic, 'The Fields of Athenry'. Not only did 2FM refuse to play the song, but when it entered Ireland's Top 10, presenter Larry Gogan mentioned that it was at number 8 but didn't play the track. One year and five months after its release, 'The Fields of Athenry' was still in the Irish charts. What has become probably the most famous song in Irish popular music history, the alternative nation anthem, was deemed not good enough for RTÉ Radio. As Phil Coulter told me, 'If I wrote a classic song today like 'The Town I Loved so Well', it would simply disappear without a trace. That is how bad things have become for my own music on Irish radio.'

Almost forty years on from Jim Hand's now-infamous bashing of 2FM, not only has nothing changed, it's got a whole lot worse for new Irish songs and musicians. Due to the withdrawal of funds from IMRO (the Irish Music Rights Organisation), the demise in early 2021 of Play Irish, the online all-Irish station brilliantly managed by Sinead Troy, is yet another nail in the coffin for Irish artists and home-produced music. This would not be the case if the collective will of the industry came together and demanded from government access to our own airways for our own people.

So let's jump from Jim Hand's outrage in 1982 to 2018 and a singer and song I had a direct connection with – Donna Taggart's 'Jealous of the Angels'. The song, a heart-breaking tale of a mother's love, struck a chord with so many millions who had lost loved ones. Donna's stunning vocal raised the song to a higher spiritual level, perhaps because she had experienced a deep personal loss. She really was singing directly to the angels. Donna, from Omagh, called me for advice a few weeks after putting her recording of the Jenn Bostic song online. Donna had lost a child, and without mentioning the circumstances posted the song as a personal remembrance. Almost instantly, the Facebook hits passed one million, within a week there were ten million, and on and on it went, reaching an astonishing 200 million. Within weeks of its release, the song and Donna's album *Celtic Woman* was number 1 on the American Billboard World Music and Easy Listening charts. Yet amazingly, no one at RTÉ Radio or the commercial stations wanted to know. I got on my knees to my old pal Ronan Collins to give 'Jealous of the Angels' an airing on his popular RTÉ Radio 1 show. Ronan and I go back a long way together and he is a dear friend, but that cuts no ice when it comes to what he plays on his radio show, so that one play was a real concession. Music producer Dermot McEvoy at RTÉ stuck his neck out and put Donna on *The Late Late Show*, but RTÉ Radio and the commercial stations just blanked her. *What the fuck is going on here?* I thought. Here was a singer with class written all over her and with the most captivating voice imaginable. One of the best, if not the best ever female Irish singers, certainly since Mary Black, and all I was getting was two fingers from radio. Not even the few stations that give Irish music a fair crack – even if it is that dreaded depressing country & Irish tripe – gave Donna any kind of priority play listing.

To support the single and album, I promoted the first Irish tour for Donna, and once again MD Eugene McCarthy delivered a great band for her concerts. We sold out a number of shows, including the 900-seater Ulster Hall, where I was proud to present Donna with a platinum disc for worldwide sales of her *Celtic Woman* album. Following Donna's world-wide success with the song, at least six other acts did cover versions of it, including Katherine Jenkins and Nathan Carter. None had the magical sincerity of Donna's performance, which remains by a mile the definitive version of this great but very sad song.

The reason Irish music can't get its foot in the door at our commercial stations is threefold.

1. The strength of the commercial stations' financial clout coupled with the political lobbying power of their highly paid PR agencies.
2. The total lack of political will by continuing ministers of communications to tackle the commercial sector and introduce percentage airplay, which was originally promised when commercial radio licences were being granted.
3. The failure of a properly co-ordinated approach by the Irish music community to establish an Irish music board along the same lines as the film and theatre business.

The reality is that Irish commercial radio has never helped develop young Irish songwriters and performers. It's incredible to think that 200 million people across the globe could be listening to your song, but in your own broadcasters in your own country are oblivious to your success. Donna Taggart is just one of dozens of talented young Irish songwriters who are victims of commercial radio's 'war on talent'.

RTE Radio One and RTE television are the only major supporters of local talent. The problem is that on Radio One the music content is so strictly limited and fragmented you simply can't build any rotation airplay, which means your song is never going to be heard more than three times in one week. You need twenty plays a week to turn a new song into a hit.

On television, thanks to guys like Alan Byrne, Dermot McEvoy and Philip King, we regularly get to see some of the best new acts in the country. The problem with 2FM and the commercial radio stations is that they wait for you to make your own waves and then jump on board when the shiny press kits arrive from British record companies. Irish commercial stations' playlists never feature emerging local talent and are a continuing slap in the face to all Irish artists. Their hidden policy is along the lines of 'Feck off and prove yourself in some other territory and then we will look at playing your music.' Will someone please tell me why we have always had to wait for British and American approval before our own radio stations can pick winners?

RTE television spends big money far too often on Country & Irish *Late Late* specials, which can often be an embarrassment with acts that are amateurish and very poorly rehearsed. The reality is that Irish country music is of such low quality that in its fifty-year history it has never produced one, not one, original song of merit. It was the brilliant contemporary songwriter Mick Hanley, who penned 'Past the Point of Rescue', which still remains Ireland's only true international country classic.

I am sure all the Country & Irish folk are lovely, kind, warm people, and certainly the ones I know personally, are indeed that and more. But does anyone out there really believe that Daniel O'Donnell, Margo, Declan Nerney or Jimmy Buckley can actually sing? Because I don't.

If that's what folk want, by all means let them have it. But not on a regular basis on the country's flagship TV show. When I watch Ireland's most talented television presenter, Ryan Tubridy, a guy who loves Sinatra and the kings of swing, attempting to talk up a bunch of musicians and singers, some of whom find it difficult to sing and play in tune, I am not sure he's very convincing. I almost feel sorry for him.

Am I out of line here? I agree there is and should be room across the airways for everyone's musical tastes, but to ignore a vast pool of original talent and give priority prime-time coverage again and again to such a bland and uninspiring bunch of cover artists is a grave injustice to our talented young songwriters and singers, of whom there are thousands.

It's important to state at this point, before I continue my rant at the injustices of the Irish airplay system, that the future of terrestrial radio is looking bleak. While the industry will say this is not the case, all the indicators say differently. One person who seemed to believe the truth in this was multi-millionaire businessman Denis O'Brien. After selling his radio

• •

'I don't like the suite – it's old-fashioned and the carpets and wallpaper are depressing.' – One-time American heart-throb Jack Jones to me after checking out his room at the Burlington Hotel.

• •

empire in 2020, he said, 'I just don't know whether a twelve-year-old today, who is going to be fifteen in three years' time, is going to be listening to Spin 103fm.' The outlook in America appears much worse. No one under twenty in America is listening to terrestrial radio. People no longer want to listen to a bunch of advertisements – that day has passed. SiriusXM, the biggest satellite station in the USA, costs just $13 a month and gives access to 300 channels, with no commercials on music channels.

The country does not need RTÉ's 2FM. Were it to disappear overnight very few would notice. Just flick the dial to Today FM or FM104, Spin or Nova and you have a direct replica. I am sick and tired of the lip service spouted by 2FM and the commercial sector about what they are doing for Irish acts. It's bullshit and a complete whitewash of the facts. The figures speak for themselves: less than 15 per cent of what is played on our radio stations is Irish, and 70 per cent of that is by established acts such as U2, Westlife, Hozier, Kodaline, Dermot Kennedy, Gavin James and the Script. The rest is played when virtually no one is listening. One in every seven radio plays is an Irish act and the majority of those are in off-peak airtime hours. The current situation with 2FM is that in order for an Irish music act to get rotation airplay, the music has to come from a British or American record company. In other words, any local Irish-based act lucky enough to fit into 2FM's required genres must, in nine out of ten cases, export its music to the UK or USA and have it reimported into Ireland to get on the playlist. As journalist Kevin Courtney asked in the *Irish Times*, 'why does Irish music on the radio have to begin and end with Hozier?'

It's not just the new kids on the block who are discriminated against in terms of radio airplay. Some of our greatest and most established artists can't get any kind of sustained radio play, and many have just ceased releasing new music to Irish radio. In 2020, I released a single by Colm Wilkinson, one of his original songs, 'Harcourt Street', and it was a brilliant high-quality recording. It received a total of seven plays on RTÉ Radio 1 and was not put on the playlist of even one commercial station. A new release from Colm Wilkinson, a giant in musical theatre across the globe, should be automatically playlisted on Irish radio. Even if he is past his sell by date he is still a major Irish and international star. If we won't play our successful acts, what chance have the newcomers got? In any other business sector of Irish life, this would not be tolerated. The fault is not entirely 100 per cent that of the commercial radio stations – it's as much a fault of the Irish music fraternity, which is driven by a collective self-interest and not by the greater good of Irish music. Too many of the star names, both young and old, have adopted an 'I'm all right, Jack' attitude and couldn't care less about their less privileged colleagues. Would the Irish film and theatre family stand by and have their industry trampled into obscurity? Like hell they would. But that is exactly what is happening to Irish music.

To create a vibrant home-based Irish music community speaking with one voice, we need four or five powerful music establishment figures to step forward and be counted. We need to confront the Taoiseach and the Arts Minister with the bare facts: that Irish radio continues to shaft its own young people by refusing to play Irish music in favour of imported British and American product. Artist managers and promoters of stature, who have become highly successful financially through their popularity with generations of Irish fans, need to give something back to the younger generation of Irish musicians in their quest for a fair share of our national airways. I'm talking about people with money, like Enya, Bono, The Edge, Adam Clayton and Larry Mullen Jr, Christy Moore, Mary Black, Paul Brady, Sinead O'Connor, Paddy Moloney, John Sheahan, Hozier, Phil Coulter, Colm Wilkinson, Imelda May, Daniel O'Donnell, Van Morrison, and powerful industry players like Denis and Caroline Desmond, Peter Aiken, Tommy Swarbrigg, Philip King, Nicky and Roma Ryan, and more.

Big names and established stars fronting a proactive, progressive Irish music board could demand from the government that any Irish act who produces quality music has the right to have their work played on their national radio in their own land. It's time to bury the self-interest bullshit and pussyfooting that has been going on for generations. The big names in the Irish and international music business need to come forward and use their political clout and money to establish a powerful Irish music board, properly funded and with a small dedicated staff, that will look after the interests of our young ultra-talented generation. It's also time for the government to introduce legislation for percentage airplay and cease hiding behind imaginary European restrictions. A 30 per cent prime time Irish music policy across the commercial radio sector is a small ask that needs to be implemented without further delay. There are a number of ways this can be done without affecting or disadvantaging the current playlist policy of the commercial stations. All it would take is a ministerial order to force the commercial sector to sit down with a powerful Irish music board and hammer out a percentage airplay policy. After all, why should lining the pockets of the ultra-rich foreign owners of the commercial radio sector take priority over the interests of our young people? As things stand at the moment that is exactly what is happening. Denis O'Brien gave millions to the Football Association of Ireland to fund the wages of a foreign football manager yet at the same time his radio stations appeared to be turning their backs by refusing to playlist the young Irish musical talent on his own radio stations. He's a guy I greatly admire, he gave my concert business great support in the 1980s, and without 98fm my gigs would not have been so successful, and for that I will always be grateful. But when it came to playing Irish acts on his many radio platforms his Communicorp group was found seriously wanting.

In 2018, myself and the former Granny's Intentions front man and classic songwriter of The Voyage, Johnny Duhan, along with Phil Coulter and folk singer Danny McCarthy, met with Minister of Communications, Alex White. A guy with a sizable ego, which is evident from his first meaningful sentence: 'I'm the Minister and I call the shots with the Broadcasting Authority of Ireland!' In reality, Alex White had no interest in our efforts to highlight the damage being done to Irish talent - young and old - by the lack of airplay on our own airways. It was just a lip service meeting. The kind politicians give in their sleep. Loads of excuses and false promises to look into the matter came to nothing. The only reason we were given the appointment in the first place was that the Minister did not wish to be seen to ignore Phil Coulter's legendary status as Ireland's Ambassador of music. Until we get a Minister with some real awareness of the damage done to the Irish music family by our commercial radio sector, I regret to say nothing will change.

Nothing in my 50-plus years in this business irks me more than the injustice of the Irish airplay system. While radio may no longer be king in terms of having your music heard, it will, I believe, survive and experience a rebirth in popularity among the younger generations. I'm well aware that my career as a music promoter is in its twilight years, but I feel strongly that I owe something to the business that has given me a very comfortable standard of living. Putting my money where my mouth is, €10,000 is on the table as the first contribution.

I hope that sum will be matched (and bettered!) by our ultra-rich stars in the setting up of a powerful Irish music board – to ensure not just that our young artists get airplay but that they also get live performance opportunities from the major Irish promoters.

25: 'IT'S OVER FOR YOU, PAT. YOU ARE FINISHED!'

*D*enis Desmond is the most successful Irish promoter internationally, and a highly respected European CEO, with Live Nation, the world's foremost music promoters. In the early 1970s Denis, who's from Cork, was working as a trainee engineer in the UK. I had started to run my record stores and gigs in Ireland and he would ring me up occasionally asking about the music scene in Dublin and talking about the idea of doing some promotions together. I reckon we know each other longer than any other two people in the Irish music business. Denis built his MCD company into an international player way beyond anything I could ever aspire to – the company surely turns over hundreds of millions annually compared to my few single million digits. We had run a few gigs together over the years, including Black Sabbath at Dalymount Park, a Status Quo tour and Mary Black at The Point (as the 3Arena was then known). I was also involved as a partner in one of his small businesses, and yet I still never *really* knew the guy.

On a social level, Denis is charming, approachable, low-key, soft-spoken, shy, very generous and a really genuine, likeable guy. He has no visible ego whatsoever (if he does, he keeps it well hidden). I have always liked him, but being involved in business with him in any way means that the line in the sand is drawn by one person only, and that person is Denis. Fortunately or unfortunately, trying to keep your head down and steer clear of his influence is impossible. If you want to run a concert or music festival in Ireland, Denis is someone you can't avoid. If you want to run a gig at the Gaiety, the Olympia, Bord Gáis Energy Theatre, the 3Arena or the Academy, you will be dealing with his company, MCD, at one level or another.

The social Denis Desmond is a very different person from the businessman. Ultra-shrewd and uncompromising, he is a ruthless operator who thinks on his feet and consumes bit players like me in his coffee breaks. In terms of festivals and outdoor shows, he was the ultimate pioneer and survivor in this field, and now controls many of Europe's largest festivals. With massive investment and interests across the entire entertainment industry – the *Sunday Times* Rich List says he and his partner Caroline are worth in the region of €300m – you might think he would have little or no interest in the parochial goings-on in the local Dublin showbiz parish. Unquestionably, this is not true. If one of my poster staff at IPA (Irish Poster Advertising, the entertainment poster business I manage in Dublin) shifts an MCD poster from a high-profile city centre city site to a secondary site, perhaps because of pressure for space, my mobile phone will ring within a few hours and the man himself will be on the line to me. 'Why the fuck was my poster moved from Dorset Street? Aiken's and the Bord Gáis posters are still there. I give you more business than they do, so put it back up immediately.' And then my phone would go silent. The fact that we would have given him a better site somewhere else was irrelevant.

I run a lot of shows for the over-50s age group. Some are in-house productions, such as the highly successful Carpenters Love Songs; Callas, The Life and Music of Maria Callas; Mario Lanza – The Loveliest Night of the Year; and the West End's Definitive Rat Pack Show. These shows are ideally suited to the National Concert Hall as they fit like a glove the venue's more senior audiences for theatre and concerts. The NCH over-50s audiences are a very specialised bunch of windswept and interesting people. They are extremely fussy and demanding; they know what they like and they won't have the wool pulled over their eyes. They love the feel of the venue because of its attention to their requirements, and it's a very safe and secure place to enjoy great music. With its beautiful chandeliered lobby, it has a high-class ambience. That sense of occasion makes an evening at the hall more than just a concert, but rather a gala night out. Simply put, it's a joy to run an event at the NCH.

For me as a promoter, it was an ideal venue to expand my business into catering for a market that the two big Irish promoters, MCD and Aiken, were not interested in. Around 2010, when the economy was collapsing, I agreed to an arrangement with the then management of the NCH to run up to twenty-five concerts a year with named artists, as well as our own in-house-produced celebration/tribute shows. I hired the brilliant MD Eugene McCarthy and his wife, the singer Karen Black, to put together our own big band and together we produced tailor-made shows for the over-50s at the NCH. I would gladly have used one of Denis's theatres for the shows. The Gaiety was ideal but never available and the Olympia was simply not suitable for the age profile I was trying to attract – there were too many stairs to climb, very tight leg room in the rows of seating, and it's located in an area of the city that's full of hustle, bustle and continuous streams of traffic and people. Not only that, but NCH's rental deal was much more attractive.

Denis was not happy that I had deserted the Olympia, where I still ran the Christmas panto but very few other productions. 'I am going to close you down. I will put you out of business,' he told me during a telephone call in which I tried to explain the situation I was in. 'I will still be running some shows at the Olympia when I can get dates,' I argued, 'but the senior NCH audience won't go there.' His response? 'It's over for you, Pat,' at one point shouting, 'You're putting twenty-five shows a year into the National Concert Hall when you know the Olympia is suffering. Pat, you are *finished*!'

A year or so later, I met Denis at a showbiz dinner in the Burlington Hotel. To my surprise, he greeted me warmly. Maybe he had thought about his outburst and realised I had been talking sense. To be fair to him, he apologised: 'I was a bit hard on you last year. No hard feelings.' It meant a great deal to me and showed that the softer side of Denis was well worth knowing. Of course, I hope by letting this slip that I won't tarnish the man's reputation as the toughest guy in town.

26: 101 DARK NIGHTS

We are the management at the NCH and you are not going to dictate to us how we should run our venue. We do not have to answer to you in relation to why the hall was dark on any particular night. It is none of your business. You can now take your place at the back of the queue like any other promoter. Your priority rental arrangement based on the number of shows you present here every year is being withdrawn, as are all your other special privileges.
The management, NCH.

In 2018, the National Concert Hall's main room, a 1,150-seat concert auditorium, was dark for 101 nights. This included a sizeable number of prime weekend and midweek nights when business was readily available. The hall simply closed its doors and made no attempt to rent or fill the dates in question. After a long period of extreme frustration, I regularly lost my cool attempting to get answers from the venue management. I wanted to know why the dates in question were not offered to me and other promoters, and why we were left weeks and months waiting in our attempts to secure a booking. I went on RTÉ's *Prime Time* and RTÉ Radio 1's *Drive Time* to highlight the issue of the 101 dark nights at the country's principal government-funded concert venue. My frustration had boiled over when I drove past the hall on successive weekends to see it in darkness. I had written to the NCH chairperson, Maura McGrath, with whom I had a good relationship and who I found very warm and approachable, but, disappointingly, she refused to support me when the chips were down. I made my annoyance known by writing to the board, but despite a sympathetic reply to look into the matter my ongoing requests for dates were ignored or not responded to. In some instances, it took up to three months to secure a date. In a number of cases, due to long delays, I had lost the booking or act to another venue or promoter.

I simply could not understand why I was being treated in such a poor fashion. I was not a troublemaker and I had never caused problems at any of my shows. But when my position and livelihood were under threat I had no option but to fight back.

Over my 25 years promoting at the NCH I had spotted a gap in the market for high-quality, nostalgic celebration and tribute shows aimed at the over-50s, and I had grown a sizeable loyal following for up to twenty shows a year, achieving 100 per cent business on 85 per cent of the shows. I was drawing far more people to the NCH than any other promoter. Being refused dates because the venue was busy was one thing, but closing the doors and making no one aware that a bunch of good nights were available was, in my opinion, an abuse of privilege. I felt that as the venue's longest and most successful commercial promoter, I had a legitimate right to speak out against what I considered mismanagement of the venue's event calendar. The evidence was there for all to see: 101 dark nights in one year with no performances, yet business was being turned away. I calculated that the loss to the taxpayer for just 50 per cent of the period when the NCH was turning away business was in excess of €500,000. It made absolutely no sense. The NCH was receiving grants of €2.5 million a year and was still managing to lose excessive sums on top of their grants. I wrote again to the board and met with an adviser to Arts Minister Josepha Madigan, with responsibility for the NCH, yet I received no answers as to why the hall was dark for 101 nights when business was available but being turned away.

For years, NCH management has struggled to attract the ordinary middle-class Dubliner to the venue. The reason? It was perceived by most as stuffy, snobby, elitist and not somewhere you were likely to hear anything but Bach and Mozart. A number of campaigns had been rolled out in an effort to attract the ordinary Dubliner, but with little success. Nothing had done more to open up the hall to the Dublin working- and middle-class public than broadly-based popular concerts presented by Pat Egan Management. Shows featuring artists such as Billy Connolly, The Dubliners, Bonnie Tyler, the Stylistics, Dr Hook, Sir George Martin, Brendan Grace, Gene Pitney, Mike Denver, Phil Coulter, Sonny Knowles, the Sugar Cubes Big Band, Rebecca Storm, the Ronan Collins Showband

Show, Tommy Carey, Melanie McCabe, plus dozens of our own celebration shows based on the lives of recording legends such as Perry Como, Connie Francis, the Carpenters, Matt Monro, Bobby Darin, Anne Murray and more. In an effort to attract all tastes, I had Emmy-award-winner Niall Morris produce a series of excellent high-quality classical crossover shows including Callas – The Life and Music of Maria Callas (eight performances), Pavarotti – His Life and Music (four) and The Puccini Story (two). Our own Classical Crossover success with Mario Lanza also played twelve nights at the hall. President Michael D. Higgins, the Greek Ambassador and NCH chairperson Maura McGrath attended the Callas show, and Michael D. told our producer–director Niall Morris that it was one of the best and most enjoyable shows he had ever attended at the venue.

During my many years promoting shows there the NCH was, for the first time, accessible to a large working-class audience who came in their thousands to rediscover the nostalgic music of their younger years.

We have a National Opera House in Wexford that is, to some degree, a white elephant in relation to achieving its intended goals and capacity audiences. Why not shift the country's entire arts community to Wexford, including the Abbey Theatre, and create a truly dynamic national cultural quarter for heritage and the arts?

In my opinion, the NCH is seriously out of touch in terms of the bigger picture regarding the venue's core audiences. Their new contemporary diverse music plan is recreating the veil of exclusiveness around the venue and its audience that for years it had tried to lose. Ordinary Dubliners are again to be alienated and squeezed out in favour of a high-end arts and contemporary agenda. It's all very fine to introduce highbrow music platforms, new age, world music and so on, but the problem is they are rarely commercially successful. Ninety-five per cent of the acts are suited only for small venues, not a major 1,000-plus capacity venue like the NCH.

In my humble opinion, any move to introduce an in-house concert promoter as part of its new diverse package is deeply flawed. It's fine and dandy to be a concert promoter when you're playing around with someone else's money (i.e. the taxpayer) and you end up paying out way over the odds to secure acts because you don't have a track record at the highest level, and maybe not the commercial acumen about how that business operates.

The top tier international concert business is a very exclusive club controlled by a handful of great white sharks. They take no prisoners. The agents that the major acts use at the top of the contemporary rock music business are pariahs. They will strip you of every last penny and leave you with little or no margin to operate with. The days when I could buy an act for €20,000 and make double that are history. But more important from the NCH point of view, why on earth would you want to risk losing large amounts of taxpayers' money by setting up competition in Dublin with MCD and Aiken Promotions, two of the most successful worldwide event promoters? The solution for the NCH in securing top of the line artists is simple. Let our two big promoters run major names at the venue, charge them 30 per cent, plus rent, of the gross box office. By applying this rationale, the venue would walk away smiling, not just on rental but also from a capacity bar and restaurant business. The end result is no risks whatsoever and a profit to help fund developing artists.

Just because it's 'the arts' shouldn't mean every project losing millions. The NCH does not need to promote its own contemporary music events. There are enough promoters out there to hire the venue and take the risk, leaving the hall free to concentrate on its core classical business, in which it excels.

The vision for the venue's new, more diverse and integrated programming that was launched in 2017/18 has, if the accounts published in 2019 are anything to go by, been a financial disaster. The NCH lost close to €500,000 on top of a €2.5 million grant in 2018. Does anybody in government or on the NCH board ask why this is happening in a market that is desperate for live music.

Why, I ask, had the current arts minister to go to the UK to appoint a new head of the NCH in 2021? Surely we had dozens of capable, experienced Irish arts administrators lining up for such a prestigious job. The previous director of the NCH, the highly respected arts and heritage director Judith Woodworth, had the balance perfectly sussed. She remarked to me on more than one occasion during her time at the hall that it couldn't survive on classical music alone. 'It's simply not going to happen unless we have the commercial balance right. For our classical music business to thrive, we need your type of shows at the hall.'

The NCH owes me nothing. My company and career as a promoter grew enormously through association with the hall, and it is by far my favourite venue to work in. Having presented shows at London's Royal Albert Hall, the West End Lyric, the Cork Opera House and the 3Arena, I can honestly say that nothing gave me as much joy as working there. It was, however, heart-breaking and damaging to my company and my well-being to be dismissed in such a fashion. I had helped the venue open its doors to a wider audience by presenting shows that appealed to over-50s Dubliners who had few, if any, other options to hear the music they loved. I had, through the bleak recession years of 2008-2013, put my money where my mouth was, presenting dozen of shows when business at the venue was suffering a serious decline. I was drawing more people to the hall than its premier client, RTÉ. A 25-year-plus love affair working at the venue stood for nothing – not as much as a meeting over coffee to discuss the new diverse programming agenda. Because I opened my big mouth and highlighted what I perceived to be a legitimate concern regarding the venue's booking process and multiple dark nights I failed to get any new bookings at the venue in 2019. I went from having as many as eighteen shows on sale at any one time to only one in late 2019.

I want to take this opportunity to recognise and thank some of the people who made my long relationship with the NCH such a total joy: Sheila Dunne at reception; Rosita Wolfe (senior public relations executive) for her ongoing support; marketing executive Joanne Taaffe; Stage manager Paul Hunt and his crew, Jim Tate, Aran Scully, Ian Dowdall and Paul Kohlman; Managers John Nolan, Aidan Quinn, Kevin Shaw; Also Caroline Feehily; Aisling Coyle; David Lonergan; Bernie Nolan, queen of the chocolate gateaux; Kevin Summerville, the restaurant manager; and Ian Willis at the Music Box.

I greatly regret having to face the reality that the NCH may no longer have any great wish to cater for the over-50s nostalgia market of wind-swept and interesting music fans, unless their taste falls somewhere between Laurie Anderson and Branford Marsalis.

In life you win some and you lose some, and unfortunately for me this is one battle I may have lost; but I live in hope, and I don't for one minute regret fighting for our audiences.

27: THE PYRAMID OF GREED CARTELS

'Ticketmaster, just like Manchester United or Barcelona, is just a brand, a front, for the pyramid of greed cartels that now control the sports and entertainment industries' (Bob Lefsetz)

*W*hat did I learn about life and business, having spent 50 years ducking and diving, hustling my way from nowhere to a reasonably successful and comfortable lifestyle? My business and financial achievements are modest by any standards, but it's true to say that I have lived the dream. I was never tough, sharp or wise enough to build an empire, but I know some people who have, and I know I never had that fuck-you, ruthless, uncompromising streak I see in them. I always believed in the old show business saying that there's enough in this deal for everyone, and certainly in my early days as a concert and music promoter, that was the case – everyone got a piece of the action. There are, I regret to say, no such deals to be done today in music promotion. Opportunity has ceased to exist.

I have worked sometimes and in some other ways as a promoter or booking agent with all the top Irish acts and their managers. Sometimes I got fired or dropped; sometimes I just walked away from situations that were no longer doable or suitable for me. Without any natural or creative talent or college education, surviving in the dog-eat-dog Tin Pan Alley of showbiz at the highest level for fifty years was a big personal achievement for me. I learned from day one when at the age of thirteen I started work as a messenger boy for Thomas Corry and Sons in Smithfield that the one thing I had going for me was that I couldn't get enough hard work or hours on the job. I was in at 8.30 a.m. every day, thirty minutes before we opened our doors, waiting for the boss to arrive. I was still hanging around at 6.30 p.m. to help him lock up. While times have changed beyond recognition, I still believe that, regardless of circumstances, and if given the opportunity, there is a place for any kid to make their own luck by working their socks off. Although I come from the tough inner-city streets of the 1950s, I was a bit of a strategic coward in that I never got into a fight I knew I couldn't win. I was more likely to run and fight another day than to stand up to some tough guy who was going to clobber me with one punch. But what I did learn was some street smarts and how to survive the bullying and intimidation. Often, with my back to the wall, the easiest way was to fast talk and act or reason my way out of tricky situations. When you're not a tough nut, it's much better to have half your apple and no black eye. This is the belief I have carried throughout my business career, and for the best part of fifty years it has worked a treat for me. I never had any wish to have or leave tens of millions behind me. In fact, I have always wanted to do a Frank Carson and die as he did, with just one penny in his last will and testament.

The concert promoting agency and artist management business was, and still is, one of the most exciting and enjoyable occupations. It is also hugely stressful and extremely demanding. To avoid the many pitfalls of running a big concert event, attention to detail is paramount. Like a lot of other businesses, the line between failure and success is often down to the most minute detail. The changes that have taken place over the last twenty years have been monumental. The doors of opportunity for independent promoters, agents and young people hoping for a break have slammed shut, leaving little or no opportunity for a career as a promoter at any level, and certainly not in the premier leagues.

In the late 70s and 80s, I spent a lot of time in London knocking on open doors in the hope of meeting the managers of great acts. If I failed initially I called again and again. I met some of the most legendary figures in the business – Robert Stigwood, John Reid, Alec Leslie, Barry Clayman, Harvey Goldsmith, Roger Forrester, and Barrie Marshall – by just sitting and waiting in their respective reception areas in the hope of seeing them. I secured Bob Marley for the historic Dalymount Park show in 1980

• •
'I like to have a hot bath after every soundcheck. Please book me a hotel.' – Esteemed Irish songwriter Jimmy MacCarthy.
• •

by calling at the office of his agent every day for an entire week. You got a chance to make your pitch, and if nothing else they knew your name, knew you could pay the big bucks, and if they were planning a tour you were in with a shout to get the Irish shows. That type of scenario no longer exists.

Today, the only way for an aspiring promoter or agent to crack the big time is to work with one of the very few top companies for a good number of years, getting to know the business inside out and building a reputation as a smart, skilled and savvy operator. If you are an exclusive agent or promoter in a big organisation with a few big-name acts, chances are the act might not want to lose your service and may be prepared to jump ship with you if you decide to go solo. However, even that opportunity is now rapidly disappearing. The other important ingredient you will need is a million quid in the bank because without it, you simply can't run concerts, even on the secondary level at which I have been operating for the last twenty years. The risks are sizeable and you could lose as much as €200,000 or more on one show in the blink of an eye.

There are two levels of promoters operating in Ireland. On the top rung are Live Nation/MCD and Aiken Promotions, which between them take in all the major marquee names, along with 80 per cent of the festival business, the big outdoor arena gigs and the stadium shows. The secondary promoters – guys like Martin Nolan, Tommy Swarbrigg, Joe Gallagher and myself – occasionally pick up a big-name artist, but more often than not it's an act who is no longer in the mainstream, and who will work for set fees per night. If you get your numbers right, you can come out smiling, plus you won't have some nosey tour accountant looking over your shoulder and asking you to account for every empty seat and every penny spent. If the big boys read the market demand right, they'll know the major names will do 100 per cent business. The minute the show goes on sale, tickets fly out the door, often in a matter of minutes. The main Irish promoters will pay a big guarantee to the act of anything between 90 and 97.5 per cent of the projected net box office after all local costs are deducted (which include venue hire, production, Ticketmaster charges, VAT, public liability insurance, hotels, airfares, TV/radio, security, advertising, local transport and so on). In some cases, the biggest acts won't let the promoter make any money but will pay them a service fee for handling the local set-up and marketing. To give you an insight into how the deals have changed over the years, on my first Billy Connolly tour in the late 70s I was on an 80/20 split. On my very last tour in 2018, the deal was 92.5 in favour of the artist. That is an indication of how little room a promoter has to manoeuvre.

In fact, it's now at the stage where Live Nation is now giving almost all of the net ticket money to the big acts. So how and where, I hear you ask, are they making their vast profits? In 2019 Live Nation had global ticket sales of $50 billion from almost 50,000 major events, which gives you some idea of the scale of their power and control of live entertainment across the world and especially in Ireland, where Peter Aiken of Aiken Promotions is their only competition. Because the major acts are now taking all the ticket revenue, the profit for Live Nation is generated by the outlandish fees charged by Ticketmaster, a Live Nation company, and even at that, Ticketmaster is not keeping all the fee money. Not by a long shot.

As I said, I was extremely lucky to be in the business in its pioneering years when a promoter could take a risk and make a real killing, but the days when there was something for everyone in a big concert deal are dead and gone. The only way that can happen now is through promoting a specialist open-air festival, but again, once you start to eat into the big guys' market they will squeeze you out by limiting your access to major names.

The late John Reynolds is a classic case. John was a maverick who had an original and far-reaching creative vision for the future of music festivals. His invention, Electric Picnic, remains to this day. It is the crème de la crème of Europe's outdoor events, but there was no way he could remain independent. It just does not happen like that anymore. The other major problem for independent Irish promoters is that venue availability is hugely restricted. Dates are at a premium, even more so now since the coronavirus epidemic. Because the leading venues are now promoter-controlled you start at the very back of the queue when it comes to securing a date. There is also no competition in the theatre rental business in Dublin. None. All four of the main venues for stage production shows – the Olympia, the Gaiety, Bord Gáis Energy Theatre, 3Arena – are managed and run by one company. If you want to stage a major theatre musical or play, there is simply no place in the city centre for it. If you want to stay in the business you have to take the deal on offer at any of these venues, assuming you are lucky enough to have secured a date in the first place. Dublin is probably the only European capital where all the major city centre commercial theatres, excluding the Abbey Theatre, fall under the control of one company.

So how does the concert revenue break down after you buy your ticket? Let's take a rough example and pretend we are promoting two 3Arena shows for a premier international act. We have a 9,000-seat capacity and the average ticket price is €90, which gives us a potential gross box office of €1,620,000 for two nights (€810,000 per show) The deductions relating to the cost of staging the event are:

Gross Ticket Sales	18,000 x €90	€1,620,000
Ticket commissions	10%	€162,000
Credit card charges	3%	€48,600
Performing rights/IMRO	3%	€58,320
Insurance, public liability, etc.		€10,000
Venue hire	€75,000 per night	€150,000
Production, sound, lights, etc.		€30,000
Staging & crew costs		€6,000
Marketing & promotion – TV, radio, etc.		€25,000
Artist costs, hotels, flights		€20,000
Local costs		€3,000
Total costs		€512,920
Net		€1,107,080
Artist fees approx	95%	€1,051,726
Balance to promoter	5%	€55,354

As the artist is on a 95/5 per cent split of the bottom line, the promoter's share is small for such a big risk. Don't forget also that the promoter will have paid an upfront guarantee to the act of, say, €750,000 against 95 per cent of the net box office.

One way or the other, the promoter's risk is sizeable. The secret at this end of the promoting business is volume. It's all about the number of shows you run, which would explain why over the last ten years Live

Nation and, before that, SFX had been sweeping up and buying out all the world's major promoting companies in an effort to control the entire industry. Promoters like Aiken Promotions, now one of the world's leading independent promoters, have been fighting a major battle to stay independent.

It's the way of the world in 2021 and living with it is impossible for an independent promoter. If truth be told the writing is already on the wall for all independent promoters worldwide.

28: LIFE'S PLEASURES

A lifetime of memorabilia

Even though I now live near a golf course and pay a yearly membership fee, I have never really taken to the game. I have, however, been a fan of all sports, and sometimes to the disapproval of my wife, Helena, I tend to watch nothing but sport and crime on television. Alongside movie stars, my childhood teenage heroes were all great sporting icons – Ronnie Delaney, Liam Whelan, Shay Elliott and, in later years John Giles, George Best, Sean Kelly and Liam Brady, to name just a few.

My principal hobby, however, took hold in my early thirties and has continued for almost forty years. I became an entertainment memorabilia collector, graduating from music to movies and, later, to rare books and paintings. I would buy bargains at auctions in London, New York and Dublin. In recent years, I have sold off and I continue to give away many of the items to people I know have genuine interest in the magic of show business. It's sad, but it's time to realise nothing last for ever.

My favourite period in entertainment history has to be the Hollywood Golden Age – the 1950s and 1960s. It was the definitive star generation of the real beauty queens; Greta Garbo, Paulette Goddard, Grace Kelly, Ava Gardner, Audrey Hepburn, Vivien Leigh, Jean Simmons, Marilyn Monroe, Rita Hayward, Jayne Mansfield, Anita Ekberg, Lana Turner, Brigitte Bardot; It was glamorous Hollywood at its most captivating and never to be equalled or replicated, regardless of the technology available to movie makers in later years. How wonderful it was to have a bundle of letters from Garbo, shoes from Hepburn or Barbara Streisand, scarves and belts worn by Monroe, Grace Kelly's hats from her Hitchcock movies. They were each small but significant items of movie history that brought you just that little bit closer to the legendary figures on the silver screen. In music, I had Christmas cards from John Lennon, letters relating to Queen and Bob Marley, and signed photos of the great rock stars. They were valuable when originally purchased, but it's amazing how quickly the value decreases. Who will pay €500 for a signed photo of Clark Gable or Lana Turner nowadays? Very few, I regret to say. While the legacy of The Beatles and Marilyn Monroe will forever be part of pop and movie culture, the appeal of only a few others will survive more than a generation or two after their deaths. Autographs of Grace Kelly and Ava Gardner that I bought twenty years ago are losing cultural and monetary value by the day. Prices of vintage posters from Hollywood's great movies are also on the slide.

The investment in books and art has a better chance of providing a long-term return. But regardless of the value there is always a magic in owning a classic first edition book that nothing else can compete with: an original first edition of James Joyce's *Ulysses*; a signed copy of Bob Dylan's *Tarantula*; or a signed first edition of D.H. Lawrence's *Lady Chatterley's Lover*. What I have also discovered is that five thousand quid paid for a picture in 1990 seldom means the value will have increased by 2020. In fact, getting back what you originally spent on a painting is more a big miss than a big hit, unless it's a lucky strike and the artist's reputation grows out of all recognition. The highs and lows of the Irish art and book market is treacherous for amateurs like me. Among the few I have had over the years, the only paintings or rare prints that increased in value were by Irish artists at the very top of the market, such as Paul Henry, Louis Le Brocquy and Francis Bacon. I am a fan of Jack Vettriano and Roy Lichtenstein and I love John Cahill and the portraits of female faces by Ken Hamilton.

I had for many years a much-loved 1957 original clown painting by Frank Sinatra that the great man used on his personal Christmas cards of that year. By all accounts, Frank was a reasonable painter and his work only occasionally comes up for sale. One of my favourites, but of little value, is an eight-foot-high Gainsborough-style painting of Hollywood beauty Paulette Goddard from the movie set of the Academy Award-nominated *Kitty* in 1946 (the year I was born). It cost more to bring it from New York to Dublin than the $1,000 I paid for it. Collecting has never really been about making a profit – it's great if you make a few quid, but you just can't put a value on historical items. The joy is in knowing they once belonged to and were part of some famous movie stars or historical figures.

Kieran Kennedy, the former guitarist with the Black Velvet Band and husband of the brilliant singer and actress Maria Doyle Kennedy, sold me a very rare item handed down from his grand-uncle, Brian Kennedy, who in 1942, having been sentenced to three years for being a member of the IRA, had been a resident of Cell 32 in Mountjoy Prison. Kieran wanted to buy a new guitar and was short of a few quid, so he rang me one evening and asked would I be interested in this unique piece of literary history. The item was an autograph book with a shabby, faded green velvet cover. The fascinating history behind the book was that on 12 November 1942, an IRA member by the name of Maurice O'Neill was shot by firing squad at Mountjoy. In the months that followed, the prison held many IRA men including one by the name of Brendan Behan, and the autograph book was passed from cell to cell so that IRA members could write a page of tributes to their fallen comrade. At the very back of the autograph book are two full pages written in Behan's hand. The pages were titled 'Maurice O Neill, executed Mountjoy 1942', and signed 'Long Live the Workers Republic – Brendan Behan'. For me, this truly was one of the joys of being a collector. To my way of thinking, collecting memorabilia simply does not come better than that.

Life's rules

Thanks to Tommy Higgins, one of the good old boys of the Irish music business, I get the daily newsletter from Bob Lefsetz, a leading American music critic and analyst. Bob has thousands of followers and his finger is on the pulse of what is happening across the entertainment industry worldwide. It's always riveting reading and Bob pulls no punches when it comes to exposing the spoofers and chancers across the industry. A newsletter he published in 2015 still sticks in my head and relates well to my own experiences of life's lessons. I am reprinting it here because Bob says it better. If you play by these rules you won't go far wrong in life.

1. *Karma exists. It may not be instant like in that John Lennon song, but it happens. May take a long time, might not be easily seen, may not be visible to anybody but you, the one who was scathed, but it's real.*

2. *Niceness triumphs. Although no one can be nice all the time. And sometimes you have to push back. But if you have got the option, be nice, people appreciate it.*
3. *Be yourself. We're all individuals. That's what attracts us, our uniqueness. Don't try to imitate someone else, focus on your strengths and heighten them. Everyone can't do everything. Don't try to fit your square peg in a round hole. But your trapezoid will appeal, if you just let it shine.*
4. *You can't please everybody. It's a phony concept that flames out. Be thankful you're got your group, your friends, your family, your fans. There are those who would appreciate you whom you've never met, focus on meeting them, not those who don't care.*
5. *Education is everything. And it doesn't have to happen at school. But at this late date we can understand why reading, writing and arithmetic are so important. Yes, in the internet era, reading and writing are everything (typing too!) As for maths ... You can't do a deal without knowing the numbers. And everybody wants to do a deal.*
6. *Learning is lifelong. You keep gaining insight and then you die. Life is a puzzle, one in which you are constantly delivered new pieces. And you can't sort some stuff out until you get this new information. Which is why age equals wisdom and the young may have their youth, but the old have all the happiness.*
7. *Possessions mean less as you age. You can't take them with you. Furthermore, we're evolving into a no possessions era. One in which you can rent a ride and you don't even own a car. Experiences are everything.*
8. *No one has the answers when it comes to love. There's no perfect partner, if you're looking for one you're doomed. The key is to play. Relationships are the salad dressing of life, without them it tastes very bland.*
9. *Do the right thing. Not only will it make a difference. You'll feel better about yourself.*
10. *Time starts accelerating sometimes in your late thirties or forties. If you are not paying attention, if you're not steering, chances are you not going to get where you want to go.*

'A song for you'

I have spent a full sixty years of my life in music and I regularly get asked about the music that influenced me and that I most enjoy and who are my favourite artists. It is an impossible list to compile. My early years were driven by one-off single hit songs that I will simply never forget. Not a lot has changed in all that time; I am still very much a one song guy. Maybe that is why most of my album collection is made up of Greatest Hits and Best of albums.

My favourite all-time artists are Dusty Springfield, Roy Orbison, Paul Brady, the Eagles, Diana Ross, the Four Tops, Mary Chapin Carpenter, Mary Black, Rebecca Storm, Colm Wilkinson, Eric Clapton, Billy Fury, Glen Campbell and Danny Ellis. The list of songs is really endless, but here are a few of the great songs that over the years have been my all-time favourites.

1. 'Save the Last Dance for Me' – The Drifters. My mind-blowing introduction to the power of rock'n'roll.
2. 'Don't Let Me Be Misunderstood' – Nina Simone. Spellbinding vocals, simply brilliant.
3. 'Halfway to Paradise' – Billy Fury. Billy, the ultimate loser in love, sings a teen heart-breaker.
4. 'Always on My Mind' – Elvis Presley. Elvis at his supreme best.
5. 'You've Lost that Lovin' Feeling' – The Righteous Brothers. Phil Spector's wall of sound, a lover's desperation, best single production ever.
6. 'Yesterday, When I Was Young' – Glen Campbell. The best life song ever written.
7. 'Crying' – Roy Orbison and k.d. lang. Masterful duo, a heart-breaking love ballad like no other.
8. 'Layla' – Derek and The Dominos. Eric Clapton at his very best; an unforgettable opening guitar riff.
9. 'Going Back' – Dusty Springfield. Outstanding Carol King song for all seasons. No one comes near Dusty.
10. 'Across the Universe' – Noel Bridgeman. The best unreleased Irish track; one of Lennon's lost masterpieces.
11. 'You Say' – Lauren Daigle. Stunning spiritual vocal, best new song for many a long year.
12. 'Back for Good' – Take That. Brilliant recreation of a 1960s heartbreaker.

13. 'Bring Him Home' – Colm Wilkinson. Specially written for Colm's voice. A masterpiece.
14. 'Blue Bayou' – Roy Orbison and Rebecca Storm. The place we all want to return to someday, Paradise Island, Blue Bayou.
15. 'My Boy' – Richard Harris. Phil Coulter's masterpiece for the forgotten child in a broken relationship.
16. 'Brown-Eyed Girl' – Van Morrison. The kind of Van the Man song we don't get from him often enough.
17. 'The Power of Love' – Melanie McCabe. A truly underrated young vocalist singing one of the greatest love ballads.
18. 'Eleanor Rigby' – The Beatles. Classic Beatles and a brilliant George Martin arrangement.
19. 'Rock and Roll (I Gave You the Best Years of My Life)' – Kevin Johnson. Classic song for all the guys like myself who nearly made it.
20. '24 Hours from Tulsa' – Gene Pitney and Dusty Springfield. Burt Bacharach's brilliant classic tale of love at first sight.

A bunch of good old boys – reunion

One of the occasions I look forward to immensely every year is the annual get-together of another bunch of windswept and interesting, bothered and bewildered old record company and retail dinosaurs like myself. Thanks must go to Tommy Higgins for the annual bringing together of this motley crew. Tommy, like myself a retailer from the 70s in Sligo and Galway, and later the head man at Ticketmaster, went on to be a big winner with *Riverdance* and other international show investments. Tommy, always on top of his game, has dined at the top table with some of the industry's biggest movers and shakers and he wrote a wonderful book in 2015. *Just the Ticket* tells of his exciting life wheeling and dealing at the top of international showbiz. Tommy donated the book's royalties to the North West Hospice, which says a lot about the kind of guy he is.

Around the third week of December every year, I get the chance to catch up with some good old boys from the days when record shops were the real driving force of the music industry. Alas, those times have passed but the buzz and memories of standing behind a busy shop counter on a Saturday afternoon remain. The excitement of having a bunch of new release albums by Jimi Hendrix, Rory Gallagher, Deep Purple, Mike Oldfield or even brilliant pop from the Bee Gees and Abba, to offer your regular customers gave you a unique feeling of being right on top of what was happening musically in the 70s and 80s.

They were great days, when Dublin had major international offices for labels like Pye, Polydor, CBS, EMI Universal RCA and Irish distributors Ritz, Dolphin, Tara, Irish Record Factors, run by some great characters like John Woods (Pye), David Duke (CBS) and, in later years, Cathal Tully (Beaumex), Rory Golden (Virgin), Dave Pennyfeather (Universal), Jackie Hayden (CBS), Willie Kavanagh (EMI), Paul Keogh (Universal), John Cooke (Tara), Freddie Middleton (RCA) and Shay Hennessy (Crashed).

So meeting up every December is a wonderful way of saying hello and reminiscing with great old pals from the golden days of record retailing like Paul O'Reilly, Tommy Tighe, Freddie Blake, Pat Kennedy, Brian Wynn, Noel Cusack, Gerry MacDonald, Maurice Byrne, Charlie Church, Ray Quinn, Paul Egan, Seamus Hayes, Robert Young, John O Reilly, Joe Stuart, John and Richard Forde, Michael Moore, Tony McNulty, Vivien O'Rourke and of course the chairman of the board Tommy Higgins, whose great idea it was to pull the whole thing together.

29: 60,000 NEW SONGS A DAY – COVID AND BEYOND

*A*s I write this, our beloved entertainment business is hopefully now emerging from the grip of the terrible Covid plague. It is now October 2021 and hopefully we are facing into a new beginning for the live entertainment business. The importance of allowing full room capacity is paramount if the business is to recover and thrive. You can run your shows, but you can't make ends meet on a 50% to 80% event. The various one-off public relations test events by the Department of the Arts over the lockdown were merely stunts, and served no purpose at all. The Department involved was fooling no one, least of all the hundreds of musicians and production crews who have been left high and dry with no work whatsoever. Our industry also seems to be at the very bottom of the government's priority list. The amount of revenue the live music business generates for the hospitality and travel sector appeared to have been totally overlooked. The vast majority of Dublin bars and hotels would be empty every second weekend without the huge numbers of fans generated by the nationwide concert business.

I was in touch daily with music people who were trying to make the best of a bad situation, and I fear going forward that work opportunities will, for a long time, be harder to come by. Every theatre in Ireland is jammed up with rescheduled booking for the next two or three years and the longer the entertainment lockdown lasts, the bigger the problems become. 85% of the bands booked into the available venues are overseas acts. My business is only second tier, yet I am having massive problems getting a date in any of the major venues. Thanks to Stephen Fallon at the

Board Gais I have been able to pencil some Sundays in 2022. The promoter controlled venues don't want my business; they have too much of their own that they can't reschedule.

So where does that leave smaller guys like me? Up shit creek. Where are all the musicians and singers I have been hiring over the last twenty years going to get work? I have no idea, and you know what, no one cares. I am worried for the future of the top-end local market, the one that hires Irish musicians. Now more than ever is the time we need an Irish music board to protect our industry and put pressure on the Arts minister to incentivise and support working musicians.

The internet has changed everything about today's live music business and not, I believe, for the better. The biggest problem musicians have today is getting people to listen to their music. No one is listening – it really is almost impossible. With over 60,000 new songs a day being posted online, everyone is far too busy selling their own personalised hit parade, far too busy to listen to anything else. In the year 2021, it's true, anyone can be a star; in fact, everyone is having a go. You no longer need a record company or a spot on *Top of the Pops*. Today the internet is your oyster; thousands are looking to see how far having no talent can take them – which, judging by the number of social media wizards and super-star influencers, is a long way.

For real artists old and new to stay relevant, they have to directly identify and target the age profile that is most like to respond to their work – easier said than done. The best people by far at doing that are the kids on Twitter and Instagram. It's much tougher for the ponytailed senior players. The secret seems to be to stick to chasing a core market, where your chances of getting traction are more likely to pay dividends. Creating the one brilliant song exclusively for your chosen audience is the bottom line. If you can do that, the word will be on the street and your chance to grow a fan base will be up and running. Way back in the good old days of *Melody Maker*, *New Musical Express* and *Disc*, the word filtered out

• •

'Shirley, you're the greatest! Please give me something nice.' – An elderly man to Shirley Bassey at the stage door of the RDS. Shirley replied, 'Oh, you sweet thing! Kiss me, kiss me' as she threw her silk scarf around his neck. The gentleman was so shocked he broke down in tears.

• •

slowly about a great new song or act. The charts were a great barom-
eter of growing trends and new artists were given time grow a career
by record companies, with a two- or four-album deal. Of course, unlike
now, you did need genuine talent in the first place to get a record deal.
Also unlike now, radio was king and continued rotation airplay helped you
build your own constituency of devoted fans who purchased everything
you released. Now, in 2021, the album is dead. No one has time to listen
to twelve songs any more. It's all about that one song, and grabbing as
much attention as you can. It's all changing so fast that the song itself is
now more important than the artist who performs it. Radio without DJs
and commercials is becoming the norm for anyone under twenty-five.

The current Irish music scene is very tough place, especially for young
middle of the road acts trying to get ongoing work. If you don't fit into
the rock genre your options are few. There is little or no television and
radio is a total no-go area; the stations just won't play new Irish talent.
Hard to believe our own radio stations won't play our own young people's
work, but very true.

I have tried to include in my shows some very promising talent like the
terrific O'Neill Sisters from Kerry; Celtic Woman star Chloë Agnew, one of
our best female exports; and my own personal favourite, the outstanding
Melanie McCabe. Other great young voices that need to be heard include
Aoife Scott, Rachel Coyne, Sibéal Ní Chasaide. The big problem they all face
is that there is simply no work on the local Irish scene. I have great hopes
also for the second coming of young George Murphy, one of the best ballad
singers since the great days of the Dubliners. After a number of years in
the wilderness it looks like his star is rising again and George's hard work is
beginning to pay off. He is carrying on where the great ballad voices of Luke
Kelly, Jim McCann and Paddy Reilly left off. The great Irish songbook will
always have an audience for songs like 'The Fields of Athenry', 'The Town
I Love So Well' and 'The Wild Rover' – they will be sung for ever, wherever
there is an Irish flag flying. George Murphy is an excellent songwriter with
the credentials and the voice to carry on the ballad tradition and in doing so
preserve the legacy of Kelly, McCann, O'Reilly and the great Ronnie Drew.

An old rock head like me can only mourn the great days of *Top of
the Pops*, *The Old Grey Whistle Test* and a bunch of new releases every
Friday from one of a dozen record companies that sadly now no longer
exist. Unfortunately you can't hold back the future any more than you
can return to the past.

30: 'YESTERDAY, WHEN I WAS YOUNG'

*M*y troubles started during my wild years living in Cork. Until I moved to Cork, I had always lived at home with my mother, but now I was staying in the Metropole Hotel, where I lived for the first six months before moving into an apartment above the Patrick Street store. I drove back up to Dublin every Sunday morning and did my purchasing at the various record companies in the early part of the week before returning to Cork on Wednesday evening or Thursday morning. I was in a long-term relationship at the time, and my then partner was in Dublin, but I was not, I am ashamed to say, playing by the rules. I was a total disaster in my late twenties and thirties with beautiful women, and in Cork I went over the top. It's easy now, looking back, to laugh it all off, but at the time I really was not an honest or honourable person. I was living a big lie and two separate lives. In Cork I had numerous short-term affairs before falling in love with a super beautiful Cork air hostess, Fionnuala. She dumped me when she discovered I was cheating on my partner in Dublin, and later married a better man.

I had, a number of times, experienced love that I was not mature enough to appreciate. For me it was all a game, but in the end the laugh was on me. I married at 31 without any awareness of the commitment needed for such a sacred partnership. I treated the whole experience with disregard and when my first child, Graham, and then his sister, Deborah, came along, I was oblivious to my responsibilities as a father. I continued to self-destruct, living a totally irresponsible wild life, as if I had no one to answer to but my self-centred, immature ego. Tragically, I missed my children's golden childhood years when they moved to the other side of the world. The love they needed as kids and that I did not provide still hangs deeply over me. I ensured they had everything money could buy, but I know now that a father's love involves a multitude of responsibilities and that money is not one of them. The past may be gone and can't be revisited, but I have carried the guilt of my failings as a very heavy load. So much so that it destroyed my second-long term relationship.

I fought hard over the last thirty years never to lose touch with my children and to finally become a good father to Deborah and a grandfather to her children, Fiona, Farrah and Beau – a man they could be proud of. My first son, Graham, who lives with his mother in Canada, no longer talks to me. He blames me for the carnage of his early life, and rightly so. It has not been for the want of saying I am sorry or trying on my part to build a new beginning with him, but it's been to no avail. I grieve the loss of my relationship with Graham so much; it is a constant shadow on every single day of my life. Looking back now it would be easy to blame others for my mistakes, but that would be folly. No one was to blame for my wayward selfishness but me. At 32, I was a married man acting like a spoilt child, neither able nor wanting to assume the responsibilities of being a dad. What I really needed was a dad of my own to beat me about the head and tell me to grow up and be a man. I genuinely wish someone had done it. Through my own short-sightedness I hurt people I truly loved and who did not deserve it. I deeply regret it, because none of these people ever hurt me in return.

There were so many weaknesses and failures in my make-up that I had to attempt to correct, and it was hard to know where to start before it was too late. I had realised I was a long way from being what a father should be. In later years, when a 23-year relationship broke down, I eventually laid out all my weaknesses and shortcomings in front of me like one big map and I promised myself to navigate my problems one by one on my way to a better future for myself and my children. I had suffered for years with severe anxiety problems that I refused to have treated. I would insist that there was nothing wrong with me – I knew better, I thought. The mood swings, depressions and blackness were always of someone else's making, never mine. At the age of 60 I was on my own. Eventually, after much heartbreak and wasted years, and far too late to make up for the past, I gave in and sought help and medication. It was a wise move, but one I regret not making years earlier.

In my second relationship, I had two other wonderful children, David and Layla. I managed, thanks only to their mother, Caroline's, guidance and support, to make a better job of my second chance of fatherhood. I am so happy now that Deborah, Layla and David, and my grandkids, Beau, Fiona, and Farrah, are also my best and dearest friends, and I know their love and affection has made a better man of me. Not a day passes that I don't pray for forgiveness for my weaknesses and shallowness of character in my younger years. Growing up as a kid in the 50s, surrounded by priests of the Holy Roman Empire, it was easy to turn to God when it suited me. All those years of having had it drummed into me that prayer is the salvation of the soul has, finally, reaped some good for me. Over the years I may have lost my faith at times, but I never lost my belief in the power of the Lord and his goodness. Thank God for second chances.

At the ripe old age of 62, when I thought that romance was gone for ever and that I would be alone for the rest of my life, my good friend Stuart O'Connor told me that there was a beautiful young lady I should meet.

'How old is she?' I asked.

'Forty-two,' said Stuart.

'Are you joking me? What on earth would she be wanting with an old teddy boy like me?'

'I'll set you up with a blind date,' he said.

'Just one condition,' I answered. 'You tell her I'm twenty years her senior and that I'm half deaf and losing my hair, and if she's still interested, I'll give it a shot.'

So it came to pass that I arranged to meet the lady at a country house hotel for dinner. It was love at first sight. Her welcoming smile alone was enough to send me into dreamland. Helena, who is a psychotherapist and yoga therapist by profession, is, unlike me, always smiling and always looking on the brighter side of life. For thirteen years now the beautiful Helena and I have shared a life of special love together in the lovely village of Straffan. On 30 December 2019, after twelve years together, we married among family and close friends. It was a very special, joyous day and never to be forgotten. I can never thank Helena enough for loving my daughters as her own. As the saying goes 'some guys have all the luck'. I am now, as my old pal Billy Connolly so often says, 'one of the windswept and interesting survivors of the 60s'.

Now 75, I am hoping to live and keep working until 76 and beyond. I can't see the end of the road up ahead, but some days I can feel it in my bones. I regularly dream of life's express train racing faster and faster, past the stations of time on its unrelenting journey to the final destination.

I wonder if the ghost inspector will be calling for me to depart at Heaven's Gate or Hellsville. Regardless, I will have no complaints. My life has been truly blessed by God.

From my late twenties to my forties, my life mirrored the lyrics of my all-time favourite song, 'Yesterday, When I Was Young', which was written by Charles Aznavour and Herbert Kretzmer. I think it's one of the best ever 'life' songs. Written in the vein of 'My Way', but so much stronger lyrically, it's so spot-on in conveying the wastefulness of youth. Looking back now at how I lived my life in those years, I see so much of myself in the song. The best versions of the song are by Glen Campbell and Dusty Springfield. It is truly a masterclass in song lyrics.

Yesterday, when I was young
The taste of life was sweet as rain upon my tongue
I teased at life as if it were a foolish game
The way the evening breeze may tease a candle flame
The thousand dreams I dreamed, the splendid things I planned
I always built, alas, on weak and shifting sand
I lived by night and shunned the naked light of day
And only now I see how the years ran away

Yesterday when I was young
So many drinking songs were waiting to be sung
So many wayward pleasures lay in store for me
And so much pain my dazzled eyes refused to see
I ran so fast that time and youth at last ran out
I never stopped to think what life was all about
And every conversation I can now recall
Concerned itself with me, me and nothing else at all

Yesterday the moon was blue
And every crazy day brought something new to do
I used my magic age as if it were a wand
And never saw the waste and emptiness beyond
The game of love I played with arrogance and pride
And every flame I lit too quickly, quickly died
The friends I made all seemed somehow to drift away
And only I am left on stage to end the play

There are so many songs in me that won't be sung
I feel the bitter taste of tears upon my tongue
The time has come for me to pay for yesterday
When I was young.